Part Two

hands-on mathematics

Grade 3

Project Editor
Jennifer E. Lawson

Senior Author
Dianne Soltess

Mathematics Consultant
Meagan Mutchmor

Module Writers
Patricia Ashton
Joni Bowman
Betty Johns
Kara Kolson
Suzanne Mole

Winnipeg • Manitoba • Canada

Contents

Note to Teachers

While using Part 2 of ***Hands-On Mathematics, Grade Three***, you will occasionally need to refer to a page from Part 1. Please keep Part 1 close at hand for this purpose.

Module 3

Shape and Space

Books for Children (Measurement)

Barner, Bob. *Parade Day: Marching through the Calendar Year.* New York: Holiday House, 2003.

Briggs, Raymond. *Jim and the Beanstalk.* New York: Putnam & Grosset Group, 1997.

Carle, Eric. *The Grouchy Ladybug*. New York: HarperCollins, 1996.

______. *Today Is Monday*. New York: Philomel Books, 2001.

______. *The Very Hungry Caterpillar*. New York: Philomel Books, 1994.

Katz, Karen. *Twelve Hats for Lena: A Book of Months*. New York: Margaret K. McElderry Books, 2002.

Lesser, Carolyn. *What a Wonderful Day to Be a Cow.* New York: Knopf, 1995.

Sendak, Maurice. *Chicken Soup with Rice: A Book of Months*. Toronto: Scholastic, 1987.

Silverstein, Shel. *Where the Sidewalk Ends.* New York: HarperCollins, 2004.

Ye, Ting-xing. *Weighing the Elephant*. Toronto: Annick Press, 1998.

Books for Children (3-D Objects and 2-D Shapes)

Briggs, Raymond. *Jim and the Beanstalk*. New York, NY: Putnam & Grosset Group, 1997.

Feldman, Judy. *Shapes in Nature*. Chicago, IL: Childrens Press, 1991.

Hoban, Tana. *Shapes, Shapes, Shapes*. New York, NY: Greenwillow Books, 1986.

______. *Shapes and Things*. New York, NY: Macmillan, 1970.

Introduction

Measurement

Measurement concepts and skills apply directly to the students' world. Through the active, hands-on lessons in this module, students develop spatial sense and an understanding of measurement. Concrete experiences help students become familiar with different types of measures, the process of measuring, and the relationships among figures.

In lessons 1 through 9, students:

- estimate, measure, and compare, using standard units of measure for measuring length, perimeter, and mass
- select the most appropriate unit of measure
- measure the passage of time related to minutes and hours
- relate days to weeks, weeks to months, and months to a year

3-D Objects and 2-D Shapes

In grade three, students continue to investigate geometry concepts and skills that apply directly to the world in which they live. Concrete experiences will assist students in identifying and understanding the relationship between two- and three-dimensional figures, as well as in describing the relative position of objects.

In lessons 10 through 15, students:

- describe, classify, and construct three-dimensional objects and two-dimensional shapes as well as relate them to each other
- use numbers and direction words to describe the relative position of objects in one dimension and using everyday contexts

Mathematics Vocabulary

Throughout this module, teachers should use, and encourage students to use, vocabulary such as: *estimate, measure, compare, length, height, width, centimetre, metre, iteration, mass/weight, balance scale, perimeter, second(s), minute(s), hour(s), day(s), days of the week, week(s), month(s), months of the year, year(s), circle, triangle, square, rectangle, rhombus, parallelogram, angle, right angle, cube, sphere, cylinder, cone, polygon, pentagon, hexagon, octagon, rectangular prism, triangular prism, triangle-based pyramid,* and *square-based pyramid.*

Continue to use your classroom Math Word Wall as a means of reinforcing new vocabulary. As new terms are introduced in the lessons, record the words on index cards and display them under the appropriate letters of the alphabet on your Math Word Wall.

1 Measuring the Passage of Time

Materials

- action cards (included. Copy, and cut out enough sets of cards so that each pair of students gets one set.) (3.1.1)

Activity

Note: This activity is best conducted in a gymnasium or a large, open room.

Begin the activity by having students sit in a large circle. Ask them to keep their eyes on you and repeat whatever action you do. Begin to clap your hands together in a steady beat.

Once students have joined in and mastered the steady beat, change the action (e.g., tap your shoulders). Once again, it is important to maintain the same, steady beat. When students have successfully changed their action and mastered the beat, change the action once again (e.g., tap your knees).

Continue to repeat this activity with a variety of actions. Tell students that keeping a steady beat while clapping or performing another simple action is very important during this activity.

Now, hold up the action cards (3.1.1), one at a time. Read out each action. Then, randomly select one card, and ask a student to volunteer to demonstrate the action. Tell the students that, as a class, you are going to time how long it takes the student to complete this action. You will time the action by clapping your hands in a steady beat and counting the number of claps.

Note: Be sure to tell the volunteer that this is not a test to see how fast he/she can perform the action. He/she should do it at a comfortable, relaxed pace.

Ask students:

- Why is it important for us to keep a steady beat while our volunteer performs this action?

Before the student demonstrates the action, have him/her estimate how many claps it will take him/her to complete the action.

Have the volunteer demonstrate the action while the rest of the students clap together, in a steady beat. Ask:

- How many claps did it take for him/her to ____________ (action demonstrated)?

Now, ask the student who demonstrated the action:

- Was your estimate correct?
- Did you need more or less claps than you estimated?

Randomly select a second action card. Ask the same student to estimate how many claps it will take him/her to complete the action. Then, have him/her demonstrate the action while the class claps together in a steady beat. Ask:

- How many claps did it take for him/her to ____________ (action demonstrated)?

Now, ask the student who demonstrated the action:

- Was your estimate correct?
- Did you need more or less claps than you estimated?

Ask the class:

- Which action/activity took longer to complete?
- How do you know?
- How much longer did it take? (Have students respond to this question in number of claps.)

Distribute Activity Sheet A (3.1.2) and explain to students that they will now work in pairs to time how long it takes to complete each of the actions listed on the action cards. Before performing each action, students should estimate how many claps it will take to complete it, and record their estimate in the

▶

space provided. After completing the action and recording the number of claps it took, partners should switch roles and repeat the activity.

Before students begin working on the activity sheet, read the action cards once more as a class to make sure all students understand how to perform each action. Remind students to count their claps as they time their partner completing each action. Also remind them that this is not a test to see how fast they can perform the actions. They should do them at a comfortable, relaxed pace.

Activity Sheet A

Directions to students:

Working with a partner, estimate how many claps it will take you to complete each action listed on your activity sheet. Record your estimate in the space provided. Perform the action while your partner times you in claps. Record the number of claps it took you to complete the action. Switch roles, and repeat the action (3.1.2).

Problem Solving

Discuss how long students have for their morning recess. Have them draw pictures and use words to describe three activities that take less time than their morning recess and three activities that take more time than their morning recess. Then, have them record these activities on the problem solving activity sheet, "Less Time, More Time," included with this lesson (3.1.3).

Note: A reproducible adaptation of this problem can be found on page 378.

Extension

Have students create a bar graph, with your assistance, to display the results from their activity sheets.

Assessment Suggestions

- Observe students as they work together to time their actions and record their results. Use the Cooperative Skills Teacher Assessment sheet, found on page 20, to record results.
- Have students complete the Cooperative Skills Self-Assessment sheet, found on page 22, to reflect on their abilities to work together.

Action Cards

Tie your shoelace.	Put on your coat/jacket.
Do twenty-five jumping jacks.	Reach to the sky, then touch your toes, ten times.
Count to 20 by 2s.	Touch all four walls in the room.
Print your first and last names.	Sing "Happy Birthday."
Hop on one foot ten times.	Run around the room/gym.

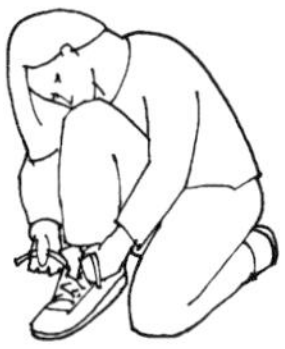

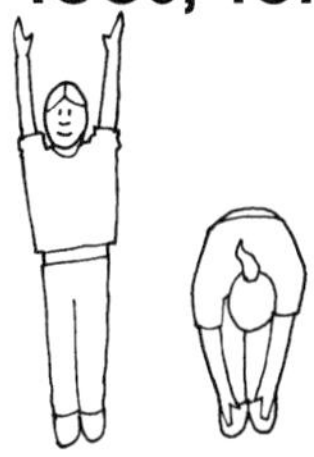

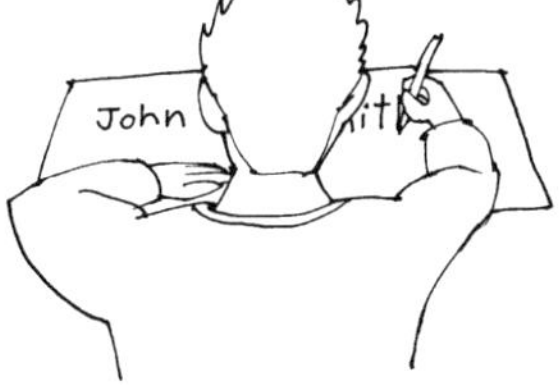

Date: ____________________ Name: ________________________________

How Many Claps?

Action to Be Measured	Estimate (Number of Claps)	Actual (Number of Claps)
Tie your shoelace.		
Put on your coat/jacket.		
Do twenty-five jumping jacks.		
Reach to the sky, then touch your toes, ten times.		
Count to 20 by 2s.		
Touch all four walls in the room.		
Print your first and last names.		
Sing "Happy Birthday."		
Hop on one foot ten times.		
Run around the room/ gym.		

Date: ____________ Name: ____________________

Less Time, More Time

These activities take less time than recess:

These activities take more time than recess:

2 Measuring the Passage of Time in Standard Units

Materials

- chart paper
- markers
- Minutes/Hours labels (included. Make one photocopy for each working group, and cut out the labels.) (3.2.1)
- Activity Cards (included. Make one photocopy of the set for each working group, and cut out the cards.) (3.2.2)
- classroom clock with secondhand
- stopwatch

Activity: Part One: How Long Is a Minute?

Have students look at the classroom clock. Point to the secondhand, and ask students:

- What does this hand on the clock tell us?
- How many seconds are there between each number on the clock?

Ask students to carefully watch the secondhand as it moves around the clock. Have students clap at each five-second interval. Stress that as the secondhand moves from one number to the next, five seconds pass. Ask:

- How many seconds pass when the secondhand makes a full circle around the clock?

As a class, count the seconds by 5s, beginning at the 12. Stress that sixty seconds pass as the secondhand completes a full circle around the clock. Ask:

- What other word do we use for sixty seconds?
- How many seconds are there in one minute?

Explain that there are sixty seconds in one minute and that one minute passes each time the secondhand completes a full circle around the clock. Point out how the minute hand moves slightly as each sixty seconds passes.

Now, have students put their heads down on their desks. Tell them that when you say the word *Go*, you will begin timing one minute on the clock, starting from when the minute hand is at the 12. Ask students to lift up their heads when they think one minute has passed and look at the minute hand on the clock. When all students have lifted their heads, ask:

- Was one minute longer than you thought? Shorter than you thought?
- What do you think you could do in one minute?

Create a list of possible things students could do in one minute. Record their suggestions on chart paper (for example, tie my shoes, count to 100, do twenty-five jumping jacks).

Activity: Part Two: How Long Is an Hour?

On chart paper, record the terms *minute* and *hour*. Ask:

- Which is longer, a minute or an hour?

Again, focus students' attention on the classroom clock. Identify the minute hand and the hour hand. Explain that as the minute hand moves from one number to the next, five minutes pass. Ask:

- How many minutes pass when the minute hand makes a full circle around the clock?

Again, have the class count by 5s, beginning at 12. Stress that sixty minutes pass as the minute hand completes a full circle around the clock. Ask:

- What is another word for sixty minutes?
- How many minutes are there in one hour?

2

Explain that there are sixty minutes in one hour, and one hour passes each time the minute hand completes a full circle around the clock. Ask:

- What do you think you could do in one hour?

Create a list of possible things students could do in one hour. Record their suggestions on chart paper (for example, bake cookies, rake the leaves).

Divide the class into working groups, and provide each group with a set of Minutes/Hours labels (3.2.1) and a set of Activity Cards (3.2.2). Have students work together to sort the activities into two groups: activities that can be completed in minutes, and activities that can be completed in hours.

Have the groups share their results of this sorting activity. As they do, record their findings on a piece of chart paper, as in the example below:

Activities Measured in Minutes	Activities Measured in Hours

Now, distribute Activity Sheet A (3.2.3), and have students list and illustrate two activities they would measure in minutes, and two activities they would measure in hours. Also have students estimate how many minutes or hours each activity would take.

Activity Sheet A

Directions to students:

List, and illustrate two activities that you would measure in minutes. Estimate how many minutes you think each activity would take.

List, and illustrate two activities that you would measure in hours. Estimate how many hours each activity would take (3.2.3).

Problem Solving

Demonstrate a series of physical education activities (actions) for students (for example, jumping jacks, hopping on one foot, squats). For each action, have students estimate how many of the action they can do in one minute, and record this estimate on the Problem Solving Sheet called "What Can You Do in One Minute?" (3.2.4). Next, time each student for one minute, and have him/her do as many of each action as he/she can. Have students record the actual number of the action they can do in one minute.

Extensions

- Add the terms *second*, *minute*, and *hour* to your classroom Math Word Wall.
- Have students use a strip of paper as a timeline and record their activities over a twenty-four hour period.
- Have students estimate how many times they can perform an action or activity (for example, tie their shoes, print their names) in one minute. Or, have students time each other to see how long it takes them to complete an action or activity (for example, tie and untie their shoes ten times, print out the alphabet).
- Have students write and draw pictures on index cards to illustrate daily classroom activities. Use the cards to create a class timeline for each hour of the school day. Use clothespins to attach the cards to a piece of string, and hang the timeline in the classroom.
- Make posters or scrapbook pages to record the passage of time. For example, "A Day in the Life of (student's name)" "A Year in the Life of (student's name)."

Minutes/Hours Labels

Minutes
Hours

Activity Cards

Brush Your Teeth

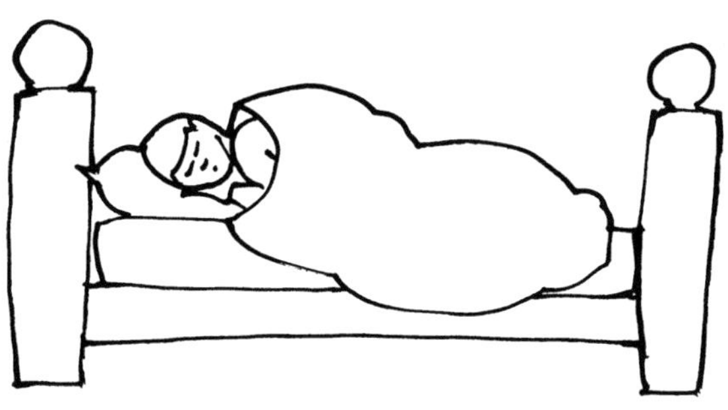

Sleep at Night

Watch a Movie

Activity Cards

Play at Recess

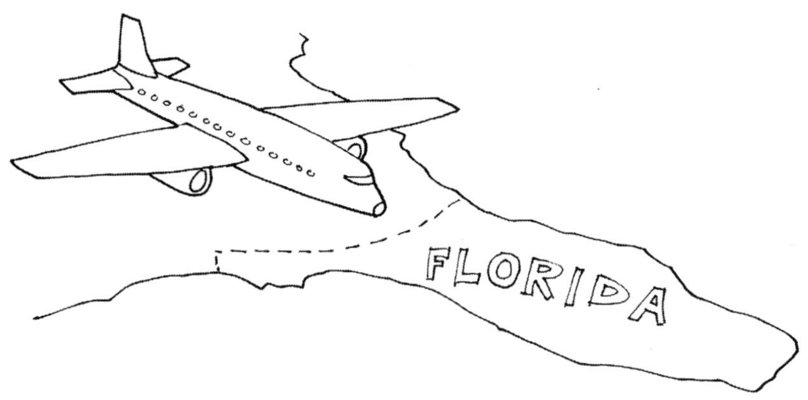

Fly on an Airplane to Florida

Eat Your Lunch

Activity Cards

Have a Shower

Read a Chapter Book

Get Dressed for School

Activity Cards

Go to School for the Day

Play a Video Game

Drive to Prince Edward Island

Date: ____________ Name: ____________________

Measuring Time

Activity Measured in Minutes: ______________________ Estimate: ________ minutes	Activity Measured in Minutes: ______________________ Estimate: ________ minutes
Activity Measured in Hours: ______________________ Estimate: ________ hours	Activity Measured in Hours: ______________________ Estimate: ________ hours

Date: ____________________ **Name:** __________________________________

What Can You Do in One Minute?

Activity	Estimate	Results
1.		
2.		
3.		
4.		
5.		
6.		
7.		
8.		
9.		
10.		

3 Days in a Month, Months of the Year

Materials

- calendar month (Photocopy the same month from a wall calendar for each student.)
- month labels (included. Copy, laminate, and cut out each label) (3.3.1)
- pocket chart
- glue
- scissors
- monthly spelling cards (3.3.4)

Activity: Part One: Reviewing the Months of the Year

Place the month labels (3.3.1) in random order in a pocket chart. Have students look at the words carefully. Ask:

- What do all of these words have in common?

Read the names of the months together as a class. Now, ask students:

- Which month comes first?

Have one student locate the January label. Place it first in the pocket chart. Now, ask:

- Which month comes after January?

Have another student find the February label. Place it after January.

Repeat this procedure until all the months are in order. Read the months together as a class.

Gather up all the month labels again. Select one label (for example, April) and place it in the middle of the pocket chart. Ask:

- Which month comes before April?
- Which month comes after April?

Repeat the questions using a different month. Then, distribute Activity Sheet A (3.3.2), and have students cut out the names of the months and glue them down in the correct order.

Activity Sheet A

Directions to students:

Cut out the names of the months, and glue them down in the correct order (3.3.2).

Activity: Part Two: A Closer Look at the Calendar

Distribute a photocopy of the same wall-calendar month to each student. Ask a number of questions to draw students' attention to the different parts of the calendar. For example:

- Which month does this calendar page show?
- How many days are there in this month?
- On which day of the week does this month begin?
- How many Fridays are there in this month?
- How many weekends are there in this month?
- Are there any holidays in this month?

Select a date on the calendar. Have students locate, and point to, the date with their fingers. Now, have them read the date aloud, together. Remind students to read the date in the correct format: day of the week first, then the month, then the number date, finally the year. For example: Thursday, March 17, 2005. Now, ask:

- What is the date of the first Tuesday of this month?
- What is the date of the last Sunday of this month?
- What is the date of the second Friday of this month?

Now, distribute Activity Sheet B (3.3.3), and have students use their calendar pages to answer the questions.

▶

Activity Sheet B

Directions to students:

Use the calendar page to answer the questions (3.3.3).

Problem Solving

- Put the month labels in order in a pocket chart. Have students close their eyes. Remove one of the months. Ask students to open their eyes and identify which month is missing.
- Distribute copies of the monthly spelling cards (3.3.4), and have students cut out each letter. Ask students to mix up their cards and then put them back in order to spell all of the months of the year. Use a clock or a watch with a second hand to time students to see how quickly they can spell the months.

Note: A reproducible master for this problem can be found on page 378.

Extensions

- Add the months of the year to your classroom Math Word Wall.
- Distribute to students photocopies of a wall-calendar month at the beginning of each month. Have students fill their calendars with notes and/or pictures of daily events, upcoming special activities, field trips, and so on.
- Make a graph that shows students' birthdays for each month of the year.
- Teach students the following verse to help them remember how many days each month has:

Note: There are many variations to this verse.

Thirty days hath September,
April, June and November.
February has twenty-eight alone,
All the rest have thirty-one.
Excepting leap year, that's the time
When February's days are twenty-nine.

- Read *Chicken Soup with Rice: A Book of Months*, by Maurice Sendak.
- Use a Venn diagram to sort the names of the months. Some sorting rule examples include: months that begin with *J*, months that end with *ber*, months that end with *y*.
- Distribute the extension activity sheet called "Monthly Jigsaw" as well as scissors and small envelopes. Ask students to cut out the jigsaw puzzle pieces, mix them up, and then put them back together again. Have students store the puzzle pieces in the envelopes (3.3.5).
- Distribute the extension activity sheet called "Monthly Word Jumble," and have students put each of the jumbled letters into the correct order and spell each of the twelve months of the year (3.3.6).

Month Labels

January	February
March	April
May	June

Month Labels

July	August
September	October
November	December

Date: ____________________ Name: ________________________________

Months of the Year

Month 1	Month 2
Month 3	Month 4
Month 5	Month 6
Month 7	Month 8
Month 9	Month 10
Month 11	Month 12

April	February
December	June
August	January
September	July
March	November
October	May

Date: ________________ Name: ____________________________

A Closer Look at the Calendar

1. What month and year does this calendar page show?

   ____

2. How many days are there in this month? ________________

3. On which day of the week does this month begin?

   ____

4. How many Fridays are there in this month? ________________

5. How many weekends are there in this month? ____________

6. What special holidays do we celebrate in this month?

   ____

7. What is the date of the first Monday of this month?

   ____

8. What is the date of the last Sunday in this month?

   ____

9. What is the date of the second Thursday in this month?

   ____

10. What month comes before this month?

    ____

11. What month comes after this month?

    ____

Monthly Spelling Cards

J	a	n	u
a	r	y	F
e	b	r	u
a	r	y	M
a	r	c	h
A	p	r	i

Monthly Spelling Cards

l	M	a	y
J	u	n	e
J	u	l	y
A	u	g	u
s	t	S	e
p	t	e	m

Monthly Spelling Cards

b	e	r	O
c	t	o	b
e	r	N	o
v	e	m	b
e	r	D	e
c	e	m	b
e	r		

Monthly Jigsaw

January
February
March
April
May
June
July
August
September
October
November
December

Date: ____________ Name: ____________________

Monthly Word Jumble

1. p l r i A ____________________

2. y u J l ____________________

3. a a u n J r y ____________________

4. t s u g u A ____________________

5. e t m e S p e b r ____________________

6. c m r D e e e b ____________________

7. y M a ____________________

8. e y F b a r r u ____________________

9. e u J n ____________________

10. o O t c r b e ____________________

11. h M r c a ____________________

12. o m b e e r v N ____________________

4 Introducing Standard Measurement: Metre and Centimetre

Materials

- chart paper
- markers
- metre sticks (one for each pair of students)
- string
- scissors
- 30-cm rulers (one for each student)
- unsharpened pencils (or other identical objects for students to measure. You will need one for each student.)
- variety of objects to measure in centimetres (for example, pencil, eraser, book, chalkboard brush, piece of chalk)

Activity: Part One: Introducing the Metre

Divide the class into working groups. Provide each group with a metre stick, and have students examine it. Ask:

- What is this called?
- What is it used for?

Print the word *metre* on chart paper. Beside the word, introduce the symbol *m*. Explain to students that the *m* represents the word *metre*.

Now, ask each group to find something in the classroom that looks like it is about one metre long, tall, or wide, to use as a referent. On chart paper, make a list of the groups' referents, which students can use for estimating or to discuss the metre unit.

Select one student from each group to measure their object (referent). Have students hold their metre sticks up to their objects. Ask:

- Is your object one metre long?
- Is your object longer than one metre?
- Is your object shorter than one metre?

Note: As each group measures their object, stress the importance of accuracy. Demonstrate how the 0 on the metre stick should be in line with the edge of the object in order to determine if the object is one metre in length. Also point out how, on some rulers, the 0 is right at the end while on other rulers, the 0 is indented from the end. In the latter case, lining up objects at the end of the ruler can lead to miscalculations.

Now, ask students:

- What are some things we could use a metre stick to measure?

On chart paper, record students' suggestions beside the word *metre*.

Divide the class into pairs of students. Provide each pair with a metre stick, a piece of string that is longer than one metre, and a pair of scissors. Have students use their rulers to measure one metre on their pieces of string and then cut the string to exactly one metre in length.

Now, distribute Activity Sheet A (3.4.1), and have students look for objects in the classroom that are:

- shorter than one metre
- longer than one metre
- equal to one metre in length

Tell students to refer to the list of metre referents on chart paper to help them estimate the length of each object. Have students use their string to measure the objects, and have them record their results on their activity sheets. Stress that for accurate measuring, they must make sure their string is flat against the object and pulled straight.

▶

4

Activity Sheet A

Directions to students:

Use your string to measure objects that are shorter than one metre, longer than one metre, and equal to one metre in length. On the chart, draw a simple illustration for, and label, each object (3.4.1).

Activity: Part Two: Introducing the Centimetre

Review students' results from Activity: Part One. Ask students:

- Which objects are equal to (or very close to) one metre in length?
- Which objects are longer than one metre?
- Which objects are shorter than one metre?
- How can we measure the objects that are shorter than one metre?

Distribute 30-cm rulers to students. Ask:

- What can you tell me about this ruler?
- What does each mark on the ruler mean?

Introduce the word *centimetre*. Print the word *centimetre* on chart paper. Beside it, introduce the symbol *cm*. Explain to students that the *cm* represents the word *centimetre*.

Note: When recording abbreviated units of measure in metric, a period is not used after the abbreviation. The correct abbreviation for ten centimetres is "10 cm".

Explain that the word *centimetre* comes from the word *cent*, which means 100 in French. Point out that there are 100 centimetres in a metre, and 100 cents in a dollar.

Now, have students use their rulers to see which of their fingers is approximately one centimetre wide.

Explain to students that they can use this "finger measure" as a referent for one centimetre. Discuss, and record, on chart paper, other possible referents for the centimetre unit.

Have students locate the number 10 on their rulers. Ask:

- What does this 10 stand for? (ten centimetres or 10 cm)

Now, display for students a variety of objects of different length. Hold up one of the objects, and ask:

- Do you think this object is shorter than ten centimetres, longer than ten centimetres, or equal to ten centimetres?

Demonstrate how to use a ruler to measure the object. Show students how to line up the 0 on the ruler with the edge of the object you are measuring. Introduce the term *iteration*, referring to the numeric line markings on a ruler.

Together with students, measure and sort the objects into three groups:

- shorter than ten centimetres
- longer than ten centimetres
- equal to ten centimetres in length

Activity: Part Three: Measuring in Centimetres

Distribute 30-cm rulers to students, and review how to accurately measure in centimetres, stressing the importance of beginning at the 0 on the ruler. Also, distribute to students identical objects such as unsharpened pencils or strips of paper. Have students examine their objects closely and estimate the length, in centimetres. Ask:

- How many centimetres long do you think your object is?

Encourage students to use the discussed centimetre referents (finger width or other objects) to help them estimate the length of their objects.

Record students' estimates on chart paper, and then have them use their rulers to measure the length of their objects. Circulate as students measure, ensuring that they are using their rulers correctly. Record students' results on chart paper.

Note: Since students are measuring identical items, their results should be the same. Discuss any discrepancies, and ensure that students are able to measure the items accurately.

Now, distribute Activity Sheet B (3.4.2), and have students find objects in the classroom that they think are shorter than thirty centimetres. Have them estimate the length of each object and then use their rulers to measure the object's actual length. Have students record their results on their charts.

Then, distribute Activity Sheet C (3.4.3), and have students use their 30-cm rulers to draw lines for each measurement shown.

Activity Sheet B

Directions to students:

Find objects in the classroom that you think are shorter than your 30-cm ruler. Estimate the length of each object, and record your estimate on the chart. Then, use your ruler to measure the actual length of each object, and record the measurement on the chart (3.4.2).

Activity Sheet C

Directions to students:

Use your ruler to draw a line for each measurement shown (3.4.3).

Activity: Part Four: Selecting Measurement Units and Measuring Instruments

Divide the class into working groups, and provide each group with a piece of chart paper, a marker, a metre stick, and a 30-cm ruler. Have each group make a list of five objects they could measure using the metre stick and five objects they could measure using the 30-cm ruler.

Now, have the groups share their ideas with the rest of the class. Discuss the appropriate selection of measurement units and measuring instruments. Ask students:

- Why would you use a metre stick to measure the length of the hallway?
- Why is a metre stick better than a 30-cm ruler for this task?
- What would you use to measure the length of a paper clip?
- Why is a 30-cm ruler better than a metre stick for this task?

Distribute Activity Sheet D (3.4.4), and have students work in their groups to decide if they should use a metre stick or a 30-cm ruler to measure each object. Then, have them estimate and then measure the length of each object.

Activity Sheet D

Directions to students:

Read each sentence. Decide if you would use a metre stick or a 30-cm ruler to measure the length of each object. Use a checkmark to show your choice. Then, estimate and measure the length of each object (3.4.4).

4

Problem Solving

Have students work with partners to complete the problem-solving activity sheet called "Choosing the Unit of Measure" (3.4.5). Have students find and record five objects in the classroom that would be measured in centimetres and five objects that would be measured in metres.

Note: A reproducible variation of this problem can be found on page 378.

Extensions

- Add the terms *metre, centimetre, estimate, measure, length*, and *iteration* to your classroom Math Word Wall.
- Have students construct paper airplanes and then measure how far their airplanes travel.
- Read the book *Jim and the Beanstalk*, by Raymond Briggs, with students. Then, have each student plant a fast-growing seed, such as a bean. On a weekly basis, have students measure the heights of their plants, in centimetres.

Assessment Suggestion

As students complete their activity sheets, observe their abilities to:

- estimate measurements
- measure accurately
- record results accurately
- select appropriate units of measurement

List these criteria on the Rubric, found on page 18, and record your results.

Date: ____________________ **Names:** ________________________________

____

Measuring: One Metre

Shorter than One Metre	Longer than One Metre	Equal to One Metre

Date: ____________ Name: ______________________

Measuring in Centimetres

Object	Estimate (Centimetres)	Length (Centimetres)

Date: ____________________ Name: ________________________________

Measuring and Drawing Lines

Draw a line that is:

10 centimetres long.

20 centimetres long.

5 centimetres long.

8 centimetres long.

17 centimetres long.

Date: ____________________ Names: ________________________________

____

____

____

Deciding How to Measure Objects

To measure the length of a shoe, we would use a: ____ metre stick ____ 30-cm ruler Our estimate: ____________ Our result: _______________	To measure the length of a door, we would use a: ____ metre stick ____ 30-cm ruler Our estimate: ____________ Our result: _______________
To measure the length of the chalkboard or whiteboard, we would use a: ____ metre stick ____ 30-cm ruler Our estimate: ____________ Our result: _______________	To measure the length of an eraser, we would use a: ____ metre stick ____ 30-cm ruler Our estimate: ____________ Our result: _______________

Date: ____________ Names: ____________

____

Choosing the Unit of Measure

Objects to Measure in Centimetres	Objects to Measure in Metres

5 Measuring Objects by Height, Length, and Width

Materials

- measuring tapes (one for each pair of students)
- chart paper
- markers
- pencils

Activity

Explain to students that they will work in pairs to measure different parts of their bodies, including:

- the length of their *entire* bodies or their height
- the length of one of their arms
- the length of one of their legs
- the distance around their heads
- the width of one of their feet
- the distance around one of their wrists
- the distance around one of their ankles

Tell students that they will use measuring tapes to accurately measure each body part. Distribute one measuring tape to each pair of students.

Note: If you do not have access to measuring tapes, have students use string to measure around each body part, and then place the string on a ruler to determine the length.

Have students look closely at their measuring tapes. Ask:

- What can you tell me about your measuring tape?
- What units are marked on your measuring tape?
- When measuring any object with a measuring tape, what number should you start at?

Gather students into a circle. Select a volunteer to stand in the centre of the circle. Ask students to estimate the height of the student, and record their estimates on chart paper. Encourage students to use the metre and centimetre referents discussed in the previous lesson to help them with their estimation. Then, select another student to measure the first student's actual height. Record this under the estimates on the chart paper. Have students compare the height estimates to the actual height measurement. Ask:

- Were any of the estimates correct?
- Were any of the estimates close to the actual height?
- How far off was this estimate? (Point to one of the estimates.)

Distribute Activity Sheet A (3.5.1) to students. Demonstrate how to measure the remaining body parts outlined on the sheet. Discuss the terms of measurement, focusing on the difference between *height, length, width*, and *distance around*.

Then, have students work in pairs to estimate and measure the height, length, or width of their own body parts.

Activity Sheet A

Directions to students:

Estimate, and measure each body part and record the actual length, width, or height in the space provided. Be sure to include the unit of measure (cm, m, or dm) (3.5.1).

Problem Solving

Have students use their results from Activity Sheet A (3.5.1) to answer the questions found on the problem solving sheet called "Measuring Up" (3.5.2).

Extensions

- Add the terms *height, length,* and *width* to your classroom Math Word Wall.

▶

5

- Measure and compare the heights of students in September, January, and again in June.
- Discuss the importance of accurate measuring in everyday life (for example, when constructing a home, when hemming a pair of pants, when building a piece of furniture, when sewing curtains for a window, when buying a pair of shoes).
- Have students make bracelets for one another based on their wrist measurements.

Assessment Suggestions

- Observe students as they work together to measure their body parts. Record your observations using the Cooperative Skills Teacher Assessment sheet, found on page 20.
- Have students complete Cooperative Skills Self-Assessment sheets, found on page 22, to reflect on their abilities to work together.

Date: ____________________ **Name:** ________________________________

Partner: ________________________________

Measuring Me

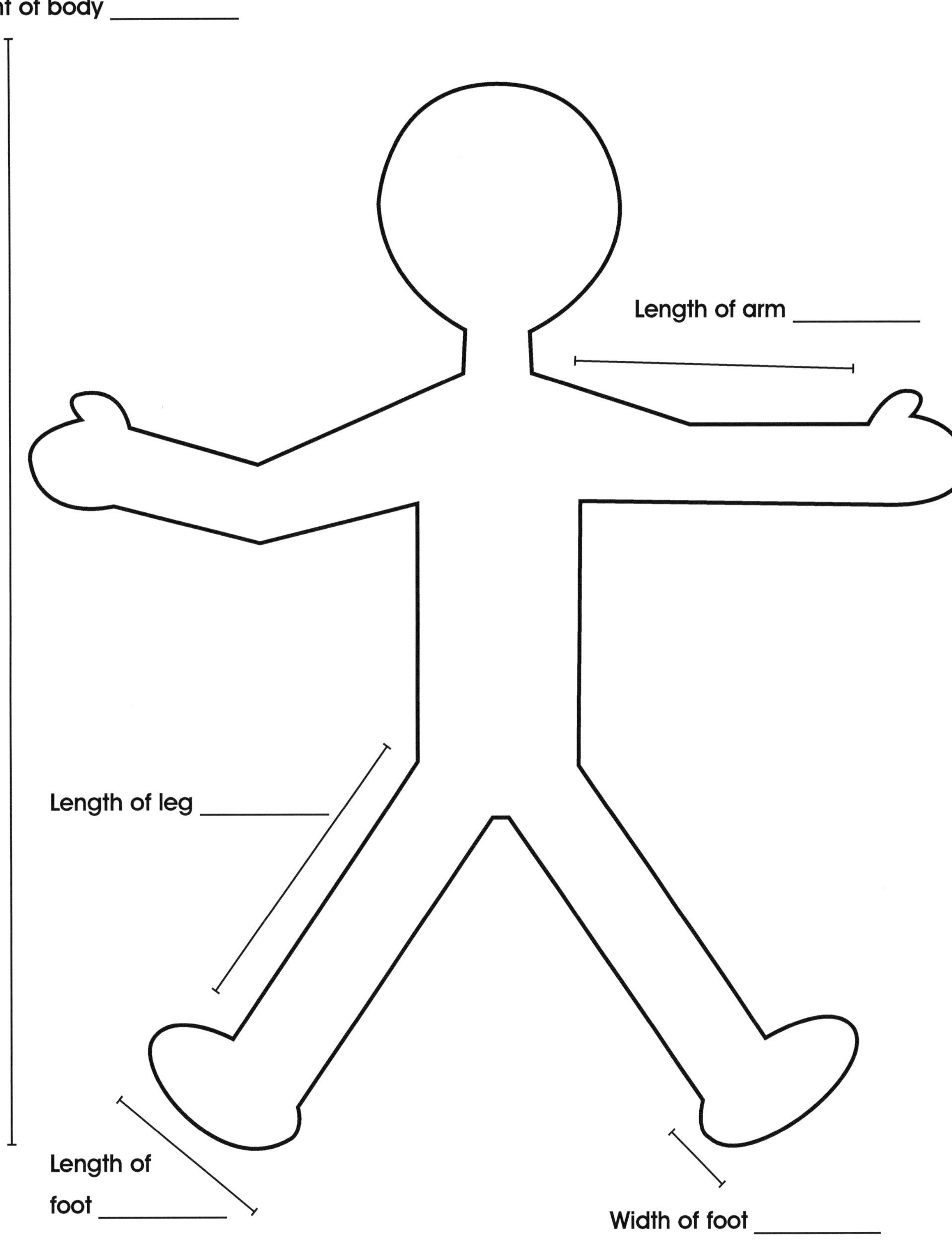

Date: ____________________ Name: ______________________________

Partner: ______________________________

Measuring Up

1. What unit of measure did you use to measure your height?

   ____

2. Record your height. ______________________________

   Record your partner's height. ______________________________

   Who is taller? ______________________________

   By how much? ______________________________

3. What is the length of your arm? ______________________________

   What is the length of your leg? ______________________________

   Which one is longer? ______________________________

   By how much? ______________________________

4. Why would you need to know the following:

   The length of your foot?

   ____

   ____

   The height of your body?

   ____

   ____

6 Comparing and Ordering Objects by Mass

Materials

- balance scales (one for each working group of students)
- chart paper
- markers
- interlocking cubes
- dried beans (for example, dried lima beans)
- several objects of different size and mass

Activity: Part One: Comparing Objects

Have eight students volunteer to take off their right shoes. Display the shoes for all students to see. Ask:

- How are these shoes the same?
- How are they different?
- How could we sort these shoes? (by size, by style, by colour)
- How could we compare these shoes? (by size, by mass)

Explain that students will now arrange the shoes in order from lightest to heaviest. Ask:

- Which shoe do you think is the lightest? Why?
- Which shoe do you think comes next?

Continue this line of questioning until all shoes have been arranged in order, from lightest to heaviest. Ask:

- How do we know if we have put the shoes in the correct order?
- What can we use to check our estimates?

Display a balance scale. Ask:

- What is this called?
- What is a balance scale used for?
- Why is it called a *balance* scale?
- How does a balance scale work?
- What do you have to do before using the scale?

Encourage students to always *zero* the scale before using it. Help student volunteers demonstrate this procedure.

Review with students how the balance scale works. For example, say:

- Put two objects on the scale, one in the right holder and one in the left holder. The scale will tilt down towards the heavier object.

Now, ask students:

- What does it mean if I put an object in each holder, but the scale does not tilt to the right or left and stays in the middle? (the objects have the same mass)

Next, tell students that you are going to use the balance scale to check their shoe mass estimates. Place the first two shoes on the scale, and observe what happens. Ask:

- Which shoe is lighter?
- Which shoe is heavier?
- How do you know?
- Were these two shoes placed in the correct order (from lightest to heaviest)?

Now, place the second and third shoes on the scale, and observe what happens. Ask:

- Which shoe is lighter?
- Which shoe is heavier?
- How do you know?
- Were these two shoes placed in the correct order?

Repeat this procedure until you have compared all eight shoes. Then, ask:

- Did we put all eight shoes in the correct order from lightest to heaviest?
- What, if any, changes should we make to our original order?
- Does the biggest shoe have the greatest mass?

- Does the smallest shoe have the lowest mass?
- Is it possible for a shoe to be bigger in size but weigh less than a shoe of a smaller size?

Reinforce that it is possible for an object to be larger but weigh less than a smaller object.

Activity: Part Two: Comparing Non-Standard Units of Measure

Note: Before beginning this activity, collect five objects of different size and mass. You will be measuring their masses using interlocking cubes or dried beans and a balance scale.

Display the five objects for students to see. Select one object, and put it on one side of the balance scale. Ask:

- How many interlocking cubes do you think I need to put in the other holder to balance the scale?

Have students share their estimates, and record these on chart paper.

Gradually place interlocking cubes on the scale, one at a time. Have students count the cubes as you add them. Once you have balanced the scale, ask:

- How many cubes did it take to balance the scale?

Compare this with the estimates recorded on the chart paper. Ask:

- Did anyone estimate the correct number of cubes?
- Which estimates were close?

Repeat this procedure using the same object on one side of the balance scale and dried beans as your unit of measure.

Ask:

- How many beans do you think I need to put in the other holder to balance the scale?

Again, have students share their estimates, and record these on chart paper.

Now, gradually place beans on the other side of the scale. Have students count the beans as you put them on the scale. Once the scale is balanced, ask:

- How many beans did it take to balance the scale?
- Did anyone estimate the correct number of beans?
- Which estimates were close?
- Did we use more cubes or more beans to balance the scale?
- From this experiment, what can you tell about the mass of one interlocking cube and the mass of one bean?
- Which has a greater mass, the cube or the bean?
- Did we need less cubes or less beans to balance the scale?

Select a different object to measure. Repeat the procedure using the interlocking cubes, and then the beans, as the unit of measure.

Activity: Part Three: Measuring Mass Using Non-Standard Units of Measure

Divide the class into working groups. Provide each group with a balance scale, interlocking cubes, beans, and several objects of different size and mass. Distribute Activity Sheet A (3.6.1) and have students work together to measure each object's mass.

Activity Sheet A

Directions to students:

In the first column of the chart, print the name of each object you will measure. For each object, estimate how many units of measure you will need to balance the scale, using both interlocking cubes and beans as the unit of measure. Find out, and record, how many cubes you actually need to balance the scale. Also find out, and record, how many beans you need to balance the scale. When you have found the mass of each object, list the objects in order from lightest to heaviest (3.6.1).

Problem Solving

Kaylee's shoe has a mass of 17 blocks. Jamie's shoe has a mass of 15 blocks. Barry's shoe has a mass of 22 blocks.

- Who has the lightest shoe?
- How much heavier is Barry's shoe than Jamie's shoe?
- How much lighter is Jamie's shoe than Kaylee's shoe?
- If you put all three shoes on one side of the balance scale at the same time, how many blocks would you need to balance the scale?

Note: A reproducible master for these problems can be found on page 379.

Activity Centre

Set up a weigh station activity centre. Provide a balance scale, a number of objects for students to weigh, and various non-standard units of measure (interlocking cubes, pennies, dried beans, and so on).

Extensions

- Add the terms *balance scale* and *mass* to your classroom Math Word Wall.
- Have each student make a balance scale using a coat hanger, string, and two milk cartons with the tops cut off, as in the following diagram:

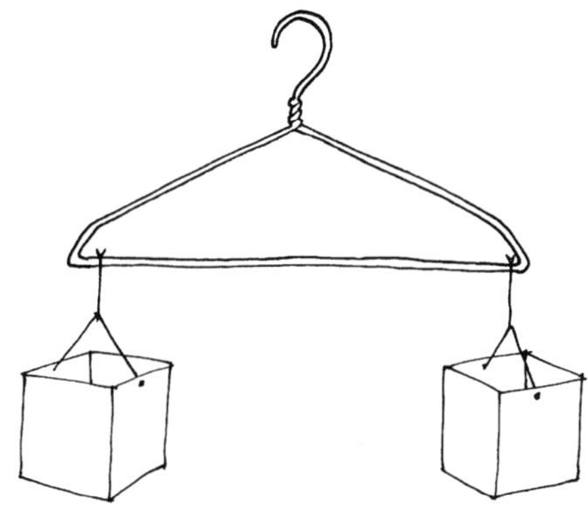

  Have students use their balance scales to compare the mass of objects around the classroom and at home.

- Discuss the various uses of scales in everyday life (a bathroom scale, a produce scale at the grocery store, a weigh-station scale for trucks, and so on).
- Integrate math and art by having students construct mobiles and then experiment with balancing objects, shapes, and materials.

Assessment Suggestions

- Observe students as they work together to measure the mass of various objects. Record your observations on a Cooperative Skills Teacher Assessment sheet, found on page 20.
- Have students complete their own Cooperative Skills Self-Assessment sheets, found on page 22, to reflect on their abilities to work together.

Date: ____________ Name: ____________

Measuring Mass

Object	Estimate (Number of Cubes)	Actual (Number of Cubes)	Estimate (Number of Beans)	Actual (Number of Beans)

List the objects in order from lightest to heaviest.

1. ____________ 6. ____________

2. ____________ 7. ____________

3. ____________ 8. ____________

4. ____________ 9. ____________

5. ____________ 10. ____________

7 Investigating Mass

Background Information for Teachers

The term *weight* refers to the pull of gravity on an object. *Mass* refers to an object's tendency to resist a change in velocity or motion. For example, it becomes clear that a refrigerator has greater mass than a kitchen chair when one tries to push each one.

In mathematics and science, the term *mass* is more accurate than *weight* when measuring objects. Be sure to discuss the two terms with students, and encourage them to use the term *mass* when conducting measurement activities.

Materials

- plastic grocery bag
- large variety of grocery produce for which mass can easily be determined (zucchini, potatoes, lemons, apples, and so on)
- selection of potatoes (approximately one dozen) of varying size and mass (total mass of all potatoes should be greater than one kilogram)
- selection of other types of fruit/vegetables (approximately one dozen of each type) of varying size and mass (total mass of all fruit/vegetables of one type should be greater than one kilogram) (optional)
- balance scale(s)
- weights (grams and kilograms)
- chart paper
- markers
- coloured pencils or markers

Activity: Part One

Have students sit in a circle, and begin the lesson by holding up an empty grocery bag. Explain that you want to carefully fill the bag with grocery items by making sure to put the lighter items on top of the heavier ones so that the heavier items do not squash the lighter ones.

Show students seven items that you want to put in the grocery bag. Ask:

- How can I find out which items are heavier and which items are lighter?

In the centre of the circle, on a low table or on the floor, place a balance scale. Ask:

- What is this called?
- What is a balance scale used for?
- Why is it called a balance scale?
- How does a balance scale work?

Review with students how the balance scale works. For example, place one grocery item in the right holder of the scale and another item in the left holder. Point out how the scale tilts down toward the heavier object. Ask:

- What does it mean if I place two objects on the scale and the scale does not tilt to the right or the left but stays balanced in the middle? (The objects have the same mass.)

Provide students with the opportunity to be "human scales." Distribute two grocery items to each student. Have students hold one item in each hand, compare the masses of the two items, and lower the hand holding the heavier item (or balance their two hands, if the items' masses feel about the same).

Now, ask students:

- What unit of measure is used on grocery-store scales in the produce or bulk-food sections?

Record the terms *gram* and *kilogram* on chart paper. Discuss the common prefix terms used in the metric system (*kilo* – *kilo*gram, *kilo*metre; *milli* – *milli*gram, *milli*metre, and so on). Ask:

- Which do you think is heavier: a gram or a kilogram?
- How many grams do you think there are in a kilogram? (1000)

7

Pass around the kilogram weight so students have an opportunity to feel its mass. Discuss ideas for referents students could use for one kilogram, and record these ideas on chart paper. Some examples include a specific classroom book, a bag of marbles, a brick, and so on. You may also consider passing around grocery items that have a mass of one kilogram (for example, a 1-kilo bag of potatoes, carrots, or onions). Ask:

- If I cut a 1-kilogram melon exactly in half, how many grams would the mass of each half be?
- If I cut a 1-kilogram melon into four equal pieces, how many grams would the mass of each piece be?
- If I cut a 1-kilogram melon into ten equal pieces, how many grams would the mass of each piece be?

Next, pass around the gram (1 gram) weight. Discuss ideas for referents students could use for one gram, and record these ideas on chart paper. Some examples include a penny, a paper clip, or other classroom manipulatives.

Pass around various other gram weights (for example, 100 g, 250 g, and 500 g). Again, have selected students hold two of the weights and be human scales to show the comparative mass of each weight.

Explain that you will now use the weights to find out the mass of each grocery item.

Demonstrate how to use the weights with the balance scale. Then, put the scale aside, and have selected students act as human scales again by holding an item in one hand and adding weights to the other hand until their hands feel balanced. Finally, help students use the balance scale and the weights to find the mass of each item. Record the mass of each item on chart paper.

Once you have determined the mass of all seven grocery items, ask students:

- Which items should I place at the bottom of my grocery bag? How do you know?
- Which items should I place next? How do you know?

Continue with this line of questioning until students have helped you place all items in the grocery bag.

Activity: Part Two

Note: Before beginning this activity, create a table like the following on chart paper:

Mass of 1 Potato	Estimate Number of Potatoes = to 1 kilogram	Actual Mass of Potatoes

Explain to students that you want to fill a grocery bag with potatoes until it has a mass of approximately 1 kilogram. Display a selection of potatoes of varying sizes and masses. Select a volunteer student to choose one of the potatoes and use the balance scale and weights to determine its mass (for example, 156 grams). Ask students:

- Do you think all the potatoes here have the same mass? (no)
- Can you find a potato that looks like it would have a greater mass than the mass of our first potato?

Have another volunteer select another potato that looks like it would have a greater mass than that of the first potato and use the scale and weights to determine its mass (for example, 205 grams).

▶

Ask:

- Does the second potato have a greater mass than that of the first?
- Which mass is greater: 156 grams or 205 grams?
- Can you find a potato that looks like it would have a mass that is less than the mass of our first potato?

Have another volunteer select another potato that looks like it would have a mass that is less than that of the first potato and use the scale and weights to determine its mass (for example, 112 grams). Ask:

- Does the third potato have a mass that is less than that of the first potato?
- Which mass is less: 156 grams or 112 grams?

Explain to students that potatoes of varying sizes, such as the selection of potatoes here, will have varying masses as well.

Now, remind students that you want to fill the grocery bag with potatoes until it has a mass of approximately 1 kilogram. Return the three potatoes for which mass has already been determined to the collection, and select a new volunteer student to choose a new potato and use the balance scale and weights to determine its mass (for example, 135 grams). Record 135 grams in the first column of the chart-paper chart, under "Mass of 1 Potato." Ask students:

- How many potatoes do you think we will need to put in the bag for a mass of 1 kilogram?

Have students offer their suggestions. Select one student to test his/her suggestion. For example, if a student suggests five potatoes, have him/her place four more potatoes on the balance scale and use the weights to determine the mass of the five potatoes (for example, 792 grams). Record 5 in the second column of the chart and 792 grams in the third column. Ask:

- Does the total mass of five potatoes equal approximately 1 kilogram? (no)
- Do we need to add potatoes or subtract potatoes from our total to get closer to 1 kilogram? (in this example, add)
- How many more potatoes do you think we need to add?

Again, have students raise their hands with their suggestions. Select one student to test his/her suggestion. For example, if a student suggests three more potatoes, have him/her place three more potatoes on the balance scale and use the weights to determine the mass of the eight potatoes together (for example, 1137 grams). Record 8 in the second row of the second column of the chart and 1137 grams in the second row of the third column. Ask:

- Does the total mass of eight potatoes equal approximately 1 kilogram? (no)
- Do we need to add potatoes or subtract potatoes from our total to get closer to 1 kilogram? (in this example, subtract)
- How many potatoes do you think we need to subtract?

Continue with the activity until you get reasonably close to 1 kilogram in mass. If desired, repeat the activity with different fruit or vegetables.

Problem Solving

Divide the class into groups of four students. Ask each student to remove one of his/her shoes, and give students an opportunity to feel the mass of each shoe in his/her group. Then, tell students to estimate the mass of each shoe in their group and arrange the shoes in order from lightest to heaviest.

Distribute the problem-solving activity sheet called "Measuring Shoe Mass" (included) as well as coloured pencils or markers, and have students draw simple illustrations of the shoes in their estimated order from lightest to heaviest. Next, ask students to use a balance scale and weights to determine the mass of each shoe in their group, and tell students to record each shoe's actual mass. Have students examine their original estimates and determine how close the estimates were as well as whether or not they put the shoes in the correct order. Tell students to rearrange the shoes (if necessary) into the actual order from lightest to heaviest and draw simple illustrations of the shoes in the correct order (3.7.1).

Activity Centre

Place a variety of objects of different sizes and masses at an activity centre, along with a balance scale and weights. Ask students to estimate the mass of the different objects in grams or kilograms. Then, have students use the balance scale and weights to test their estimates.

Extensions

- Have students make their own kilogram weights by filling Ziploc bags with any of the following materials: gravel, nuts and bolts, stones, sand, marbles, or other. Tell students to use the balance scale and a 1-kilogram weight to determine how much of the material they need to put into the bag.
- Discuss how cashiers at grocery-store checkouts find the mass of produce to determine how much money customers owe.
- Have students bring copies of their favourite recipes to school. Discuss the units of measurement for mass used in each recipe (for example, 175 g of flour).
- Do a baking activity with students to give them a real-life opportunity to test their mass-measuring skills. Have students use a balance scale and weights to measure out the necessary ingredients.
- Have students examine a variety of balls (baseball, golf ball, Ping-Pong ball, tennis ball, beach ball, and so on) and estimate which ball is the lightest and which ball is the heaviest. Have students use a balance scale and weights to determine the mass of each ball. Discuss how an item's size does not necessarily determine its mass.

Date: ____________ Name: ____________

Measuring Shoe Mass

Estimated Order (Lightest to Heaviest)			
1	2	3	4

	Estimate	Actual
Shoe 1		
Shoe 2		
Shoe 3		
Shoe 4		

Actual Order (Lightest to Heaviest)

8 Perimeter

Materials

- bags of interlocking cubes (one bag for each working group of students)
- scrap paper
- pencils
- chart paper
- markers
- large sheets of graph paper (one for each working group of students)
- rulers (one for each working group of students)

Activity: Part One

Divide the class into working groups, and provide each group with a bag of interlocking cubes. Explain to students that each group must use the cubes to find the length of a student desk (or classroom table). Once all groups have completed this task, have students compare their measurements.

Distribute scrap paper and pencils to the groups. Tell them to draw a diagram of the desktop on the scrap paper. Then, have them measure the length or width of each side of the desk and record the measurements on their diagram, as below:

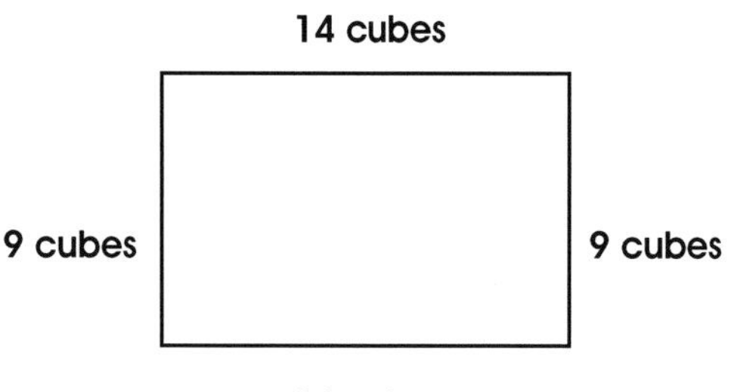

Have students look carefully at their diagrams, and ask:

- How could we figure out the total length of all four sides of the desk together?

Have students work in their groups to solve this problem, and then have them share their solutions and strategies with the rest of the class. Explain to students that the total length (and/or width) of all four sides of the desk *together* is called the *perimeter* of the desk. The perimeter is the distance around an object. Record the term *perimeter* on chart paper.

Distribute a copy of Activity Sheet A (3.8.1) to each student, and have students work in their groups to complete it. For each item, ask students to estimate the perimeter and then use interlocking cubes to measure its length and its width. Finally, have students calculate the perimeter of the item.

Activity Sheet A

Directions to students:

For each item, estimate the perimeter. Then, measure its width and its length, and calculate its perimeter. Do the same with two items of your choice (3.8.1).

Activity: Part Two

Provide each working group with a large sheet of graph paper, a ruler, and markers. Have students work together to construct a bar graph showing the comparative perimeters of the items they measured in Activity: Part One. Discuss the characteristics of a bar graph with students, and encourage them to include:

- an appropriate title
- labelled axes
- calibrations
- spaces between bars

Have each group present their completed graph to the class.

▶

Problem Solving

Farmer Brown decides to build a chicken coop to prevent his chickens from wandering off. He would like the chicken coop to be 10 metres long and 5 metres wide. What will the perimeter of the chicken coop be? If 1 metre of chicken wire costs $2, how much will chicken wire for Farmer Brown's entire chicken coop cost?

Note: A reproducible master for this problem can be found on page 379.

Extensions

- Add the term *perimeter* to your classroom Math Word Wall.
- Discuss the importance of perimeter in everyday life. For instance, when building a fence around a yard, you need to know the perimeter of the yard to determine how long the fence will be and how many boards (or metres of fencing) you must buy.

Assessment Suggestion

Assess students' bar graphs, looking for the characteristics described in Activity: Part Two. List these characteristics as criteria on a Rubric sheet, found on page 18, and record results.

Date: ____________ Name: ____________________

Measuring Perimeter

Item	Estimate of Perimeter	Length	Width	Actual Perimeter
Desk				
Sheet of Paper				
Classroom Door				
Storybook				
Seat of a Chair				
Item of Your Choice: ____________				
Item of Your Choice: ____________				

9 More About Perimeter

Materials

- chart graph paper
- chart paper
- markers
- centimetre rulers (one for each pair of students)
- metre sticks (one for each pair of students)
- geoboards (one for each student)
- elastic bands

Activity: Part One: Introducing Perimeter

Before beginning the lesson, draw a figure on chart graph paper (such as either of the two figures below):

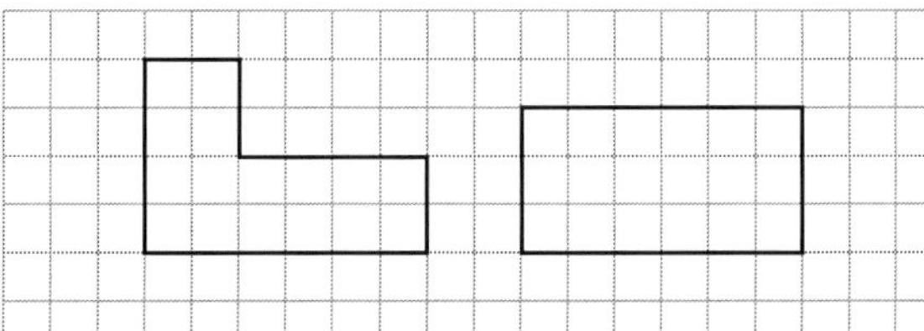

Begin the lesson by asking students to imagine a garden in which you have planted several types of vegetables. In order to protect your garden from some neighbourhood rabbits, you plan to build a small fence around it. Display the figure drawn on chart graph paper, and explain that this is a drawing of your garden. Use your finger to trace around the outside of the figure, and tell students that this is the fence you want to build. Ask:

- How can I figure out how much fencing I need? (count how many "squares" long each side of the figure is)

As a class, count the number of squares along each side of the figure. Record the number of squares next to each side.

Ask:

- How can I figure out the total amount of fencing I need? (add all the sides together)

Add the total number of squares to determine the total amount of fencing needed (in square units). Say:

- If one square on my graph paper is equal to one square metre, how many metres of fencing do I need?

Tell students they have calculated the *perimeter* of the garden. Ask:

- What does *perimeter* mean?

Explain that *perimeter* means the distance around a figure. Print the word *perimeter* on chart paper, and record the definition beside it. Read the definition together as a class.

Select a student to use his/her finger to trace around the figure on the graph paper. Select other students to use their fingers to trace the perimeters of:

- a desk
- a notebook
- a table
- a bulletin board

Distribute Activity Sheet A (3.9.1), and have students determine the perimeter for each figure and record the measurement in the corresponding blank. Remind students to include units of measurement in their answers.

Activity Sheet A

Directions to students:

Determine the perimeter for each figure, and record the measurement in the blank. Remember to include units of measurement in your answers (3.9.1).

Activity: Part Two: Perimeter of Two-Dimensional Shapes

Note: For the first part of this activity to be valuable, students' desks must be the same size. If they are not, divide the class into groups of students who have desks of the same size (for example: students in group 1 all have larger, brown desks and students in group 2 all have smaller, grey desks), and complete the activity separately with each group.

Begin this activity by asking students to use their hands as units of measure to determine the perimeter of their desks. Give students the following instructions:

- Spread out your fingers on both hands. Place the pinkie of your left hand at the edge of your desk.
- Place the thumb of your right hand next to the thumb of your left hand.
- Cross your left hand over your right hand, and place the pinkie of your left hand next to the pinkie of your right hand. Continue in this way around your desk until you have measured the perimeter in "hands." Do not forget to count "hands" as you move along.

Once students have measured the perimeter of their desks in hands, ask:

- Are all the desks the same size? (yes)
- Did each student get the same measurement for his/her desk's perimeter? (no)
- Why did some of you get different answers? (students' hands are not the same size)

Discuss the importance of having a standard unit of measurement.

Tell students they will now use two standard units of measurement, a centimetre ruler and a metre stick, to measure the perimeter of various objects around the school. Divide the class into pairs of students, and distribute a copy of Activity Sheet B (3.9.2) to each student. Have students estimate and record, and then measure and record, the perimeter of each item listed on the chart. Also, have students choose two items to add to their charts, and tell students to measure the perimeter of these items as well. Encourage students once again to use the referents for one metre and one centimetre (discussed in lesson 4) to assist with their estimation. Also, remind students to include the unit of measure (centimetres or metres) for each item they measure.

Note: Review with students the proper procedure for using a ruler to measure objects, reminding students to line up the edge of the item with the number 0 on the ruler.

Activity Sheet B

Directions to students:

Estimate and record, and then measure and record, the perimeter of each item listed on the chart. Choose two items to add to the chart, and measure the perimeter of these items as well. Remember to include the unit of measure (centimetres or metres) for each item you measure (3.9.2).

Problem Solving

Distribute to each student a geoboard and two elastic bands. Ask each student to use one elastic band to make the smallest square possible on the geoboard. Explain that you can figure out the perimeter of the square by counting how many spaces (between pegs) the elastic spans. In this case, the perimeter of the square is four units. Now, challenge students by asking questions such as:

- Can you make a square with a perimeter of 8 units?
- Can you make a figure with a perimeter of 10 units?
- Can you make two different figures, each with a perimeter of 12 units?

Extensions

- Discuss the importance of perimeter in everyday life. For example, when constructing a fence around a property, you need to know the perimeter of the property to determine how long the fence will be and how much fencing you must purchase.
- Have students use photographs of a house to calculate its perimeter and determine how many metres of lights are needed to decorate the house for the holidays. Take a digital photo of each side of a house. Assign a scale for the photograph (for example, 1 centimetre on the photograph equals 1 metre on the actual house). Have students use the photographs of the house and the scale to determine the perimeter of the house in metres and how many metres of lights are needed to decorate it.

Assessment Suggestions

- Observe students as they use centimetre rulers and metre sticks to measure perimeter (Activity Sheet B). Assess if students can accurately use standard units of measure to measure the perimeter of various objects. Record your results on the Individual Student Observations sheet, found on page 16.
- Observe students as they work together to measure perimeter (Activity Sheet B). Record your observations on the Cooperative Skills Teacher-Assessment sheet, found on page 20.
- After completing Activity Sheet B, have students complete copies of the Cooperative Skills Self-Assessment sheet, found on page 22, to reflect on their abilities to work together.

Date: ____________ **Name:** ____________

Measuring Perimeter

1.

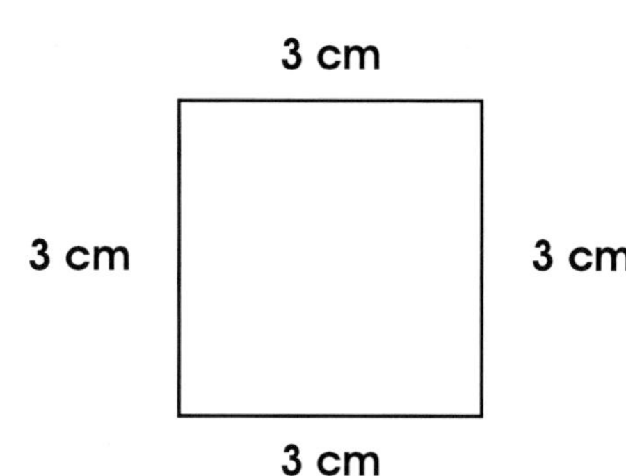

____

2.

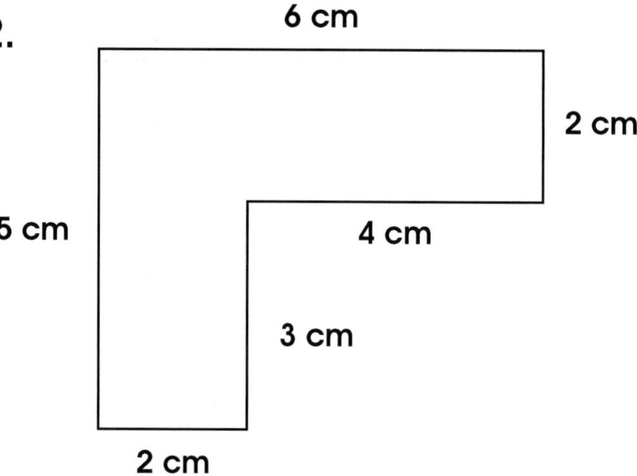

____

3.

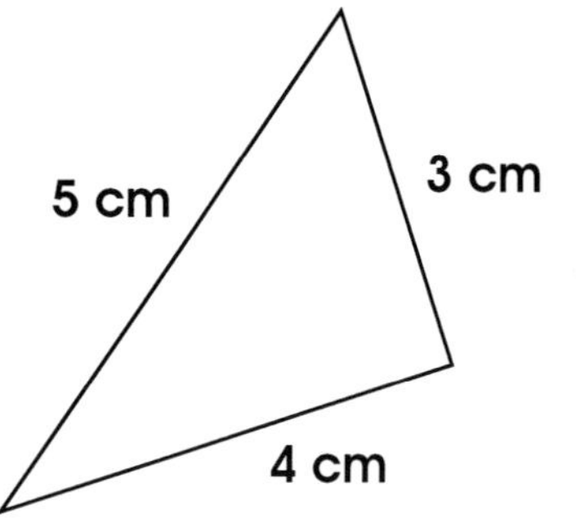

____

4.

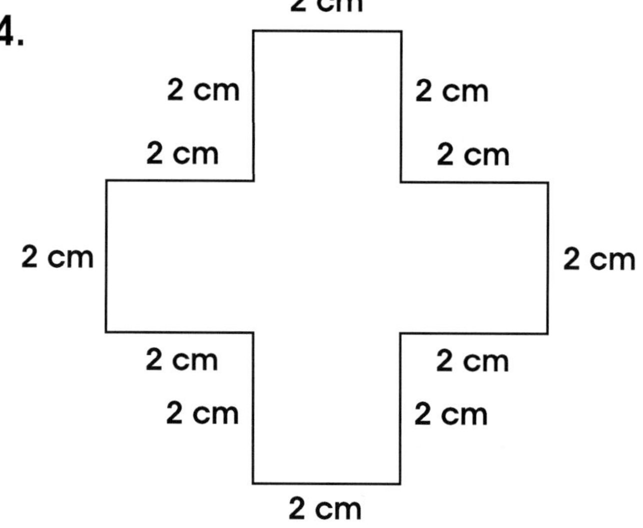

____

5.

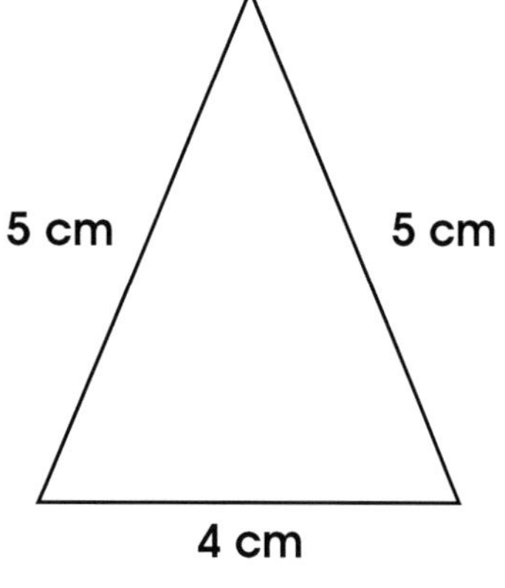

____

6.

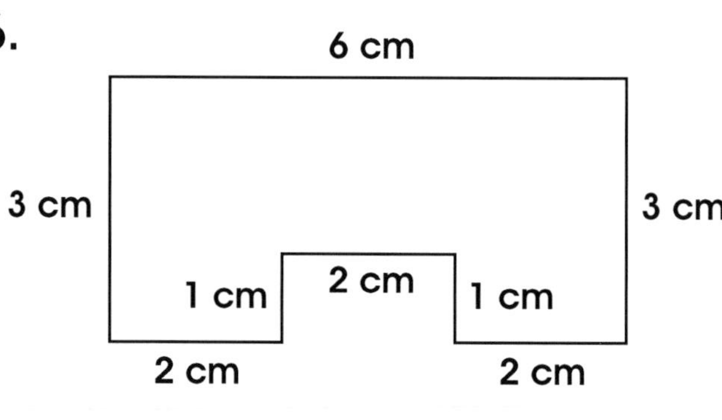

____

Date: ____________________ **Name:** ________________________________

7.

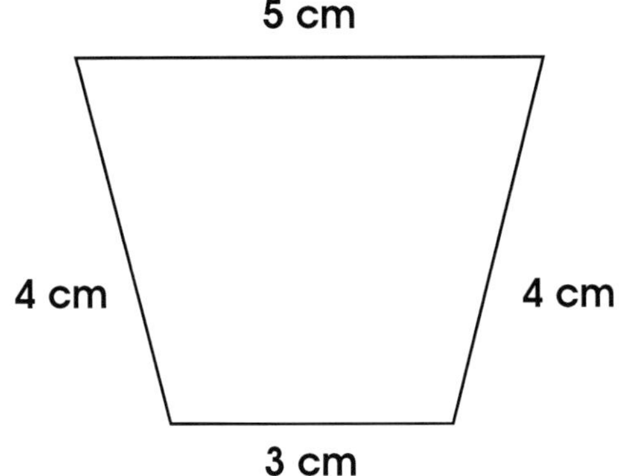

____

8.

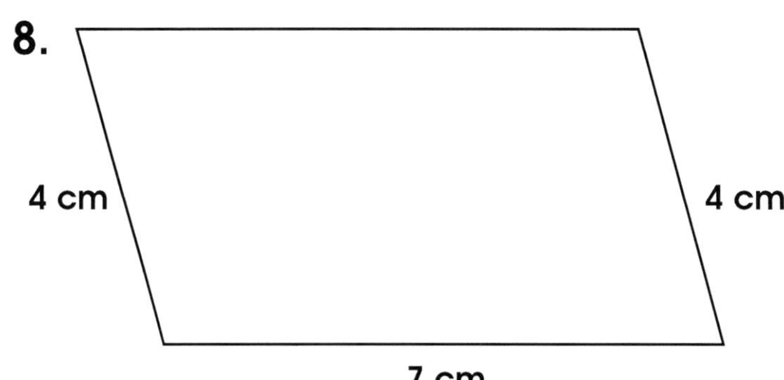

____

9.

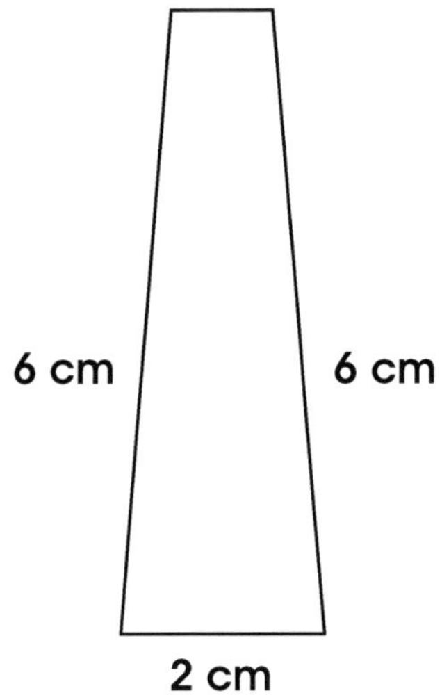

____

10.

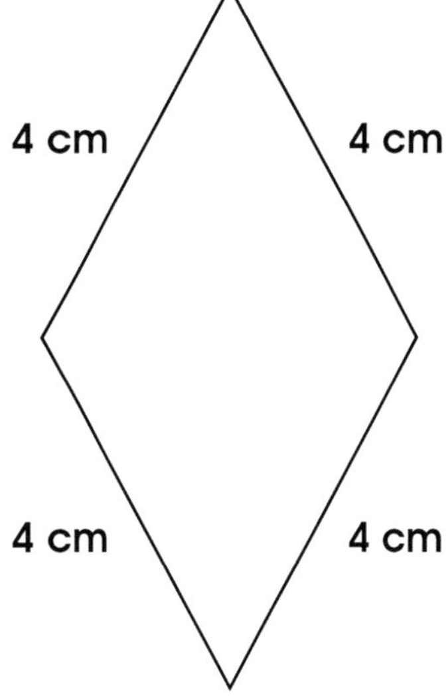

____

Date: ______________________ Name: ______________________

Perimeter Challenge

Item	Estimates			Measurements		
	Length	Width	Perimeter	Length	Width	Perimeter
Desktop						
Classroom						
Classroom Window						
Library Book						
Bulletin Board						
Painted Line around Outside of Gym Floor						

10 Exploring Two-Dimensional Shapes

Materials

- two-dimensional paper shape templates (included. Photocopy, and cut out. Consider mounting onto sturdy tagboard and laminating for future use.) (3.10.1)
- two-dimensional shape labels (included. Photocopy, and cut out. Consider mounting onto sturdy tagboard and laminating for future use.) (3.10.2)
- three Hula-Hoops or large string circles
- index cards
- scissors (one pair for each student)
- glue
- pattern blocks (one set for each student. You may also use pattern block paper shapes, included with the Patterns and Relations module, lesson 1. Photocopy each shape onto a different colour of construction paper, and cut out.) (1.1.1)
- paper
- pencils
- chart paper
- markers

Activity: Part One

Have students sit in a large circle, and place the two-dimensional paper shapes (3.10.1) in the centre. Ensure that each shape is visible to all students. Ask:

- What do all of these items have in common?

Now, place the corresponding shape labels (3.10.2) in the centre of the circle. Explain to students that they will work together to match each two-dimensional shape with its corresponding label. Select a student to find one shape and label match. Ask the student to hold up the shape and read aloud the corresponding label. Have all students repeat the name of the shape aloud, together. Then, ask students to name two characteristics about the shape. For example, a square has four straight sides and all of its sides are the same length. Repeat the process, having a different student find a shape and label match. Continue until all shapes and labels have been matched.

Distribute Activity Sheet A (3.10.3), scissors, and glue. Ask students to cut out all the two-dimensional shapes and labels. Have students match each shape with its corresponding label and glue each pair onto the activity sheet. Tell students to record two characteristics about each shape.

Activity Sheet A

Note: This is a three-page activity sheet.

Directions to students:

Cut out all the two-dimensional shapes and labels. Match each shape with its corresponding label, and glue each pair onto the activity sheet. Record two characteristics about each shape (3.10.3).

Activity: Part Two

Have students sit in a large circle, and review the names of the two-dimensional shapes looked at in Activity: Part One. Next, place two Hula-Hoops (or string circles) in the centre of the circle, and sort the two-dimensional shapes (3.10.1) in the following way:

- Hula Hoop 1: square, rectangle, triangle, rhombus, trapezoid, parallelogram
- Hula Hoop 2: circle, oval

Ask students:

- What is my sorting rule? (shapes with straight edges/shapes with no straight edges)

▶

Once students have determined the sorting rule, add a third Hula-Hoop, and resort the shapes in the following way:

- Hula Hoop 1: square, rectangle, rhombus, trapezoid, parallelogram
- Hula Hoop 2: triangle
- Hula Hoop 3: circle, oval

Ask students:

- What is my sorting rule? (shapes with four straight edges/shapes with three straight edges; shapes with no straight edges)

Distribute Activity Sheet B (3.10.4), and tell students they will now sort shapes according to their own sorting rules. Ask students to decide on a sorting rule for the shapes they see at the top of the activity sheet. Then, tell students to draw a Venn or a Carroll diagram in the space below and redraw the shapes in the appropriate places based on their sorting rule. Finally, have students describe their sorting rules in the space at the bottom of the sheet.

Activity Sheet B

Directions to students:

Decide on a sorting rule for the shapes at the top of the activity sheet. Draw a Venn or a Carroll diagram in the space below, and redraw the shapes in the appropriate places based on your sorting rule. Describe your sorting rule in the space at the bottom of the sheet (3.10.4).

Activity: Part Three

Divide the class into pairs of students, and provide each pair with a set of pattern blocks (or pattern-block paper shapes). Allow students a few moments to examine the blocks. Then, hold up one block (for example, a trapezoid), and ask:

- What can you tell me about this shape?
- How many sides does it have?
- What is this shape called?
- Could you make this shape by combining any of the other blocks? Which ones?

Repeat a similar line of questioning for each of the pattern blocks.

Tell students they will now work with their partners and use pattern blocks to cover figures. Hold up the first page of Activity Sheet C (3.10.5), and explain that students must use pattern blocks to cover the entire figure and then record how many of each type of block they used. Have students repeat the process for each of the other two figures. Consider encouraging students to find more than one way to cover each figure.

Activity Sheet C

Note: This is a three-page activity sheet.

Directions to students:

Use pattern blocks to cover the entire figure on the first page of the activity sheet. At the bottom of the sheet, record how many of each type of block you used to cover the figure. Repeat for each of the other two figures (3.10.5).

Problem Solving

Distribute pattern blocks, paper, and pencils to students, and have students use the blocks to create their own figures or pictures on the paper. Tell students to trace the outlines of their pictures onto the paper and record how many of each type of block they used. Then, have pairs of students exchange their pictures and try to cover each other's picture with pattern blocks.

Note: A reproducible master for this problem can be found on page 380.

10

Activity Centre

Place several sets of tangram pieces at a centre along with paper, pencils, and coloured pencils or markers. Encourage students to experiment freely with the tangram pieces. Then, have students use the tangram pieces to make creative designs, trace them onto paper, and then colour them. Consider also providing tangram figure outlines (similar to the figures from Activity Sheet C) for students to solve using tangram pieces.

Extensions

- Add the terms *circle, square, triangle, oval, rhombus, rectangle, trapezoid*, and *parallelogram* to your classroom Math Word Wall.

Note: You will need the memory game cards (templates included, 3.10.6) for the following extension activity. Photocopy, and cut out a set of shapes and shape names for each pair of students. Glue each shape and each shape name onto a separate index card. You may consider laminating the cards as well.

- Divide the class into pairs of students, and give each pair a set of 16 memory game cards. Have students shuffle the cards and then place them, facedown, onto the playing surface. Ask students to take turns turning over two cards and trying to find a match between a shape and its name. If a player finds a match, tell him/her to keep the cards and take another turn. When all the cards have been matched, the student with the most cards wins (3.10.6).
- Take students on a two-dimensional sign hunt through the community. Explain that many of the signs found on the roadsides are two-dimensional shapes with which they are familiar. Some of these include yield signs, stop signs, men-working signs, pedestrian-crossing signs, school-zone signs, and deer-crossing signs.
- Have students examine the washing-instruction symbols on clothing labels. Point out the various two-dimensional shapes used on the symbols.
- Discuss playing surfaces and equipment used in various indoor and outdoor sports and games. Many of these surfaces and pieces of equipment are examples of two-dimensional shapes. For example, a baseball diamond, home plate, a base; a curling rink, a curling rock; an ice-hockey rink; a tennis court; a hopscotch pattern, and so on.

Assessment Suggestion

Observe students as they sort the two-dimensional shapes (Activity Sheet B). Focus on students' abilities to sort their shapes based on two (or more) attributes, as well as their abilities to communicate their sorting rules. Use the Anecdotal Record sheet, found on page 15, to record your results.

Two-Dimensional Paper Shape Templates

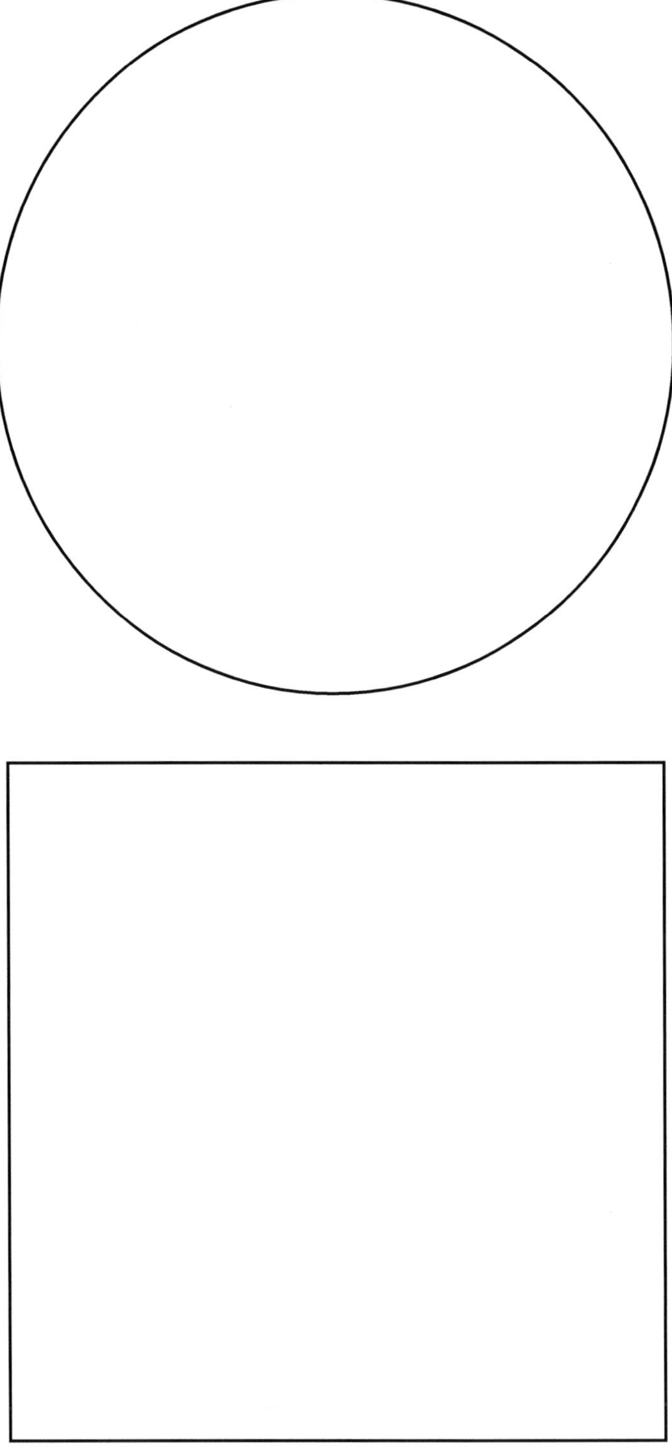

Two-Dimensional Paper Shape Templates

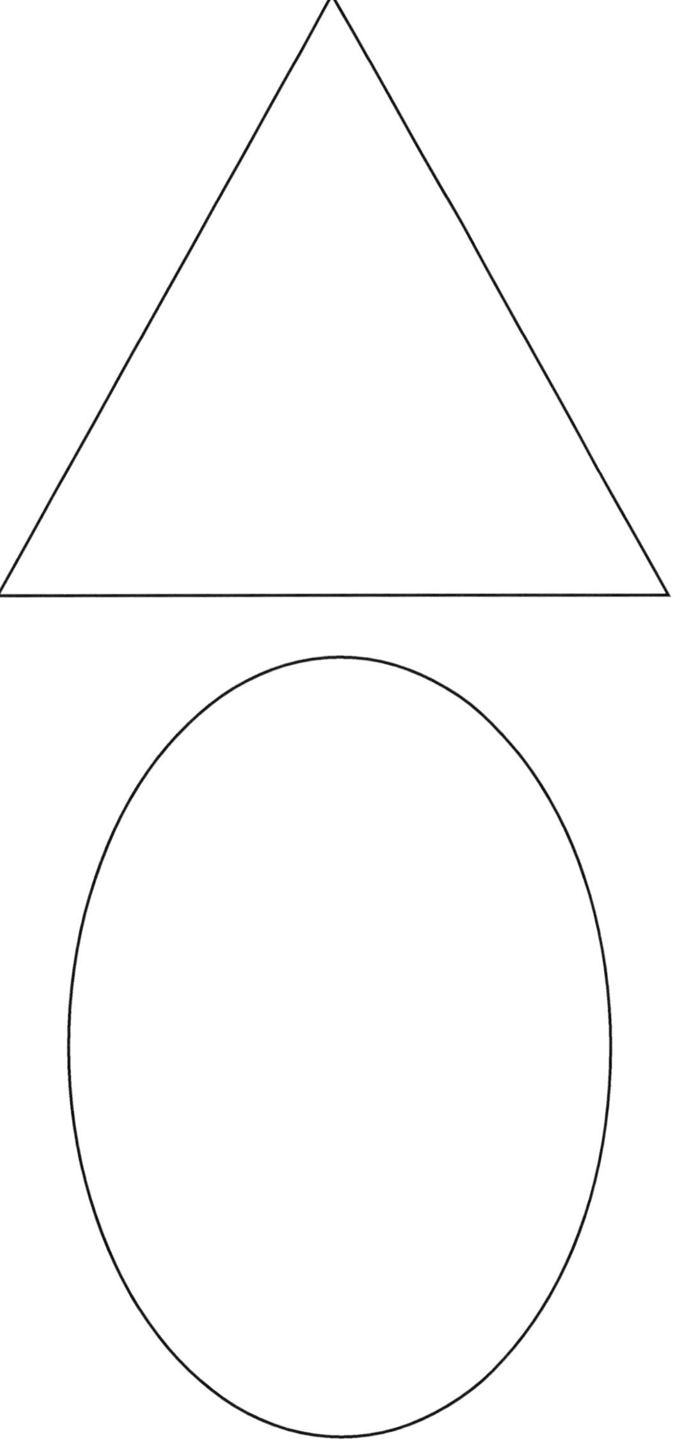

Two-Dimensional Paper Shape Templates

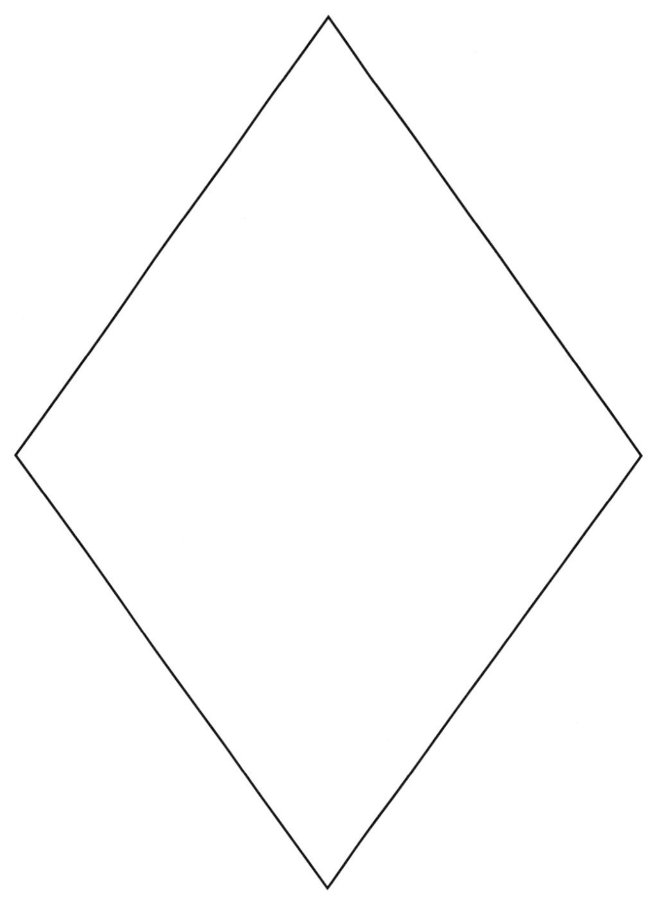

Two-Dimensional Paper Shape Templates

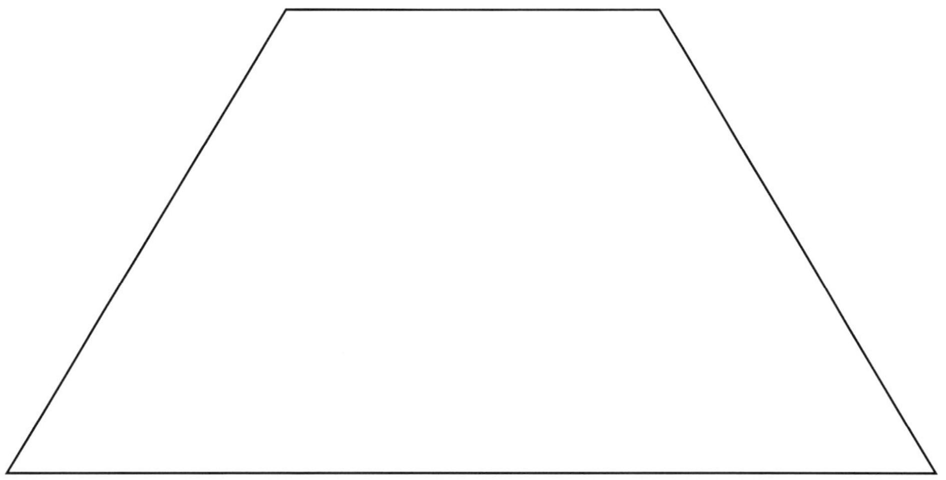

Two-Dimensional Shape Labels

Circle
Square
Triangle
Oval

Two-Dimensional Shape Labels

Rhombus
Rectangle
Trapezoid
Parallelogram

Date: ______________ Name: ______________________

Naming and Describing Two-Dimensional Shapes

Date: ____________________ **Name:** ________________________________

Two-Dimensional Shapes

Parallelogram	Oval	Circle	Trapezoid
Square	Rhombus	Rectangle	Triangle

Date: ____________ Name: ____________

Sorting Two-Dimensional Shapes

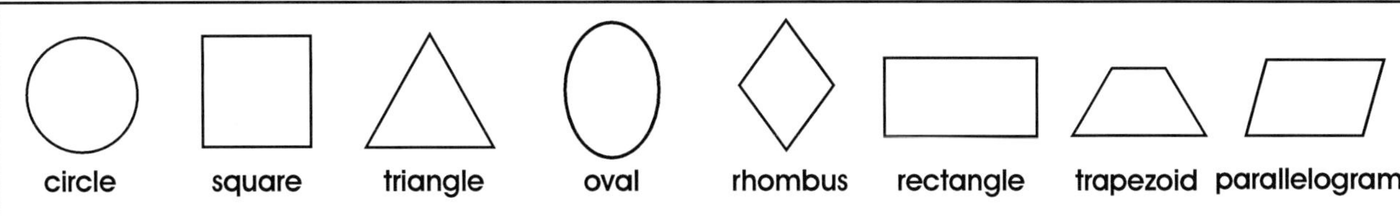

Sorting Diagram

My sorting rule:

____

____

Date: ____________ Name: ____________

Pattern Block Puzzle

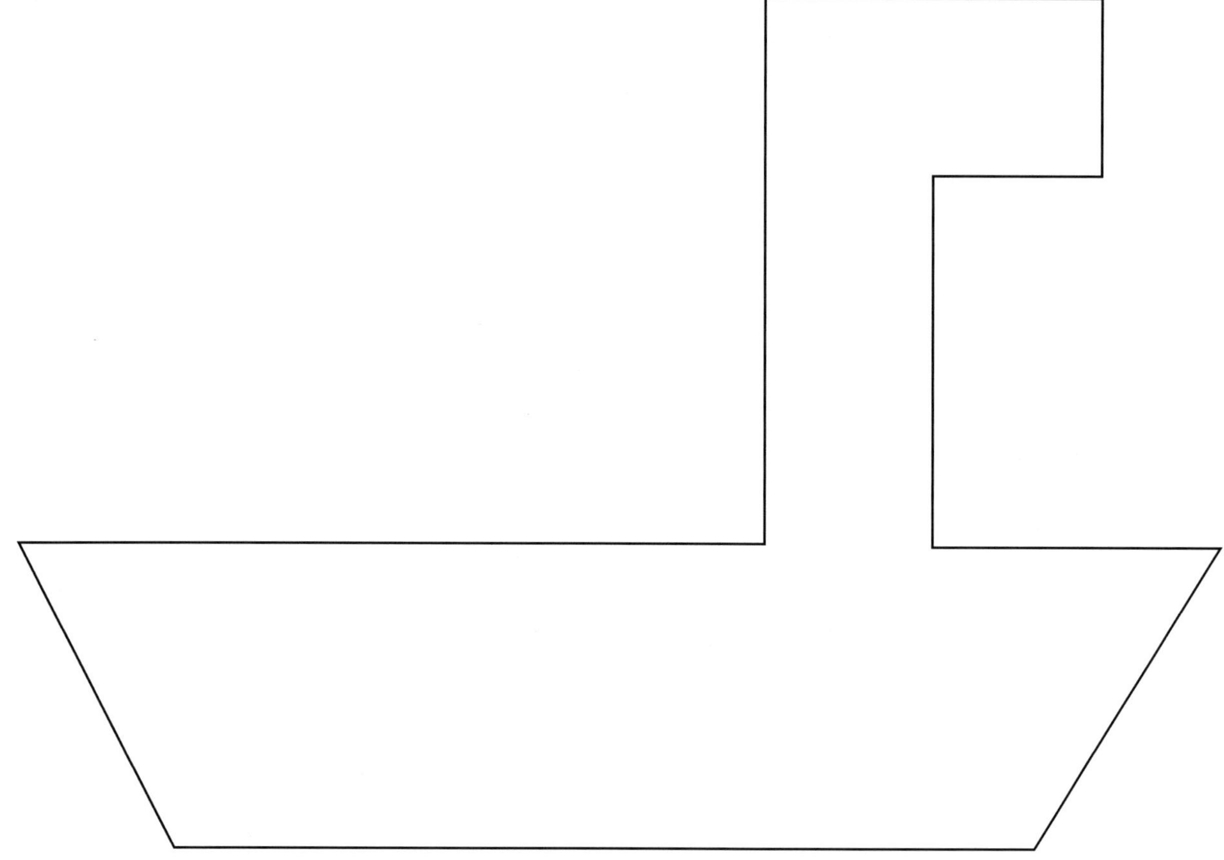

I used ____________ ____________

number name of shape

I used ____________ ____________

I used ____________ ____________

I used ____________ ____________

I used ____________ ____________

I used ____________ ____________

Date: ____________________ **Name:** ________________________________

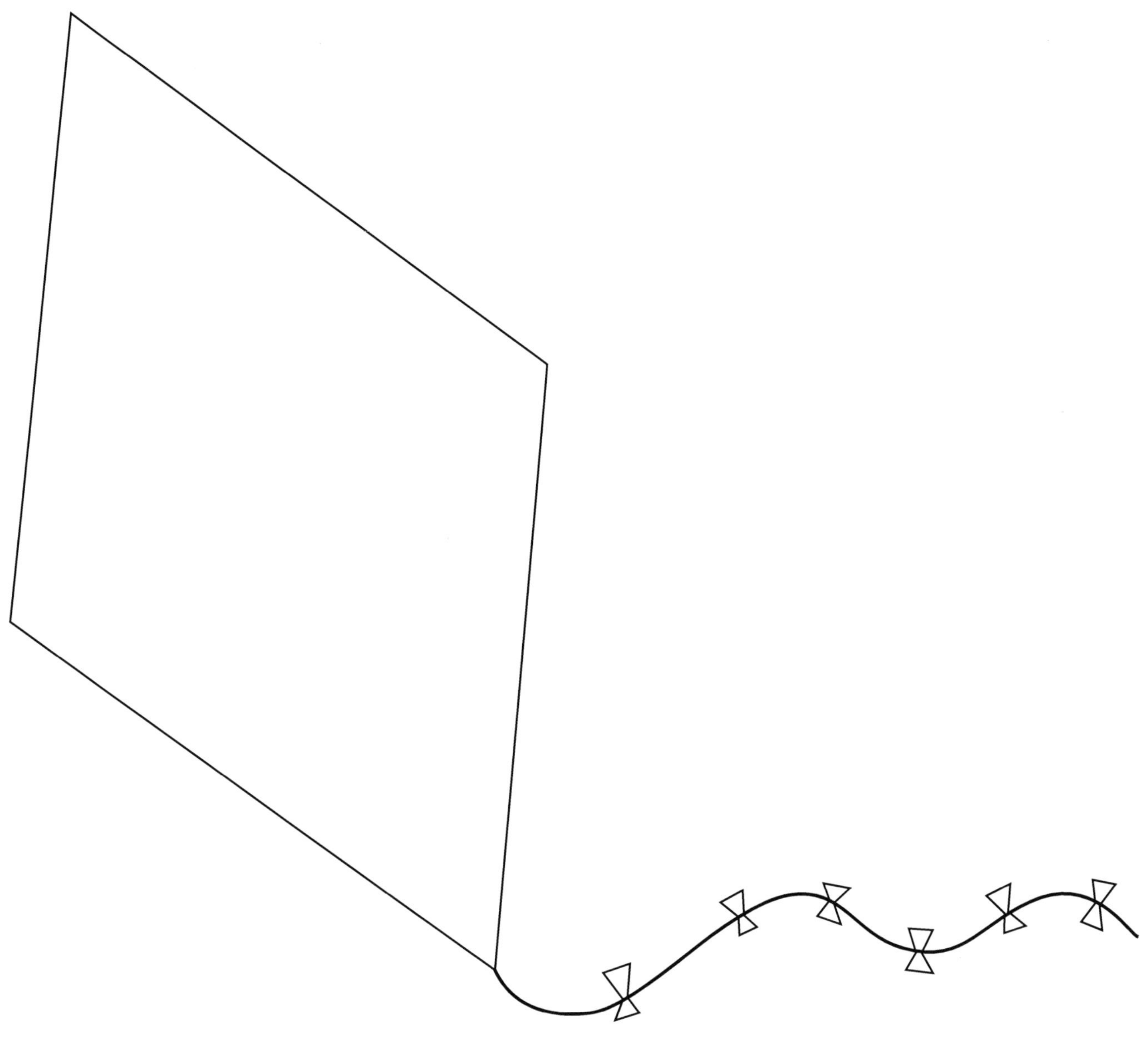

I used ______________ ____

number name of shape

I used ______________ ____

I used ______________ ____

I used ______________ ____

I used ______________ ____

I used ______________ ____

Date: ____________________ **Name:** ________________________________

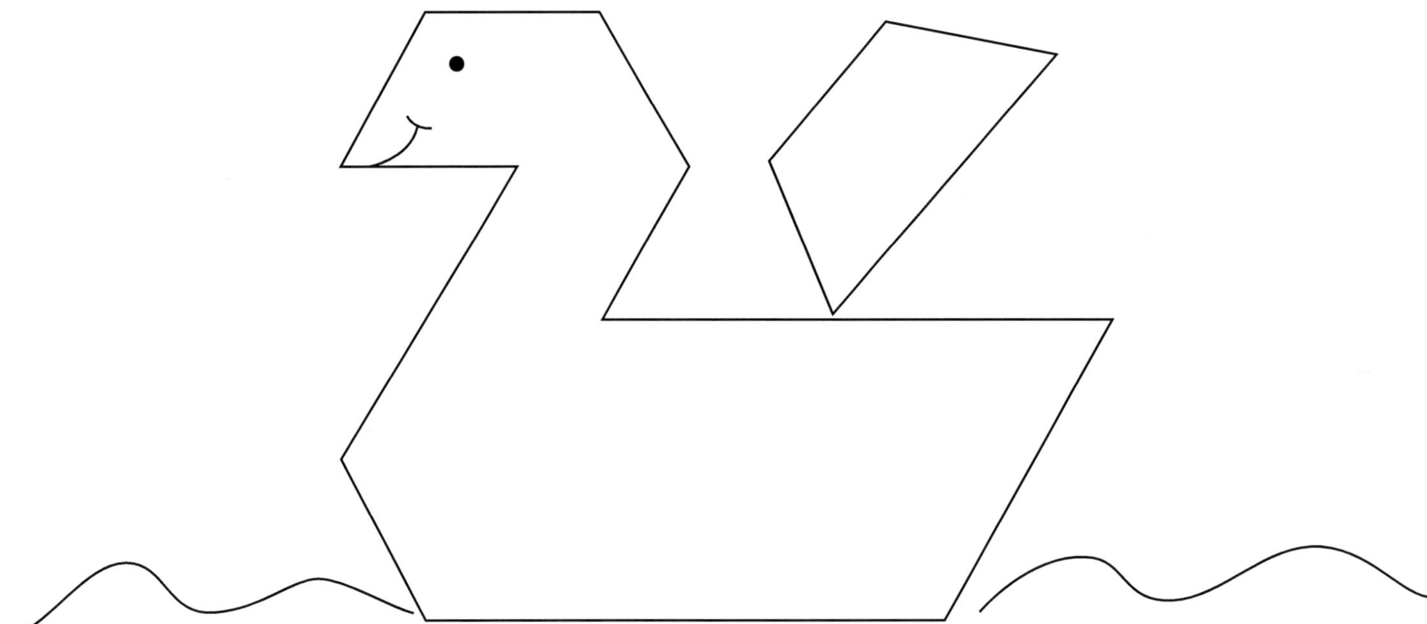

I used ______________ ____

number name of shape

I used ______________ ____

I used ______________ ____

I used ______________ ____

I used ______________ ____

I used ______________ ____

Memory Game Card Templates – Shapes

Memory Game Card Templates – Shape Names

Circle	Square
Rhombus	Triangle
Oval	Trapezoid
Rectangle	Parallelogram

11 Regular and Irregular Polygons

Background Information for Teachers

In this lesson students are introduced to the following polygons: triangle, quadrilateral, pentagon, hexagon, and octagon. These polygons are three- to eight-sided figures, respectively.

Note that on a *regular polygon*, all sides and all interior angles are equal. An *irregular polygon* is any polygon whose sides are not all the same length and/or whose interior angles do not all have the same measure.

Materials

- regular polygons (included. Photocopy, and cut out two of each shape). (3.11.1)
- pocket chart
- chart paper
- markers
- irregular polygons (included. Photocopy, and cut out two of each figure.) (3.11.2)
- scissors
- glue
- pattern blocks (one set for each student)
- geoboards (one for each student)
- elastic bands
- dot paper (included, 3.11.3)
- pencils

Activity: Part One

Have students sit in a circle on the floor. In the pocket chart, display one set of regular polygons (3.11.1). As a class, discuss each shape, identifying it by its name and features.

On chart paper, record the term *polygon*. Explain to students that the shapes they just looked at are all polygons. Ask:

- What do all the shapes have in common?

Explain that a polygon is a closed shape made up of straight lines.

Spread out the second set of regular polygons on the floor in the centre of the circle. Select a student volunteer to choose a shape from the second set, and hold it up for the class to see. Ask students:

- Can you find a polygon in the pocket chart that is exactly the same as this one?

Emphasize that the matching polygons must be the same size so that one shape fits exactly on top of the other shape.

Repeat this activity several times. As students find matching polygons, have them confirm the match by placing one shape on top of the other.

Activity: Part Two

Display one set of regular polygons in the pocket chart, and have students identify each one by name. Then, place the irregular polygons into a separate pocket of the chart. Ask:

- How are the two sets of shapes different?
- How are the two sets of shapes the same? (they both have sides and corners)
- Can you sort the two sets of polygons by number of sides?

As a class, first sort the regular polygons, and then the irregular polygons by number of sides. Then, put the sets of regular and irregular polygons together, mix them up, and sort them all by number of sides.

Distribute scissors, glue, and Activity Sheet A (3.11.4), and have students carefully cut out all the figures. Tell students to sort the figures by the number of sides, and glue them onto the chart.

Activity Sheet A

Note: This is a two-page activity sheet.

Directions to students

Carefully cut out all the figures. Sort the figures by the number of sides, and glue them onto the chart (3.11.4).

Problem Solving

Divide the class into groups of four students. Provide each student with a geoboard, three elastic bands, a piece of dot paper (3.11.3), and a pencil. Ask students to use their elastic bands to make one triangle, one rectangle, and one pentagon on their geoboards. Then, have students use pencils to copy each of their shapes onto the isometric-dot paper.

Next, have students exchange their dot-paper sheets with another member of their group. Ask students to study the triangle on the dot paper in front of them for about 15 seconds. Then, tell students to turn the dot paper facedown and, from memory, recreate on their geoboard a triangle that is congruent to the one on the dot paper. Have students check the dot-paper picture to see if the two triangles are, in fact, congruent. Repeat the activity for the remaining two shapes. For even more practice, have students exchange their dot-paper shapes with a second and even a third student from their group. Continue this activity with various regular and irregular polygons.

Extensions

- Add the terms *polygon, pentagon, hexagon,* and *octagon* to your classroom math word wall.

Polygons

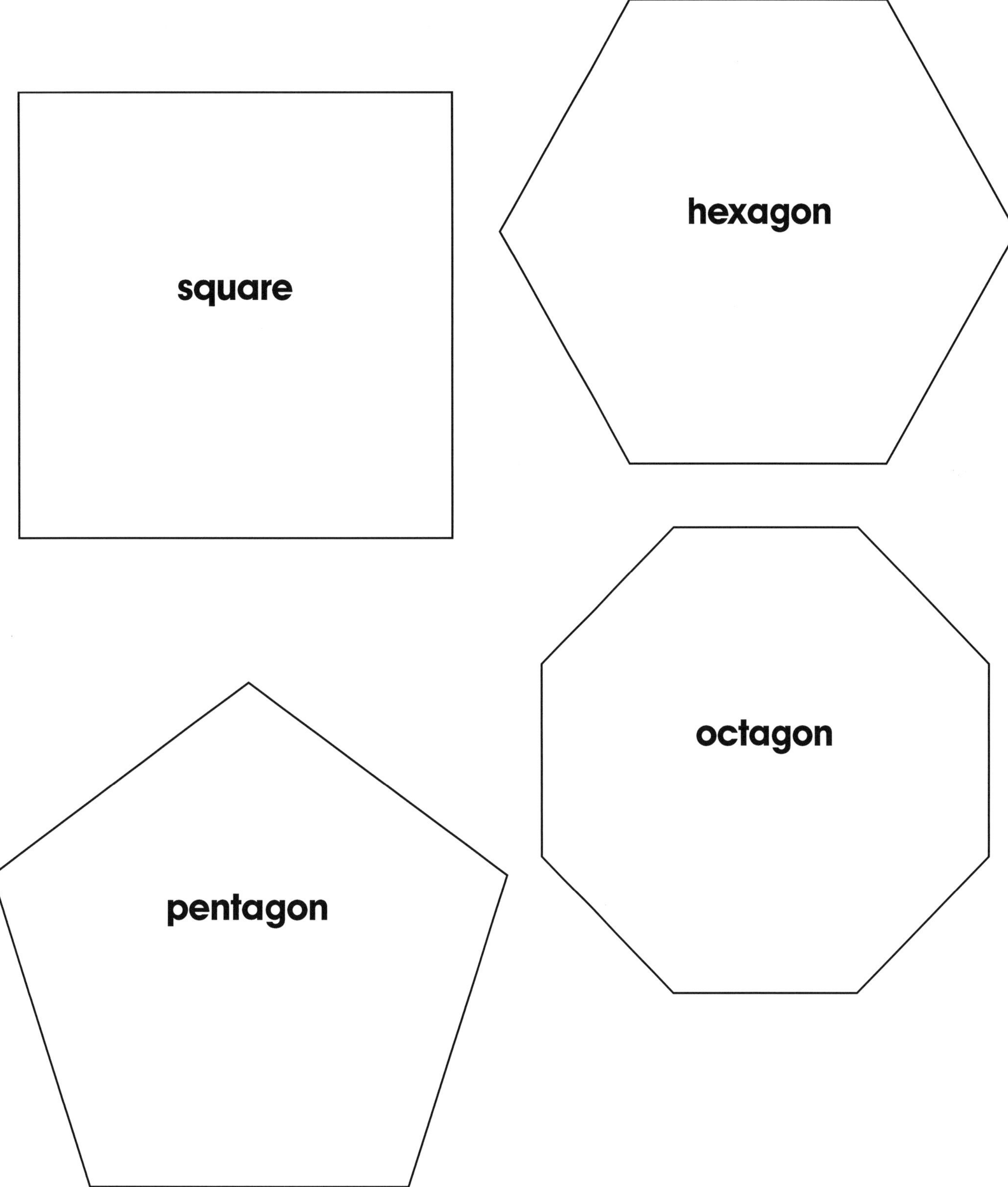

Irregular Polygons

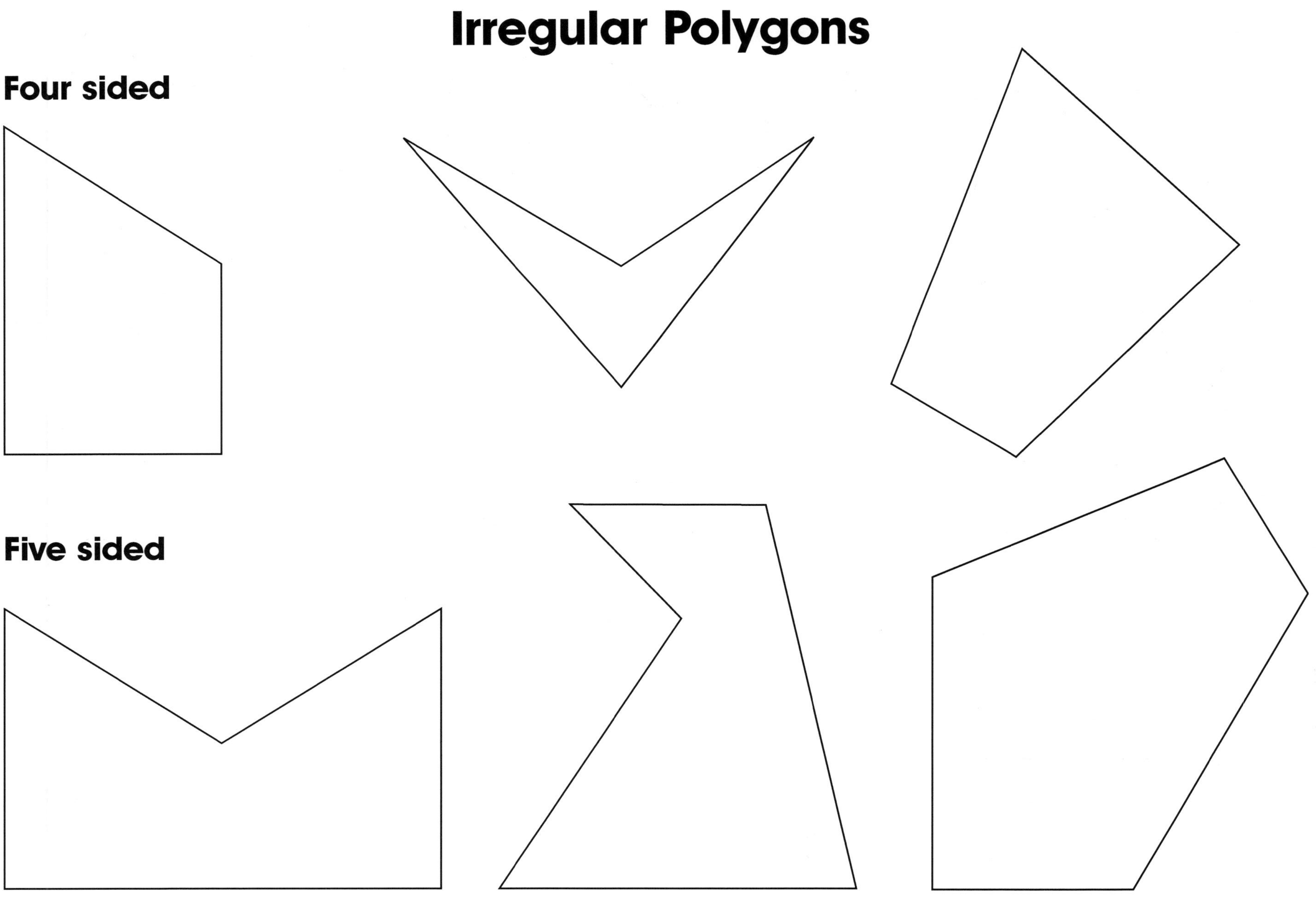

Irregular Polygons

Six sided

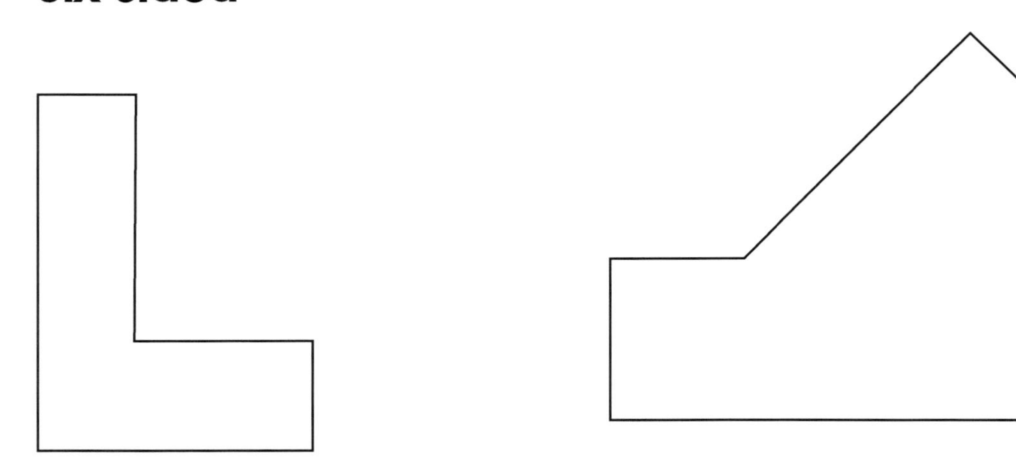

Eight sided

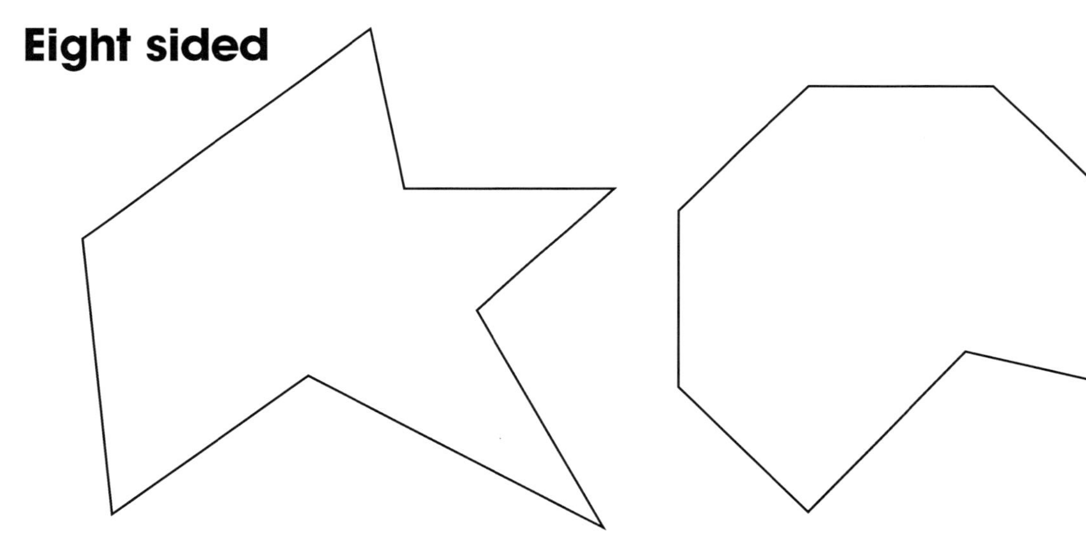

Dot Paper

Date: ____________________ Name: ____________________

Sorting Polygons

4 sides	5 sides	6 sides	8 sides

Regular and Irregular Polygons

12 Identifying the Faces of Geometric Solids (Three-Dimensional Objects)

Background Information for Teachers

In this lesson, students review and/or are introduced to a variety of geometric solids including the sphere, the cylinder, the cone, the cube, the rectangular prism, the triangular prism, the triangle-based pyramid, and the square-based pyramid.

Materials

- two-dimensional shapes (one set, included with lesson 10) (3.10.1)
- pocket chart
- geometric solids (spheres, cylinders, cones, cubes, prisms, pyramids)
- drawing paper
- pencils
- number cubes (you will need one six-sided number cube for each student as well as some other multi-faced number cubes)
- chart paper
- markers
- sorting labels for prisms and pyramids (included. Photocopy, mount onto sturdy tagboard, and cut out.) (3.12.1)

Activity: Part One

Begin the activity by reviewing the names of two-dimensional shapes. In the pocket chart, display the two-dimensional shapes. Point to one of the shapes, and ask:

- What is the name of this two-dimensional shape?
- What makes this shape different from the other two-dimensional shapes?

Repeat the questions for each shape. Then, ask:

- How is a square different from a rectangle?
- How is a pentagon different from a hexagon?
- How is a triangle different from rectangle?

Now, display the geometric solids. Pass them around among students, and allow students time to examine and manipulate each solid. Have students identify any solid with which they are familiar. Ask:

- How are these geometric solids different from the two-dimensional shapes in the pocket chart?
- Do you notice any similarities between the solids and the shapes?
- Can you find some of the shapes on the solids?

Review with students that on a geometric solid, a flat surface is called a *face*. Display one of the geometric solids (other than the sphere), and ask:

- How many faces does this geometric solid have?
- Can you describe the shape of each face? (it is a two-dimensional shape: a circle/square/rectangle/triangle)

Repeat for each of the geometric solids (except the sphere).

Divide the class into working groups, and provide each group with several geometric solids, drawing paper, and pencils. Have students trace the face(s) of each solid onto the paper and record the name of the two-dimensional shape they traced.

Activity: Part Two

Provide each student with a six-sided number cube. Have students examine and describe their cubes. Ask:

- How many different numbers are shown (or represented by dots) on your cube? (six)
- What do we call each flat area that has a number (or dots) on it? (a face)
- How many faces does your number cube have?

Review that each face of the number cube has a number assigned to it. There are six faces, and, therefore, six numbers, on (or represented on) each number cube.

Display several other multi-faced number cubes. Discuss how the numbers on each cube reflect the number of faces the cube has. A 10-sided number cube has the numbers 1 through 10 on its faces.

Activity: Part Three

Display the geometric solids for students to examine and describe. Discuss the similarities and differences between the solids, focusing on each solid's shape and face(s). On chart paper, record the name of each solid along with the shape(s) of its face(s). Also, record how many faces the solid has. For example:

Solid	Face(s)	Number of Faces
cone	circle	1
cube	squares	6
sphere	–	0
cylinder	circles	2

Students may find it more difficult to identify three-dimensional solids such as prisms and pyramids due to the complexity of their shape and faces. Be sure to spend adequate time focusing on these solids.

Have students sit in a large circle. Place a triangular prism, a rectangular prism, a triangle-based pyramid, and a square-based pyramid in the middle of the circle. Discuss various ways of sorting the geometric solids (for example, prism/pyramid; triangular faces/no triangular faces; rectangular bases/no rectangular bases, and so on). Sort the solids several times based on suggestions from students.

One at a time, hold up each of the four sorting labels for prisms and pyramids (3.12.1), and read the label. Spread out the labels in the middle of the circle. Ask:

- Who can match one of the geometric solids to its label?

Select a student to match a solid and a label. After a correct match has been made, ask:

- How did you know that this geometric solid is a _________ (pyramid/prism)?
- What do all _________ (pyramids/prisms) have in common? How are they all the same? (all pyramids come to a vertex/point at the top; all prisms consist only of faces and do not come to a vertex)

Select another student to match a different geometric solid with its label. Ask:

- How did you know that this geometric solid is a _________ (pyramid/prism)?
- How can we tell the difference between a pyramid and a prism? (a pyramid comes to a vertex at the top; a prism consists only of faces and does not come to a vertex at the top)

Select two students to make the last two matches.

Explain to students that they can differentiate between a triangle-based pyramid and a square-based pyramid by looking at the solid's base. Hold up the triangle-based pyramid, and ask:

- What is the shape of the base on this geometric solid? (triangle)

Say:

- Since the base of this solid is a triangle and all of its edges come to a point (vertex) at the top, this shape is called the triangle-based pyramid.

Hold up the square-based pyramid. Ask:

- What is the shape of the base on this geometric solid? (square)

Say:

- Since the base of this solid is a square and all of its edges come to a point at the top, this shape is called the square-based pyramid.

Finally, hold up the triangular prism and the rectangular prism. Tell students that they can differentiate between these two prisms by looking at the solid's faces: a triangular prism has both triangular faces and rectangular faces while a rectangular prism has only rectangular faces.

Distribute Activity Sheet A (3.12.2), and have students record the number and shape of faces for each solid.

Activity Sheet A

Directions to students:

For each solid, record the number and shape of its faces (3.12.2).

Problem Solving

Read each of the following riddles, and have students identify the geometric solid described in each one.

- I have six square faces. What geometric solid am I? (cube)
- I have five faces. My base is a square. I have four triangular faces. What geometric solid am I? (square-based pyramid)
- I have two faces that are circles. I have two edges but no vertices. I have one curved surface. What geometric solid am I? (cylinder)

Note: Reproducible masters for these problems can be found on page 380.

Consider creating more of your own riddles, or challenge students to create their own.

Extensions

- As they are introduced, add the names of the geometric solids to your classroom math word wall.
- Introduce the pentagonal prism, the hexagonal prism and the pentagon-based pyramid. Discuss how these prisms and pyramids get their names by the shape of their bases.

Sorting Labels for Prisms and Pyramids

triangular prism 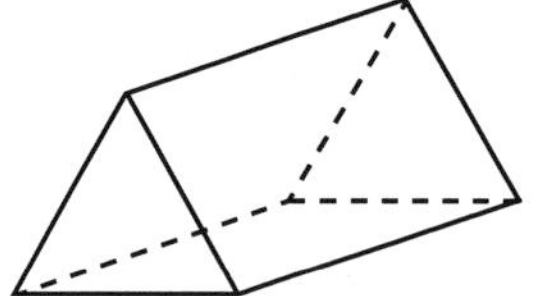
rectangular prism 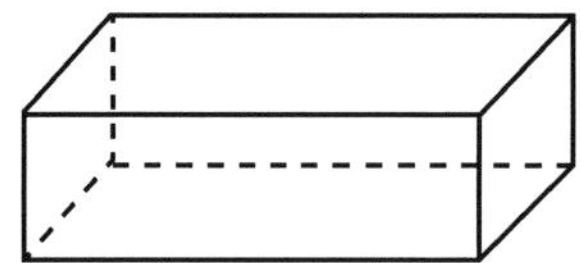
triangle-based pyramid 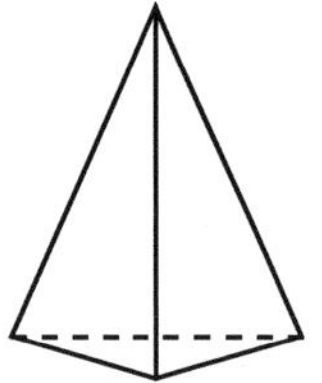
square-based pyramid 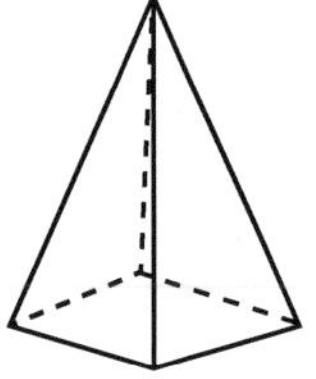

Date: ____________________ Name: ________________________________

Three-Dimensional Solids and Two-Dimensional Faces

Solid	Number and Shape of Faces
Sphere	
Cylinder	
Cone	
Cube	
Rectangular Prism	
Triangular Prism	
Triangle-based Pyramid	
Square-based Pyramid	

13 Identifying, Comparing, and Contrasting Geometric Solids

Background Information for Teachers

In this lesson, students review characteristics of the sphere, the cylinder, the cone, the cube, the prism, and the pyramid. Students also describe features of these geometric solids, including:

- face: flat planes or surfaces on a solid. A cube has six faces.
- base: the face that is supporting a solid
- edge: the line where two faces on a solid meet. A cube has 12 edges.
- vertex: the point where the edges/lines of a solid meet. A cube has eight vertices.

Materials

- geometric solids (spheres, cylinders, cones, cubes, prisms, pyramids)
- "feely bag" (any bag that is not transparent. For example, a pillowcase.)
- chart paper
- markers
- scrap paper

Activity: Part One

Divide the class into pairs or groups of three, and distribute two different geometric solids to each group. Begin by asking students to run a finger along the edge of their table or desk. Ask:

- Do you have a geometric solid with an edge like the edge on your desk/table?
- How many edges does your geometric solid have?

Now, have students find a vertex (corner point) on their desk/table. Review with students that the point where two or more edges meet is called the *vertex*. The plural of vertex is *vertices*.

Ask:

- Do you have a geometric solid with a vertex?
- Do you have a solid with more than one vertex?
- How many vertices does your solid have?

Have students run a hand over the top of their desk/table top. Remind students that on a geometric solid, a flat surface like the top of their desk/table is called a *face*. Ask:

- How many faces does your geometric solid have?

Tell students they will now determine the number of faces, vertices, and edges for each of the different geometric solids. Distribute a copy of Activity Sheet A (3.13.1) to each student, and place the geometric solids in different locations throughout the classroom. Have students rotate in their pairs/groups to each solid and use the solids as reference for completing the chart. Encourage students to touch the solids in order to help them determine the number of faces, vertices, and edges.

Activity Sheet A

Directions to students:

Use geometric solids to help you determine the number of faces, edges, and vertices for each solid shown on the chart. Record your responses on the chart. Also, draw pictures of the face shape(s) for each geometric solid (3.13.1).

When students have completed their activity sheets, have each pair/group compare their results with another pair/group. If there are any discrepancies, ask students to revisit the models of the geometric solids in question and recount the edges, faces, and vertices.

Activity: Part Two

Have students sit in a large circle, and place the geometric solids in the centre. Hold up the geometric solids, one at a time, and have students identify each one.

Put all the geometric solids into a feely bag. Select a student to reach into the bag and pull out two solids. Place the two solids in the middle of the circle, and ask:

- What are the names of these two solids?
- In what ways are these two solids the same?
- In what ways are these two solids different?

Return the solids to the bag. Repeat the process until several solids have been compared.

As a class, brainstorm a list of ways solids can be compared. Record the list on chart paper. For example:

- number of faces
- number of vertices
- number of edges
- shape of face(s)
- congruent face(s)/no congruent face(s)

Explain to students that they will now revisit their activity sheets (Activity Sheet A), compare different geometric solids, and list how various pairs of solids are the same/different. Distribute students' completed activity sheets and scrap paper, and encourage students to use the list created on chart paper to help them compare and contrast the solids.

Note: Remind students how to recognize prisms and pyramids, which can be especially challenging for students. For example, ask questions such as:

- How is a prism different from a pyramid?
- How can we tell the difference between a square-based pyramid and a triangle-based pyramid?

Problem Solving

Place three solids in front of students, and have students explain which solid does not belong with the other two and why.

Note: There are several ways to solve each problem. Encourage students to support their answers. A reproducible variation of this problem can be found on page 381.

Extensions

- Add the terms *face, base, edge*, and *vertex* (*vertices*) to your classroom math word wall.
- Have students go on a geometric solid scavenger hunt in the classroom. Ask students to find objects that have the same shape as the geometric solids introduced.
- Have students sit in a large circle, and place the geometric solids in the middle of the circle. Review the name of each geometric solid with students. Now, ask students to close their eyes. Remove one of the geometric solids, and hide it behind your back. Have students open their eyes and see if they can name the missing shape. Repeat the activity several times, hiding a different solid each time.
- Sort geometric solids into two groups (for example, solids that stack/solids that do not stack; solids that roll/solids that do not roll). Have students determine your sorting rule. Once students are comfortable with the activity, divide the class into pairs of students, and have one student in each pair do the sorting and the other determine the sorting rule.

13

Assessment Suggestions

- As students complete Activity Sheet A (3.13.1), observe their abilities to work productively in pairs/groups. Use the Cooperative Skills Teacher-Assessment sheet, found on page 20, to record your results.
- Have students complete a Cooperative Skills Self-Assessment sheet, found on page 22, to reflect on their abilities to work together with their classmates.

Date: ____________________ Name: ________________________________

Characteristics of Geometric Solids

Geometric Solid	Number of Faces	Picture(s) of Face Shape(s)	Number of Edges	Number of Vertices
Cube				
Rectangular Prism				
Sphere				
Cylinder				
Triangular Prism				
Cone				
Triangle-Based Pyramid				
Square-Based Pyramid				

14 Investigating Nets

Materials

- flattened cereal or cracker box (take box apart by cutting along several seams, but keep it in one piece. Flatten the box to form a net.)
- scissors
- tape
- rectangular prism net templates (1, 2, and 3, included. Photocopy all three sheets for each student.) (3.14.1)
- geometric solids
- experience chart paper or squared paper (squares should be at least four centimetres)

Activity

Display the flattened, cardboard box for students to see. Ask:

- What can you tell me about this object? (it is a box, it once held food, it has been folded down)
- What different shapes were used to create this box?

Explain to students that when a box like this one is broken down flat, it is called a net. A net is a pattern or outline used to make a three-dimensional object like a box. It shows all the faces of the three-dimensional object. Ask students:

- How many faces does this box have?
- Can you name the different faces? (for example, square, rectangle)
- If I put this box back together, what type of three-dimensional object would it be? (rectangular prism)

Use tape to put the box back together.

Distribute to each student copies of the three rectangular prism net templates (3.14.1) as well as a copy of Activity Sheet A (3.14.2). Have students examine the nets closely and then draw diagrams of them on their activity sheets. Ask:

- Are the three nets the same?
- What can you tell me about the faces of each net?
- What type of three-dimensional model (object) do you think the first net will make? The second net? The third net?

Distribute scissors and tape, and ask students to cut out each net and use it to create a three-dimensional model. Have students complete their activity sheets.

Activity Sheet A

Directions to students:

Draw a picture of each net. Answer the first two questions at the bottom of the page. Cut out each net, and build the three-dimensional model. Answer the third question (3.14.2).

When all students have finished making their three-dimensional models and have completed their activity sheets, ask:

- What can you tell me about the models you created? (they are all rectangular prisms)
- Were the three nets you used to create the three models the same? (no)
- Did each net have the same number of faces? (yes)
- Did each net have faces of the same shape? (yes)
- What does this activity show you? (a rectangular solid can have more than one net)

14

Problem Solving

Challenge students to find several different ways of arranging six squares so they can be folded into a cube. Have students draw their nets on experience chart paper or squared paper, cut them out, and fold them into cubes.

Note: A reproducible master for this problem can be found on page 381.

Activity Centre

Have students use net templates of triangular prisms, cubes, triangle-based pyramids, and square-based pyramids (included) as well as scissors and tape to construct three-dimensional models. Then, have students use straws and Plasticine, toothpicks and mini marshmallows, or pipe cleaners, to create replicas of their models (3.14.3-3.14.6).

Extensions

- Add the term *net* to your classroom math word wall.
- Have students use cardboard and their own net designs to construct gift boxes without lids (five faces) or with lids (six faces).
- Invite a guest speaker from a cardboard box company into your classroom. Ask the guest to bring in a variety of box samples and explain how nets are developed and how they are changed into useable, three-dimensional boxes.

Assessment Suggestions

- Have students complete Student Self-Assessment sheets, found on page 21, to reflect on their learning about nets and three-dimensional objects.
- Take photographs of students as they build their three-dimensional models from the nets. Have students document their experience on Portfolio Entry Record sheets, found on page 25, and include the sheets as well as the photos in their math portfolios.

Rectangular Prism Net Template 1

Rectangular Prism Net Template 2

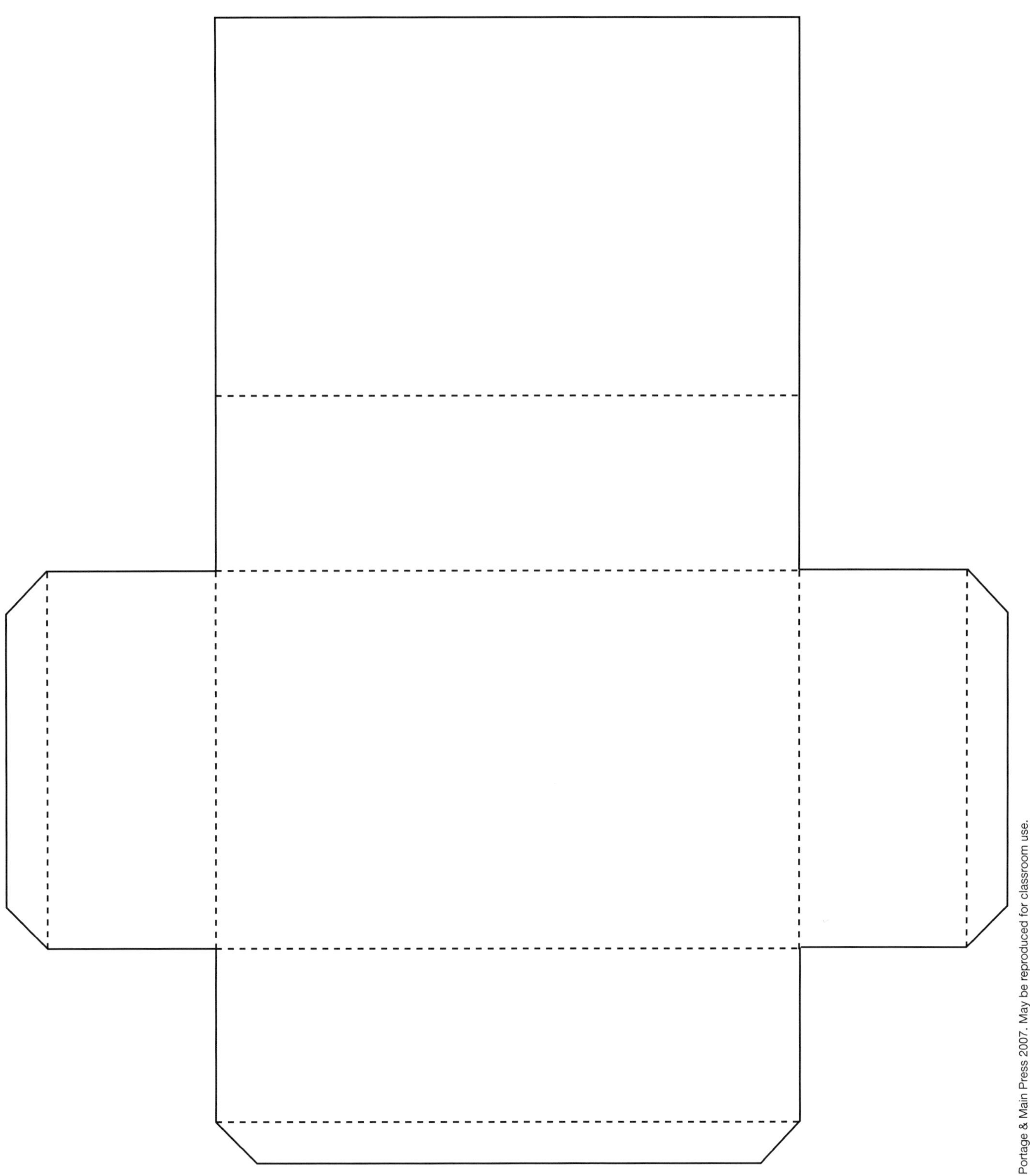

Rectangular Prism Net Template 3

Date: ______________________ Name: ______________________

A Closer Look at Nets

Net 1	Net 2	Net 3

How are the three nets the same? ______________________

How are the three nets different? ______________________

Describe the steps involved in using a net to make a model. ______________________

____

____

14A

Triangular Prism Net Template

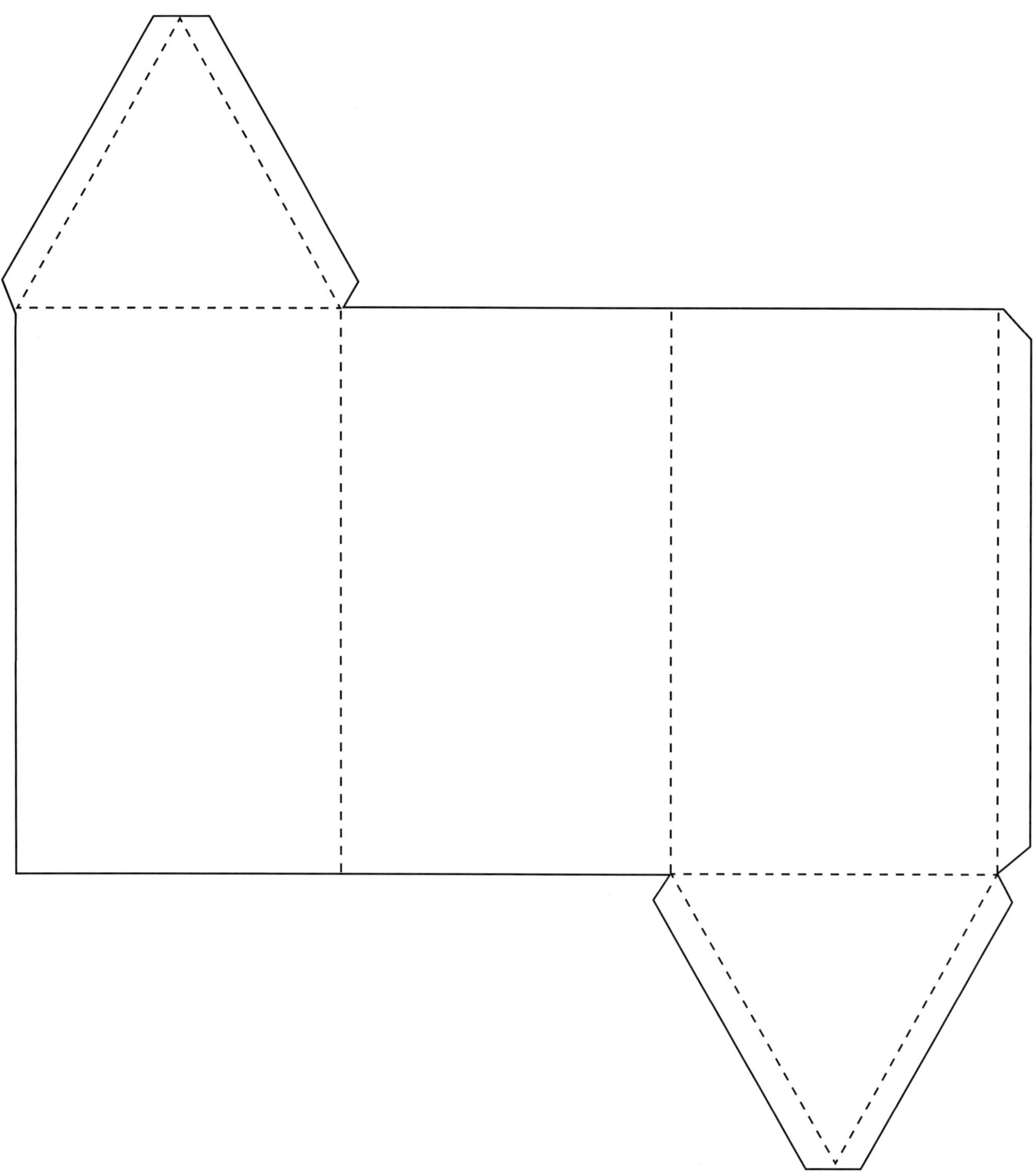

Cube Net Template

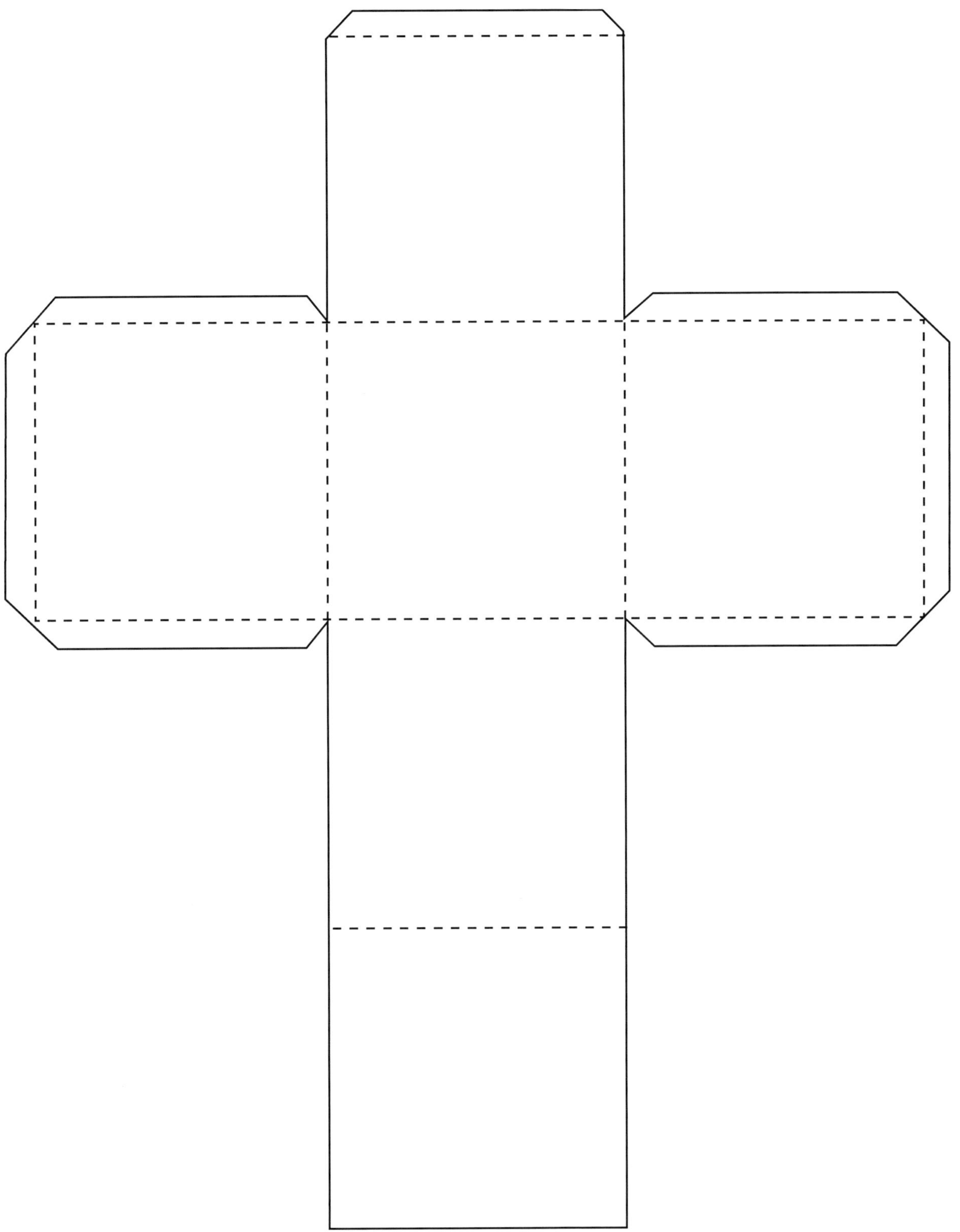

Triangle-Based Pyramid Net Template

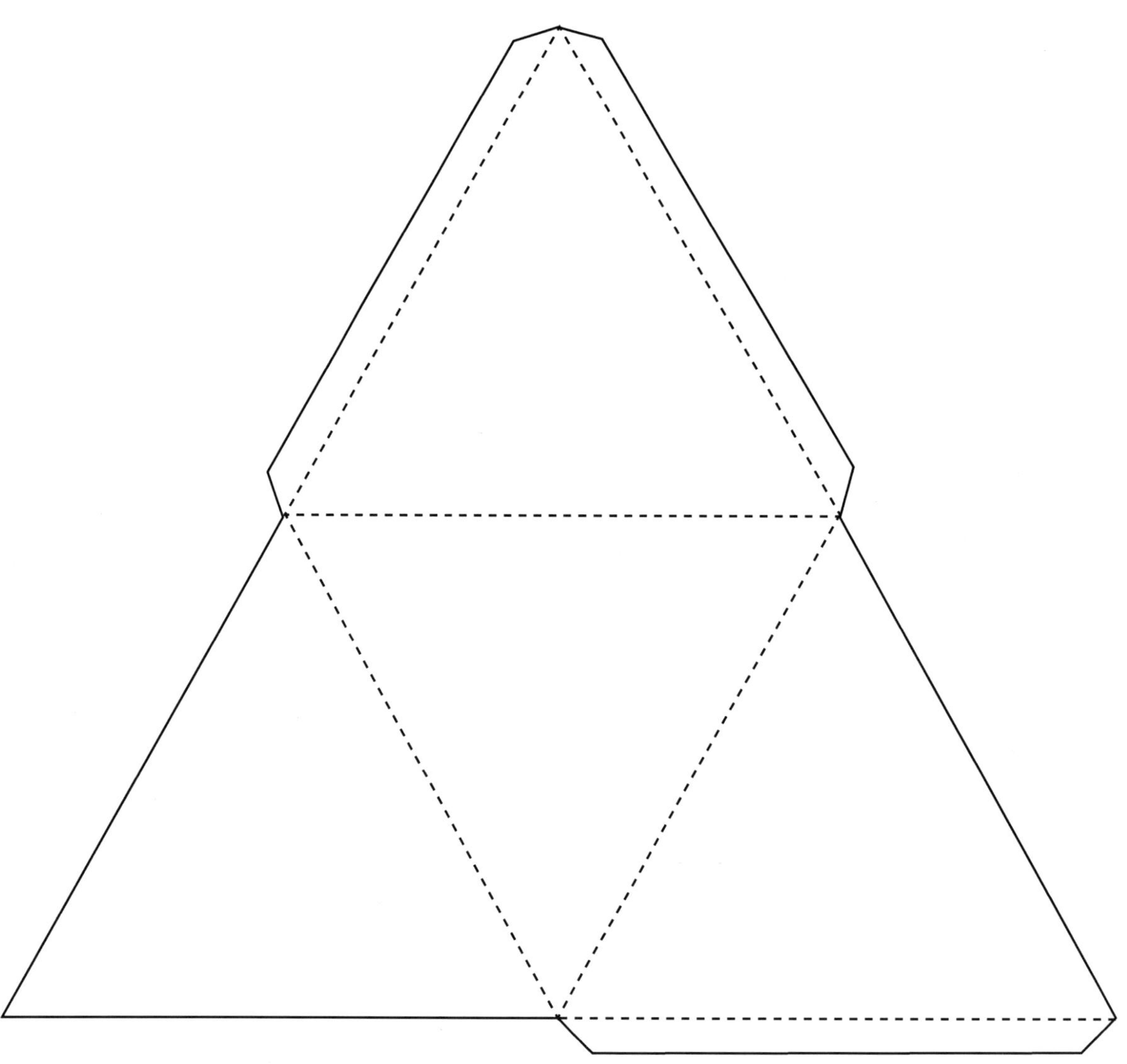

Square-Based Pyramid Net Template

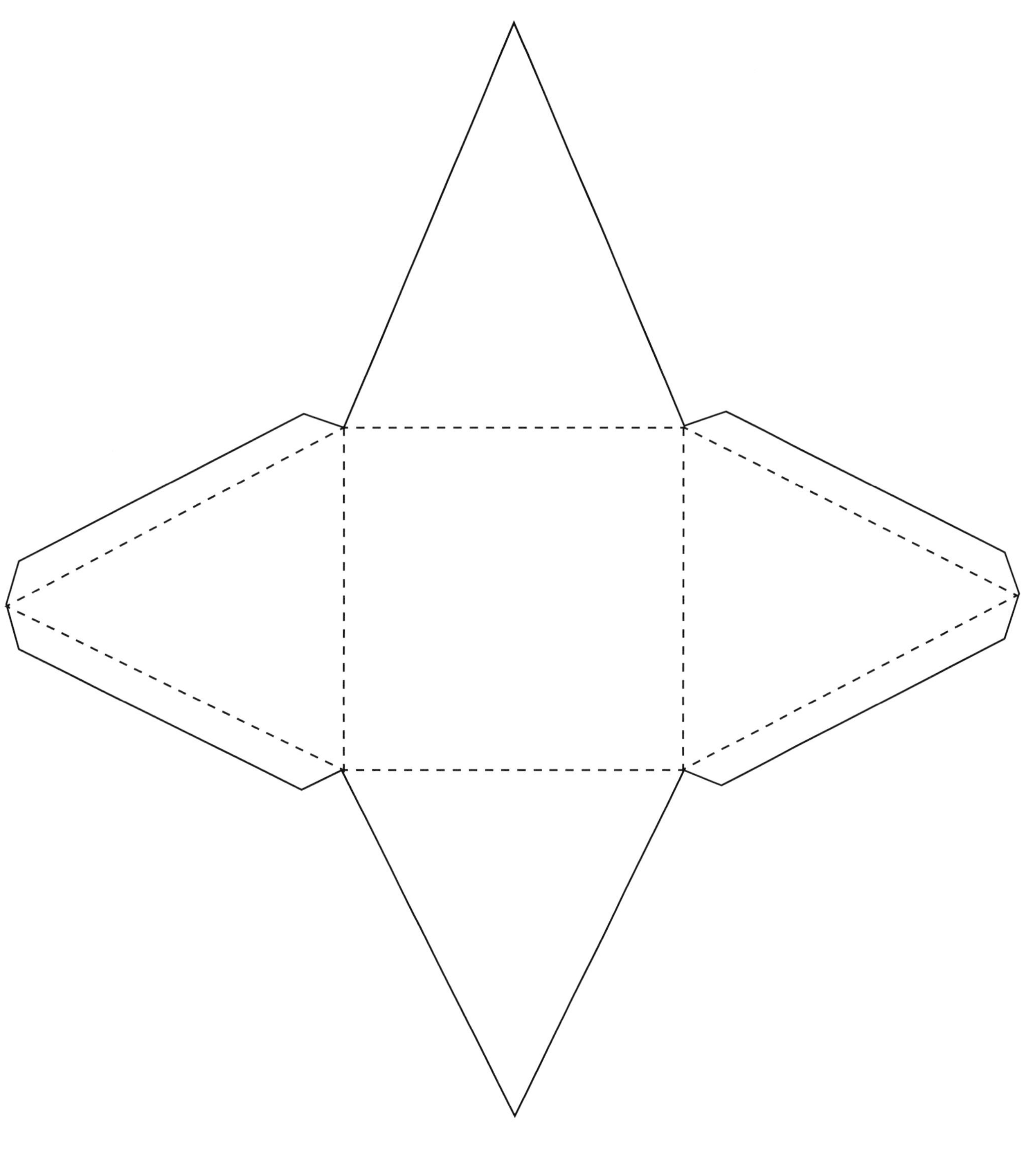

15 Skeletons and Pictorial Representations of Three-Dimensional Solids

Background Information for Teachers

Once students are comfortable working with concrete, three-dimensional solids as well as nets, they can be introduced to pictorial representations of three-dimensional solids.

Materials

- geometric solids (sphere, cylinder, cone, triangular prism, rectangular prism, cube, pentagonal prism, hexagonal prism, triangle-based pyramid, square-based pyramid, pentagon-based pyramid)
- pocket chart
- large 3-D solid cards (included. Photocopy, mount onto sturdy tagboard, and cut apart.) (3.15.1)
- magazines and flyers
- mural paper
- tape
- glue
- scissors
- feely bag or box
- small 3-D solid cards (included. Photocopy two sets of cards for each pair of students, mount onto sturdy tagboard, and cut apart. Put cards into envelopes, two sets per envelope.) (3.15.2)
- toothpicks
- straws
- modeling clay or play dough

Activity: Part One

Display a variety of geometric solids. Place the large 3-D solid cards in the pocket chart. Have students match each 3-D solid card to one of the geometric solids.

Next, distribute toothpicks and modeling clay or play dough, and have students use them to build models of cubes. Show students how to use the toothpicks to represent the edges of the cube and the modeling clay to join two edges together, as in the following diagram:

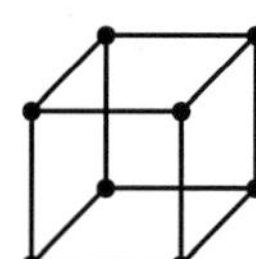

Have the geometric solids on display while students are building their models, and encourage students to refer to the cube as well as to the large 3-D solid card of the cube, focusing particularly on the edges/lines represented by the toothpicks. Later, challenge students to cut straws to various lengths and to use these along with the modeling clay to make other straight-sided 3-D skeletons such as prisms and pyramids.

Tape a large sheet of mural paper to the wall, and tape the large 3-D solid cards onto the mural paper, spreading them out across the sheet. Distribute magazines, flyers, scissors, and glue, and have students cut out pictures of everyday objects with the same shapes as the various geometric solids. Ask students to sort the pictures and glue them onto the mural paper.

Activity: Part Two

Have students sit in a large circle on the floor. Place all the geometric solids into a feely bag (or box), and put the bag in the centre of the circle. Spread out the large 3-D solid cards, facedown, around the bag. Have students take turns turning over a 3-D solid card and then using their hands (but not their eyes) to find a matching geometric solid in the feely bag. When students make a match, have them return the geometric solid to the bag. Discuss which solid is the easiest to find using the sense of touch, which solid is the most difficult to find, and why.

15

Activity: Part Three

Divide the class into pairs of students, and have them play 3-D Memory. Give each pair an envelope containing two sets of small 3-D solid cards. Have the pairs examine the cards and identify the geometric solid shown on each card.

Tell students to shuffle the cards and place them, facedown, in four rows of six. Have players take turns turning over two cards. If the cards are a match, the player keeps the cards. If the cards do not match, they are turned over again. The player with the most matches at the end of the game wins.

Large 3-D Solid Cards

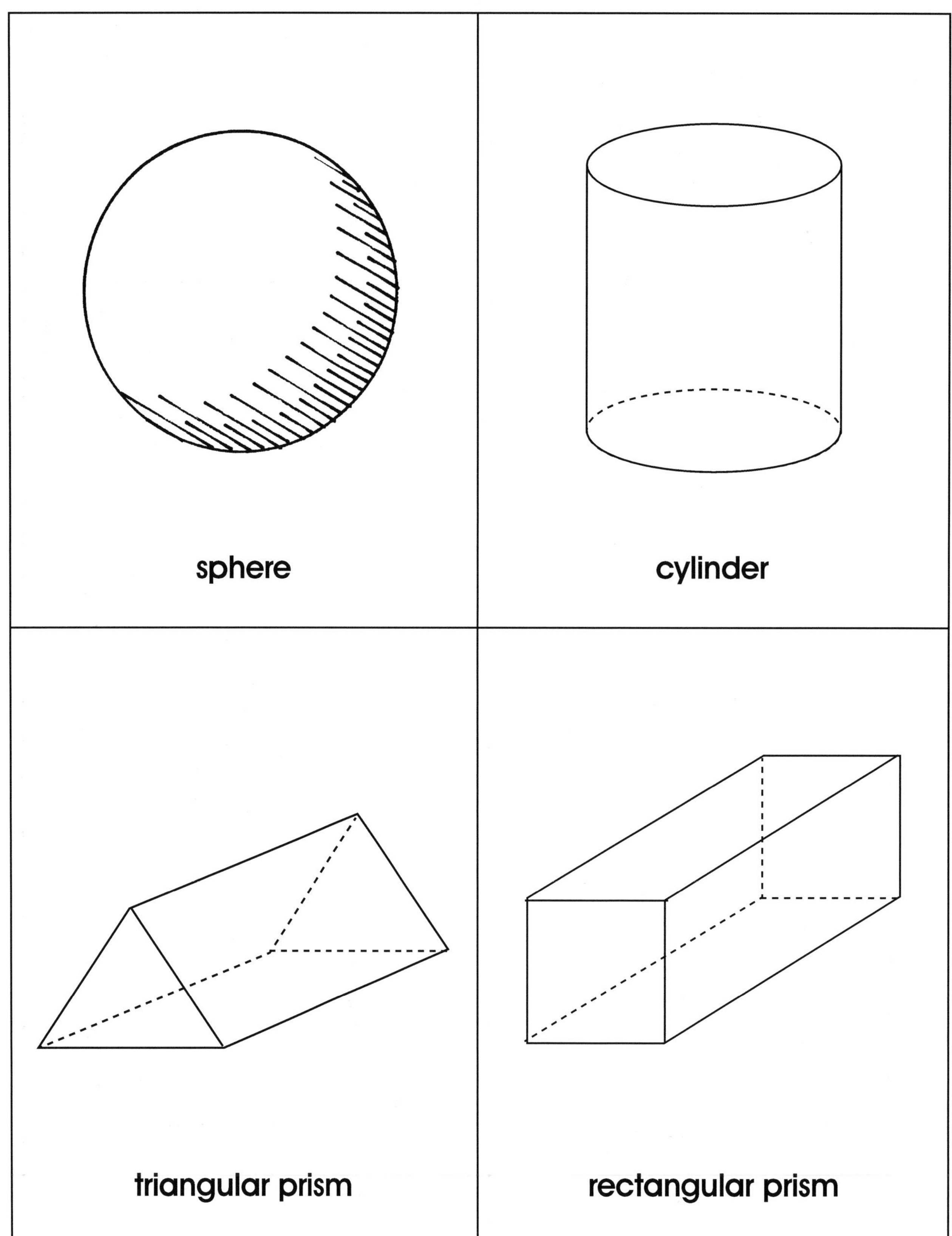

Large 3-D Solid Cards

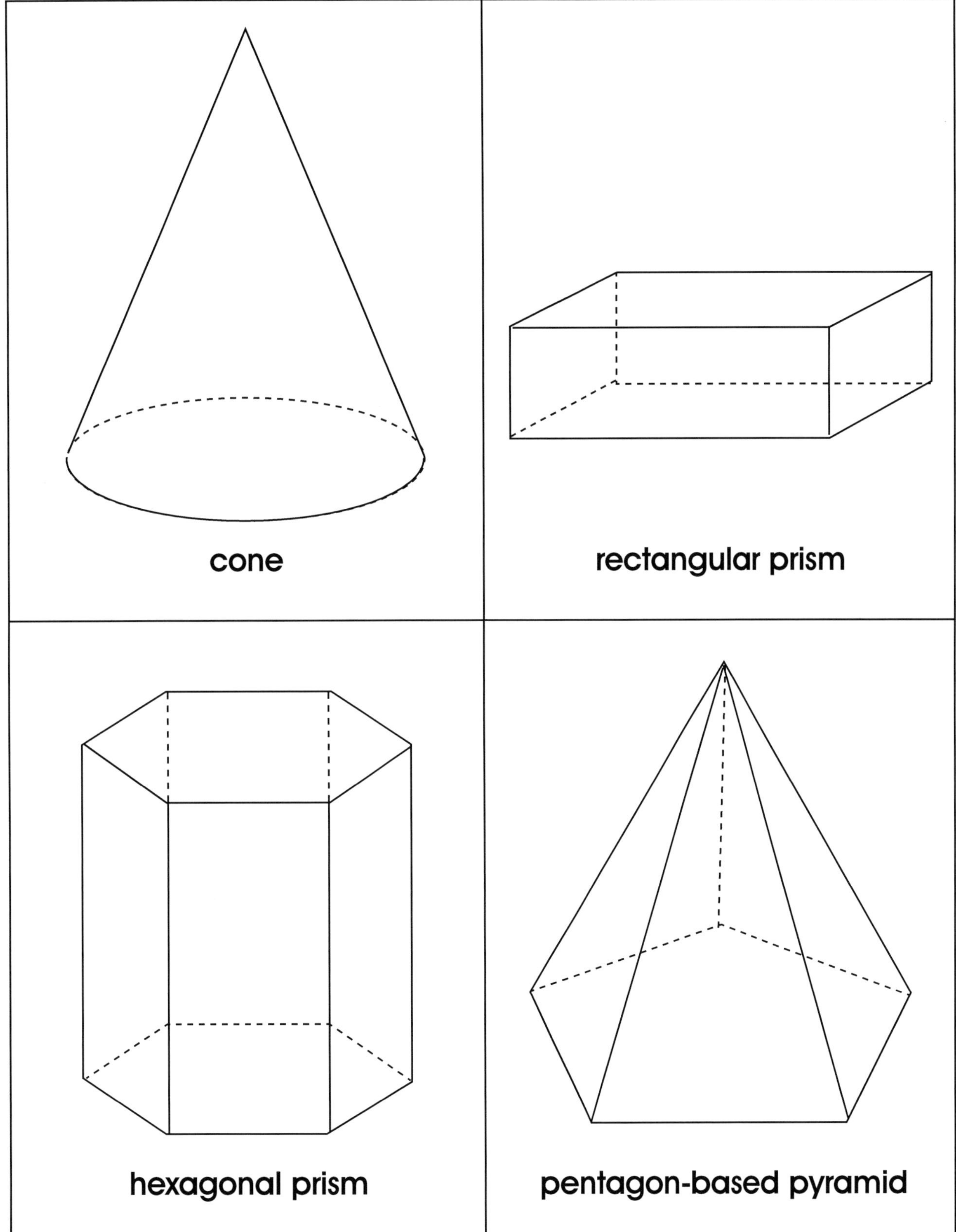

Large 3-D Solid Cards

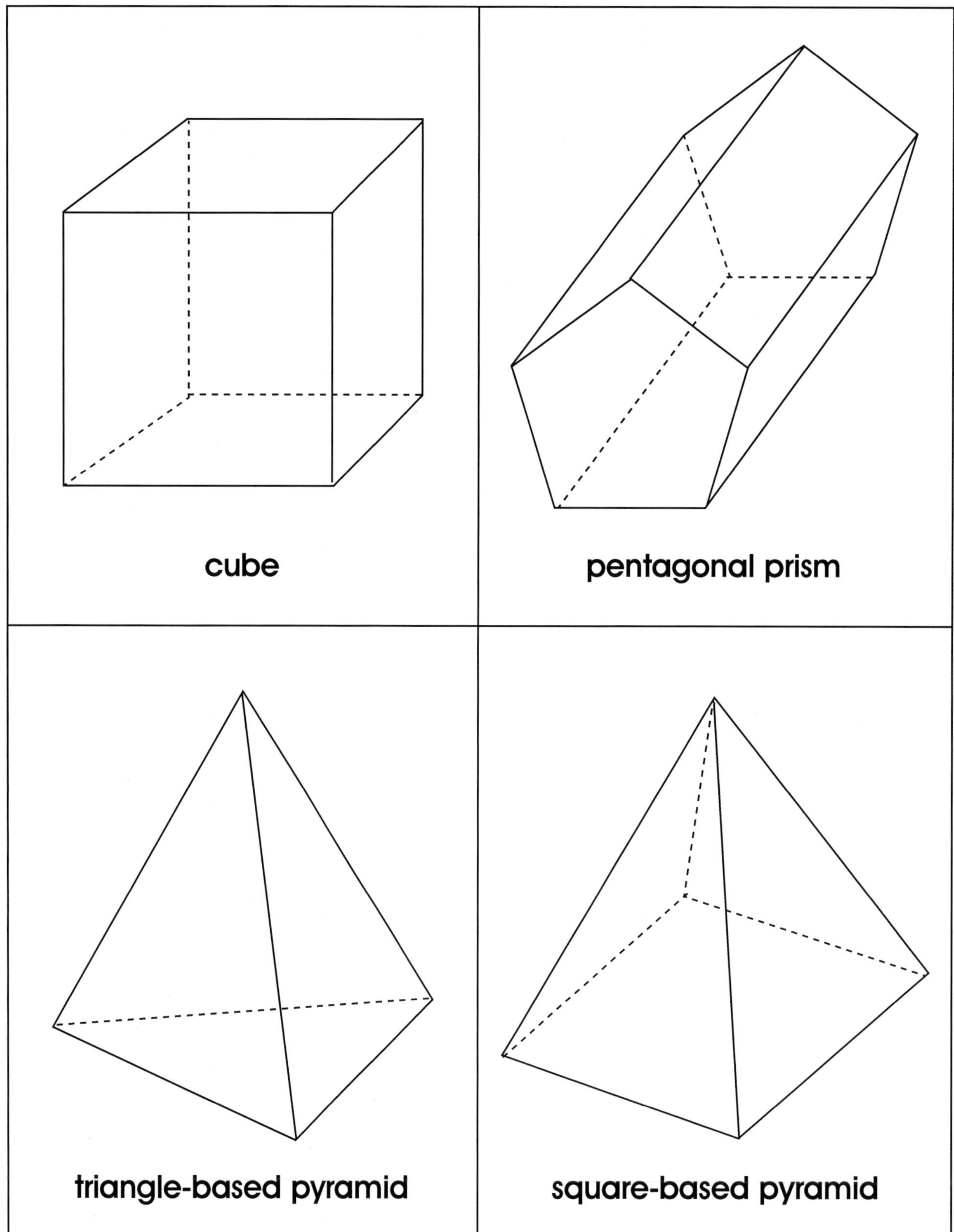

Small 3-D Solid Cards

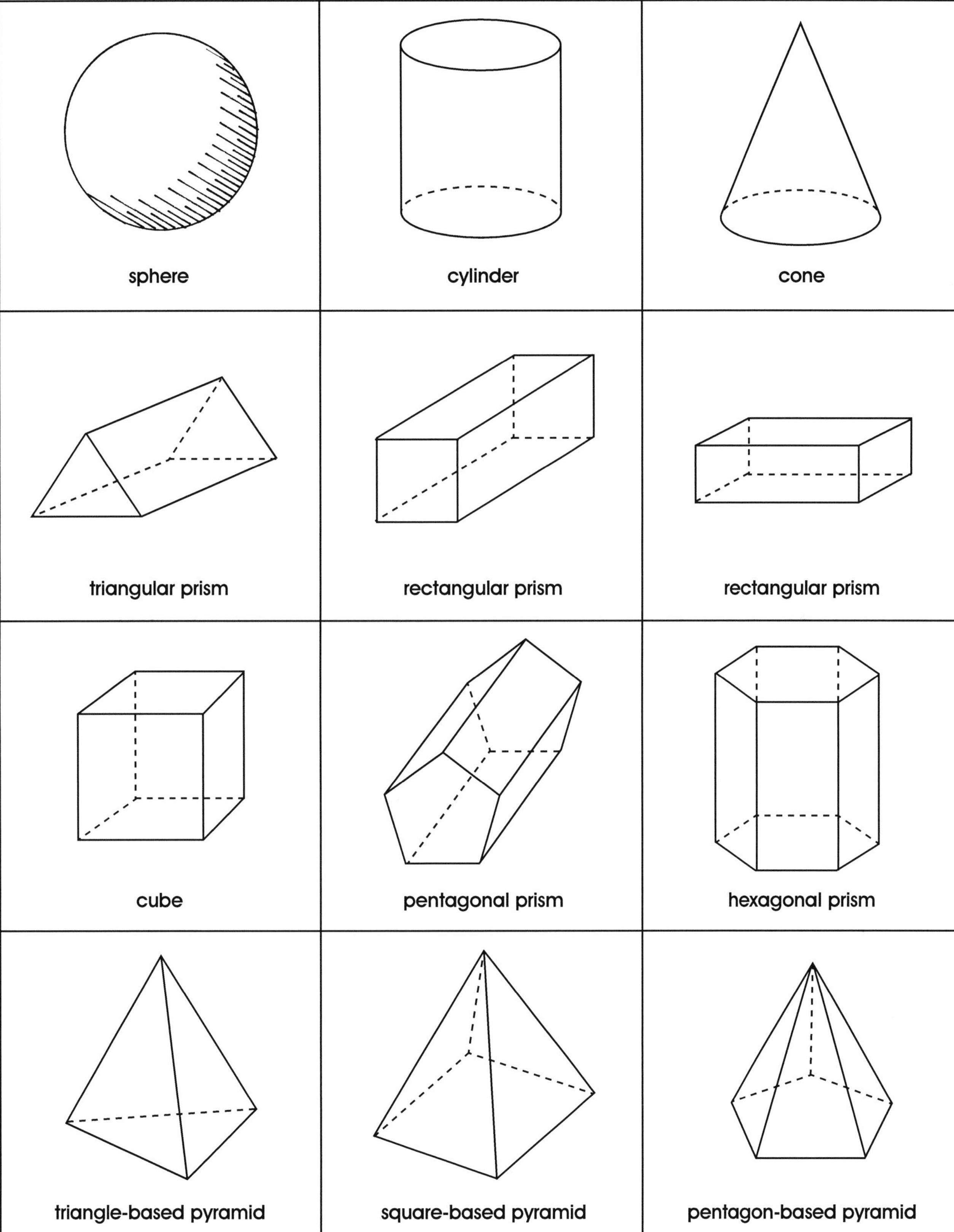

Problem-Solving Black Line Master: Shape and Space

Copy the following 4 sheets onto overhead transparencies to present to students as daily problem-solving activities. Or, photocopy the pages, and cut them apart for students, problem by problem. Have students paste the problems into their math journals or agendas for completion independently.

✂ ---

Draw pictures and use words to describe:

- three activities that take less time than morning recess
- three activities that take more time than morning recess

Adapted from module 3, lesson 1, page 272

✂ ---

Use a clock with a second hand to measure 60 seconds/one minute. Then, think of three to five actions that you could measure in one minute, such as skipping rope or touching your toes. Estimate how many of each action you could complete in one minute. Record your estimate, and then measure by timing yourself as you do the action. You may consider having a family member or a friend time or count for you. Design a chart to record your results.

Module 3, lesson 2

✂ ---

Cut out each letter from the monthly spelling cards (3.3.4), and mix them up. Then, try to put the cards back in order to spell all of the months of the year. Use a clock or watch with a second hand to time yourself to see how quickly you can spell the months.

From module 3, lesson 3, page 286

✂ ---

Find and record five objects at home that would be measured in centimetres and five objects that would be measured in metres. Make a chart to show your work.

Adapted from module 3, lesson 4, page 299

▶

Estimate the length of each finger and the thumb on your left hand. Record each estimate. Use a 30-cm ruler to measure the actual length of each finger and your thumb. Figure out the difference between each estimate and actual measurement. Make a chart to record your results.

Module 3, lesson 5

Kaylee's shoe has a mass of 17 blocks. Jamie's shoe has a mass of 15 blocks. Barry's shoe has a mass of 22 blocks.

- Who has the lightest shoe?
- How much heavier is Barry's shoe than Jamie's shoe?
- How much lighter is Jamie's shoe than Kaylee's shoe?
- If you put all three shoes on one side of the balance scale at the same time, how many blocks would you need to balance the scale?

From module 3, lesson 6, page 311

Find one of your favourite books. Now, find three things that are heavier than the book and three things that are lighter than the book. Record all examples that you find.

Module 3, lesson 7

Farmer Brown decides to build a chicken coop to prevent his chickens from wandering off. He would like the chicken coop to be 10 metres long and 5 metres wide. What will the perimeter of the chicken coop be? If 1 metre of chicken wire costs $2, how much will chicken wire for Farmer Brown's entire chicken coop cost?

From module 3, lesson 8, page 319

▶

Use toothpicks to make the following figures:

- A square with a perimeter of 8 toothpicks
- A figure with a perimeter of 10 toothpicks
- Two different figures, each with a perimeter of 12 toothpicks

Draw each figure, showing how you used toothpicks to construct it.

Module 3, lesson 9

✂ ---

Use pattern blocks to create a figure or picture on a piece of paper. Trace the outline of your picture onto the paper, and record how many of each type of block you used. Then, exchange your traced outline with a friend, and try to cover each other's picture with pattern blocks.

From module 3, lesson 10, page 328

✂ ---

Use two elastic bands to make a polygon on a geoboard. On dot paper, draw a second polygon that is different in shape but has the same number of sides as the first. Try making other polygons on the geoboard and dot paper, such as rectangles, pentagons, and hexagons.

From module 3, lesson 11

✂ ---

I have six square faces. What geometric solid am I?

From module 3, lesson 12, page 355

✂ ---

I have five faces. My base is a square. I have four triangular faces. What geometric solid am I?

From module 3, lesson 12, page 355

✂ ---

I have two faces that are circles. I have two edges but no vertices. I have one curved surface. What geometric solid am I?

From module 3, lesson 12, page 355

▶

Create your own riddles about geometric solids and their faces, edges, and/or vertices.

Module 3, lesson 12

Find a real-life example of each of the geometric solids named below. Then, for each group of three solids below, decide which one does not belong with the other two, and explain why. (There are many ways to solve each problem, so be sure to explain your answers.)

- **cylinder, cube, cone**
- **rectangular prism, cube, square-based pyramid**
- **sphere, cone, triangular prism**
- **triangle-based pyramid, cylinder, triangular prism**

Adapted from module 3, lesson 13, page 359

Find several different ways of arranging six squares so they can be folded into a cube. Draw your nets on squared paper, cut them out, and fold them into cubes.

From module 3, lesson 14, page 363

References for Teachers

Burns, Marilyn. *About Teaching Mathematics, A K-8 Resource*. Sausalito, CA: Math Solutions Publications, 1992.

Burns, Marilyn and Bonnie Tank. *A Collection of Math Lessons from Grades 1 through 3*. Sausalito, CA: Math Solutions Publications, 1988.

Burns, Marilyn, and Robyn Silbey. *So You Have to Teach Math? Sound Advice for K-6 Teachers*. Sausalito, CA: Math Solutions Publications, 2000.

Coombs, Betty, et al. *Explorations 2*. Don Mills, ON: Addison-Wesley, 1987.

Cross, Marion. *Active Achievement Grade 2*. Barrie, ON: Exclusive Educational Products, 2000.

Cross, Marion, and Monica Stevenson. *Take Shape: Solids, Faces, Lines, and Points* (Active Learning series). Barrie, ON: Exclusive Educational Products, 1991.

Fennell, Francis et al. *Connect to NCTM Standards 2000: Making the Standards work at Grade 3*. Chicago, IL: Creative Publications, 2000.

Lawson, Jennifer E. *Hands-On Mathematics: Grade Two*. Winnipeg, MB: Portage & Main Press, 2005.

______. *Hands-On Mathematics: Grade One*. Winnipeg, MB: Portage & Main Press, 2004.

Lawson, Jennifer E. *Hands-On Social Studies: Grade One*. Winnipeg, MB: Portage & Main Press, 2001.

______. *Hands-On Social Studies: Grade Two*. Winnipeg, MB: Portage & Main Press, 2001.

______. *Hands-On Science and Technology: Grade One*. Winnipeg, MB: Portage & Main Press, 2000.

Ministry of Education, Ontario. *Curriculum Ideas for Teachers: Geometry Junior Division*. Toronto, ON: 1987.

Reys, Robert E., et al. *Helping Children Learn Mathematics, 2nd Edition*. Englewood Cliffs, NJ: Prentice Hall, 1989.

Ronfeldt, Suzy. *Third Grade Math: A Month to Month Guide*. Sausalito, CA: Math Solutions Publications, 2003.

Van de Walle, John. *Elementary and Middle School Mathematics*. Toronto, ON: Addison Wesley Longman, 2001.

Western Canadian Protocol for Collaboration in Basic Education. The Common Curriculum Framework for K-12 Mathematics – Grade 3, 1995.

Western Canadian Protocol for Collaboration in Basic Education. *The Common Curriculum Framework for K-12 Mathematics – Grade 2*, 1995.

Module 4

Number Concepts

Books for Children

Anno, Mitsumasa. *Anno's Magic Seeds*. New York, NY: Philomel Books, 1995.

Anno, Mitsumasa, and Masaichiro Anno. *Anno's Mysterious Multiplying Jar*. New York, NY: Philomel Books, 1983.

Barry, David (adapted by). *The Rajah's Rice: A Mathematical Folktale from India*. New York, NY: Scientific America Books for Young Readers, 1994.

Berenstain, Stan, and Jan Berentain. *The Berenstain Bears' Trouble with Money*. New York, NY: Random House, 1983.

Birch, David. *The King's Chessboard*. New York, NY: Puffin Books, 1993.

Demi. *One Grain of Rice: A Mathematical Folktale*. New York, NY: Scholastic Press, 1997.

Fitch, Sheree. *If You Could Wear My Sneakers*. Toronto, ON: Doubleday, 1997.

Hulme, Joy N. *Sea Squares*. New York, NY: Hyperion Books for Children, 1991.

Mathis, Sharon Bell. *The Hundred Penny Box*. New York, NY: Puffin Books, 1986.

Murphy, Stuart. *Betcha!* New York, NY: HarperCollins, 1997.

Nolan, Helen. *How Much, How Many, How Far, How Heavy, How Long, How Tall Is 1000?* Toronto, ON: Kids Can Press, 2001.

Yolen, Jane. *Miz Berlin Walks*. New York, NY: Philomel Books, 1997.

Introduction

At the grade-three level, the focus of the number concepts module is on number manipulation and place value recognition of numbers to 1000. Lessons in this module concentrate on students' abilities to build sets of items to 1000 as well as their abilities to give meaning to these numbers by using place-value concepts.

In this module, students read, count, and write numbers to 1 000, build sets of items, and compare sets to note differences. Students are also introduced to fractions.

As with any academic subject, students must learn to recognize the relation of each math concept they study to the world around them. The lessons in this module provide students with many opportunities to recognize numbers as they occur in their own lives.

Most of the lessons found in this module involve numerous steps and should be completed over the course of several days. Lessons provide opportunities for students of all aptitudes to contribute and to be challenged.

Mathematics Vocabulary

Continue to use your classroom mathematics word wall to display new vocabulary as it is introduced. Throughout this module, teachers should use, and encourage students to use, vocabulary such as: *place value, doubles, multiples, ones, tens, hundreds, thousands, (empty) number line, fractions,* and *whole*. Use, and encourage students to use, this vocabulary both orally and in writing, and continue to review all vocabulary previously introduced.

Depending on your students' writing skills, consider having them begin mathematics logbooks for recording:

- new math vocabulary
- mental-math strategies
- problem-solving strategies
- graphic organizers

1 Personal Numbers

Materials

- overhead copy of Activity Sheet A (4.1.1)
- overhead projector
- nonpermanent overhead markers
- local telephone book(s)
- atlas(es)
- Internet access
- scissors
- glue
- collection of store flyers and catalogues

Note: Review items 6 and 10 on Activity Sheet B (4.1.2) for details on the types of store flyers and catalogues you will need.

Activity: Part One

On the overhead copy of Activity Sheet A (4.1.1), record some of your own personal numbers (phone number, address, height, licence-plate number, date of birth, and so on). Ask students:

- What do you think each of these numbers might represent?
- What helped you to guess what this number represents? (point to one of the numbers on the overhead)
- What numbers could you put on your own list of personal numbers?
- How will your personal numbers be different from my numbers, your friends' numbers, or your grandparents' numbers?
- How will your numbers be similar to my numbers, to your friends' numbers, and to your grandparents' numbers?

Distribute Activity Sheet A, and have students record their own personal numbers.

Activity Sheet A

Directions to students:

Fill in the boxes on the activity sheet with your own personal numbers. Be as creative as you can be when thinking of examples (4.1.1).

Have students share their personal numbers with each other in one of two ways:

- Divide the class into pairs or small groups of students, and have students take turns sharing their personal numbers with each other.
- Each day, as a math warm up, have one student present his/her personal numbers to the rest of the class.

Note: Take this opportunity to remind students that although it is appropriate to share personal numbers like addresses, phone numbers, and birthdates with friends and to record them for a school activity, they should never share these numbers with strangers, even online, without parental consent. There are special circumstances when it might be necessary to share these numbers with strangers (for example, when ordering a magazine subscription) but students should always check with a parent or guardian first.

Activity: Part Two

Explain that students will now take part in a number scavenger hunt. Divide the class into pairs of students, and give each pair a copy of Activity Sheet B (4.1.2) as well as a pair of scissors and some glue. Have students review their activity sheets, and ask:

- Where could you look to find the information you need to complete the activity sheet? (online, store flyers/catologues, phone book, atlas, and so on)
- How could you work effectively with your partner to complete this task?

1

Have the pairs of students work together to complete their activity sheets. Then, have students share their strategies and successes with each other.

Activity Sheet B

Note: This is a two-page activity sheet.

Directions to students:

Work with your partner to find all the required information, and record it on the activity sheet (4.1.2).

Problem Solving

Add together the digits in each of your personal numbers from Activity Sheet A (4.1.1). (For example, if your street address was 1422 Smith Street, you would record "1 + 4 + 2 + 2 = 9.) Then, sequence these sums from the lowest number to the highest number.

Activity Centre

Place a large selection of fairytales at an activity centre along with scrap paper and pencils. Ask students to choose a fairytale character and then record personal number(s) for that character. For example, Snow White had 7 dwarf friends, Goldilocks tasted 3 bowls of porridge, and so on.

Later, ask students to take turns presenting their characters' personal number(s) to the rest of the class without revealing who the character is. Have the rest of the class try to guess what the fairytale is, who the character is, and what the numbers represent in the story. Once several students have presented their characters' personal numbers, the class may begin to see a pattern in the numbers often used in fairytales: 3 is a recurring number in these types of stories (for example, *Three Little Pigs; Goldilocks and the Three Bears; Three Billy Goats Gruff*; the three golden apples in *Golden Bird*, and so on).

Extensions

- Have students enter their largest personal numbers on calculators. Then, tell students to add 10 to that number twelve times. Discuss with students the number patterns that emerge.
- Have students enter their lowest personal numbers on calculators. Then, tell students to predict what the number will be if they add 5 to this number eight times. Have students use their calculators to check their answers.

Date: ____________________ **Name:** ______________________________

My Personal Numbers

Date: ____________ Name: ____________________

Number Scavenger Hunt

1. Find the mailing address, the telephone number, and the fax number for the Prime Minister of Canada.

____

____

____

2. Find out how many interlocking cubes you have if you gather together three "bakers-dozens"-worth of cubes.

____

3. Find the copyright date for *Rakkety Tam*, a book by Brian Jacques.

____

4. Find the distance between Winnipeg, Manitoba, and Toronto, Ontario.

____

5. Find the phone number for your favourite video store.

____

6. From a store flyer or catalogue, cut out three items with prices whose total equals between $100 and $125. Glue each item onto the back of this sheet, record the price of each item underneath it, and record the total of the three prices here:

____

Date: ________________ **Name:** ____________________________

7. Find out how many words there are in your favourite poem from the book *Where the Sidewalk Ends*, by Shel Silverstein.

____

8. Find the date of birth of one of your favourite authors (record the author's name too!)

____

9. Find out how many steps it takes you to walk from your classroom to the gymnasium.

____

10. Find a nutritious snack in a grocery-store flyer that is between $3 and $4. Cut out the picture of the snack, glue it below, and record the price of the snack beside it.

2 Rote Counting to 1 000

Background Information for Teachers

In this lesson, students count by 1s to 1 000, both orally and in writing, using random starting points. It is appropriate for students to practice rote counting to 1 000 even if their understanding of place value is not consolidated.

Encourage students to say numbers without saying the word *and*. For example: *two hundred eighty-seven*; not *two hundred* and *eighty seven*. In mathematics, the word *and* is used to indicate a decimal point and separate the whole number from the part of the number that is less than one.

Also, encourage students to practice using backward number sequences in conjunction with forward number sequences, to help them understand the relationship between the two number patterns.

It is important to note that when writing numbers that include three or more digits, it is inappropriate to use a comma to separate the thousands place from the hundreds place. The metric system (SI) uses a space before (to the left of) every third digit (1 000), although it is also common to express numbers without the space (1000). Once the number includes the ten thousands place (i.e., five-digit numbers), a space is required (10 000).

Materials

- *How Much, How Many, How Far, How Heavy, How Long, How Tall Is 1000?* a book by Helen Nolan
- chart paper
- 10 x 10 grid on chart graph paper (you will need ten 10 x 10 grids)
- calculators (one for each student)
- number cubes (one for each student. Ten-sided cubes are preferable but any number cubes will work.)
- pencils (one for each group of three students)
- number response cards (included. Photocopy three sets for each student. Cut out the cards, punch a hole at the top of each card, and collate them on binder rings. You may consider different coloured paper for the ones cards [first set], tens cards [second set], and hundreds cards [third set]. You can also attach the three sets of cards to a plastic 30-cm ruler with binder holes for each student (see diagram below). This allows students to keep the three sets of cards separate and yet in place to represent ones, tens, and hundreds.) (4.2.1)

Activity: Part One

Read with students the book *How Much, How Many, How Far, How Heavy, How Long, How Tall Is 1000* to give them some qualitative background of the concept of 1000.

Activity: Part Two

Write the numbers 1 to 100 on one of the chart-paper grids. Have students count aloud as you record the numbers 1 through 100. Then, have students read together several forward number sequences, using various random starting points on the grid. Also, have students read several backward number sequences, using random starting points.

Remove the grid, and encourage students to rote count without use of the chart.

Encourage students to look for patterns and discuss what happens when counting over decades (series of tens).

Next Step

Over time, construct chart-paper grids from 101-200, 201-300, and so on to 1000. Have students use the grids to practice forward and backward number sequences.

Encourage students to look for patterns and discuss what happens when counting over decades and over hundreds. Have students count orally from random starting points. Encourage students to clap when the decade changes (349, 350) and stamp their feet when the century changes (399, 400).

Note: You may wish to introduce a new hundred grid each month, beginning in September. With ten months in the school year, the class could progressively work toward 1 000 by year's end. This would give students an opportunity to practice counting and examining patterns for each hundred, and allow for a developmentally appropriate progression of activities.

The following activities can be completed throughout the year, using the numbers with which your class is comfortable. For example, if students have been rote counting to 600, all subsequent activities can be conducted with numbers to 600.

Activity: Part Three

Use a number line to demonstrate rote counting. Draw a horizontal line on chart paper. Record the numbers 0 through 20 on the number line while students count aloud.

Extend this activity by drawing a number line beginning with the number 45. Have students count aloud as you record the next 20 numbers.

Then, encourage students to repeat the number sequence, both forward and backward.

Continue using number lines to have students rote count number sequences to 1 000, both forward and backward.

Activity: Part Four

Distribute three sets of number response cards (4.2.1) to each student. As a class, select a random starting number between 1 and 999. Have students create that number with their cards. Then, have students count slowly by 1s, flipping their number response cards to show each number.

Tell students to stop just before they flip to a new decade (for example, 359). Ask:

- What do you think happens now? (the ones cards go back to 0 and the tens cards go up by 1)

Continue counting with students, and have them flip their number response cards to represent each number until you reach a new century (for example, 400). Ask students:

- What do you think happens now? (both the ones cards and the tens cards go back to 0, and the hundreds cards go up by one)

Have students use the number response cards to count backward as well. Select random starting points, and count aloud with students as they flip the cards to represent the numbers in the sequence.

Note: Using the number response cards throughout this module will encourage students to create and visualize numbers and number sequences. This allows for each student to be fully engaged in all activities.

2

Activity: Part Five

Use a piece of scrap paper to screen (cover) one of the numbers on one of the chart paper number sequence grids. Have students use their number response cards to create the missing number.

201	202	203	204	205	206	207	208	209	210
211	212	213	214	215	216	217	218	219	220
221	222	223	224	225	226	227	228		230
231	232	233	234	235	236	237	238	239	240
241	242	243	244	245	246	247	248	249	250
251	252	253	254	255	256	257	258	259	260
261	262	263	264	265	266	267	268	269	270
271	272	273	274	275	276	277	278	279	280
281	282	283	284	285	286	287	288	289	290
291	292	293	294	295	296	297	298	299	300

Activity: Part Six

Note: In this lesson, students use the constant feature on their calculators. Different calculators activate this feature in different ways. On some, pressing "=" twice will engage the feature. On others, you must press "+, 1, =" and then continue to press the "=". On others still, you must press "1, +, +" and then continue to press the "=" sign. Before beginning this lesson, be sure to experiment with the calculators students will be using.

Show students how to use the constant feature on their calculators. Count slowly with students as they press the equal sign, stopping to draw their attention to number patterns. Ask students:

- What number do you think will come after 549?

Have students enter 540 on their calculators, engage the constant feature, and then press the equal sign ten times. Ask:

- What happened?
- What changed?

Activity: Part Seven

Distribute number cubes and copies of Activity Sheet A (4.2.2), and have students create three-digit numbers by rolling their number cubes three times. Ask students to count-on from their three-digit numbers, recording the next ten numbers they say. Then, have students make new numbers by rearranging the three digits they rolled earlier. Ask them to count-on from their new numbers, recording the next ten numbers they say. Finally, have students rearrange the three digits again, count-on from the new numbers they create, and record the next ten numbers they say.

Activity Sheet A

Directions to students:

Roll the number cube. In the first box, record the number you rolled. Roll the number cube again, and record that number in the second box. Roll the number cube a third time, and record that number in the last box. Now, count-on from the three-digit number you created. Record the next ten numbers that you say.

Make a new three-digit number by mixing up the three numbers you rolled before. Write the new number in the boxes. Count-on from the new three-digit number you created. Record the next ten numbers that you say.

Make a third three-digit number using the same three numbers. Count-on from that number, and record the next ten numbers that you say (4.2.2).

2

Activity: Part Eight

Divide the class into groups of three to play "Pass the Pencil." Provide each group with a number cube, a pencil, and a copy of Activity Sheet B (4.2.3). Have the first player in each group roll the number cube three times, each time recording the number rolled until he/she has a three-digit number recorded on the first stepping stone on the activity sheet. Have that player say the number aloud and then pass the pencil to the next player. Ask the second player to say the number that comes next, record it on the second stepping stone, and then pass the pencil to the third player. Have the third player say the next number, record it, and pass the pencil back to the first player. Play continues until students complete the activity sheet.

Activity Sheet B

Directions to students:

Have Player *A* roll the number cube three times and record each number rolled on the first stepping stone. Have this player say the recorded three-digit number aloud and then pass the pencil to Player *B*. Have Player *B* say the number that comes next, record it on the second stepping stone, and then pass the pencil to Player *C*. Have Player *C* say the next number, record it, and pass the pencil back to Player *A*. Continue in this way until you complete the activity sheet (4.2.3).

Problem Solving

Distribute the Problem-Solving activity sheet called "Number Line Train" (4.2.4), and have students record the numbers in sequence on the train.

Note: You can do this problem-solving activity together with the whole class by making an overhead transparency of the activity sheet. You can also modify and repeat the problem by using a different sequence of numbers.

Extensions

- Add the terms *forward, backward*, and *sequence* to your classroom Math Word Wall.
- Challenge students to use adding machine/ cash register tape on which to create a number line from 1 to 1 000. Display the number line on walls in the classroom so that students can see the number sequence grow.
- Alter commercial connect-the-dot activity sheets so that all numbers include a hundreds digit. For example, change 23, 24, 25 to 223, 224, 225 by adding the hundreds digit.

Assessment Suggestion

In one-on-one meetings, assess each student's performance on the following tasks:

- Start at 95 and count as high as he/she can.
- Start at 245 and count until you say "stop." (Stop the student at 250, and note how easily he/she crossed the decade from 249 to 250.)
- Start at 695 and count until you say "stop." (Stop the student at 701, and note how easily he/she crossed the century from 699 to 700.)

Use the Individual Student Observations sheet, found on page 16, to record your results.

Number Response Cards

0	1	2
3	4	5
6	7	8
9		

Date: ____________ Name: ____________________

Counting-On

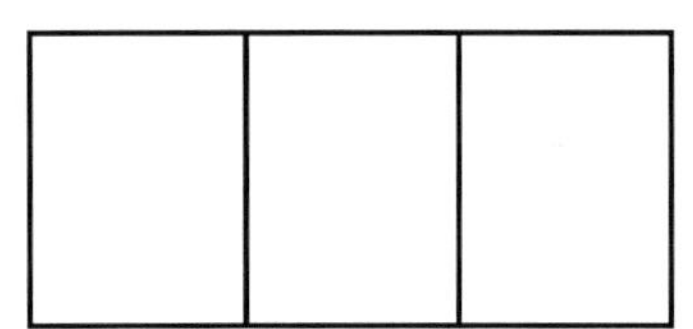

Date: ____________________ **Names:** ________________________________

____

____

Pass the Pencil

Number Line Train

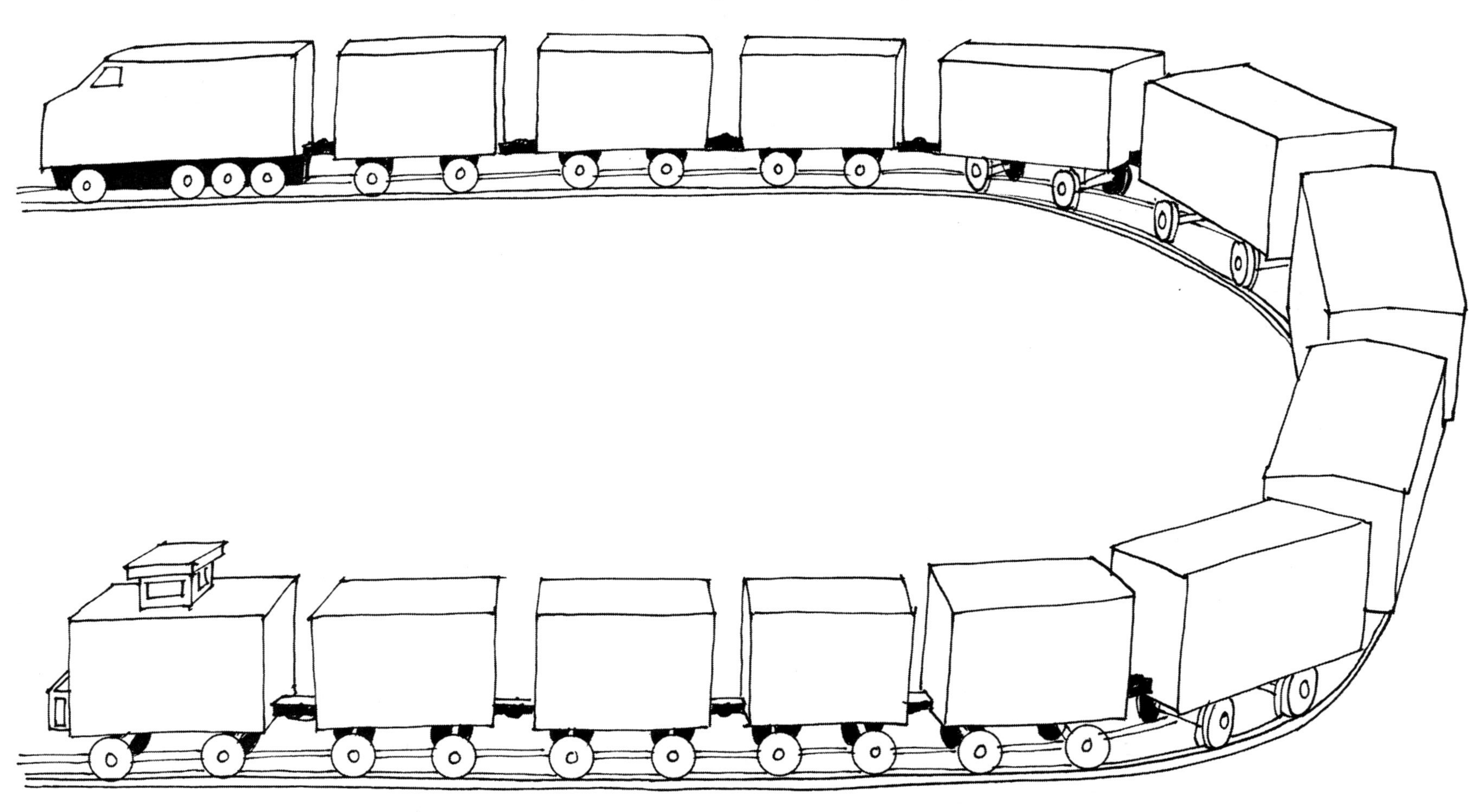

397, 400, 399, 405, 407, 406, 403, 410, 398, 402, 401, 408, 404, 409

3 Number Paths and Number Charts

Materials

- 1-100 hundred chart (included. Make a photocopy for each student as well as an overhead transparency.) (4.3.1)
- pencils
- overhead projector
- overhead markers
- overhead transparency of Activity Sheet A (4.3.2)
- bingo chips (several for each student)
- 1-300 number chart (included. Photocopy onto 11" x 17" paper for each student.) (4.3.3) – have
- various other number charts (included. Make a photocopy of each number chart for each student.) (4.3.5-4.3.23)
- overhead transparency of Activity Sheet B (4.3.4)
- nonpermanent overhead markers
- scissors
- envelopes

Activity: Part One

Distribute 1-100 hundred charts (4.3.1) and pencils to students, and place the 1-100 hundred-chart transparency on the overhead. Explain that students will create secret pathways through number charts and then share information about the pathways to see if their classmates can recreate them.

Beginning with a number along the top row (for example, 3), use bingo chips to trace a path through the chart. Use only vertical and horizontal lines, and have the path end at one of the chart edges, as in the following example:

1	2	(3)	4	5	6	7	8	9	10
11	12	(13)	14	15	16	17	18	19	20
21	22	(23)	24	25	26	27	28	29	30
31	(32)	(33)	34	35	36	37	38	39	40
41	(42)	43	44	45	46	47	48	49	50
(51)	(52)	53	54	55	56	57	58	59	60
61	62	63	64	65	66	67	68	69	70
71	72	73	74	75	76	77	78	79	80
81	82	83	84	85	86	87	88	89	90
91	92	93	94	95	96	97	98	99	100

Now, have students use arrows to recreate your path on their own hundred charts. For example, the move from 3 to 13 would be represented by a ↓, and the move from 33 to 32 would be represented by a ←.

Place the overhead copy of Activity Sheet A (4.3.2) on the overhead, and show students how to record the arrow path of the number path, as below:

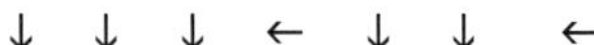

Ask students:

- How could this number path be represented with just numbers? (Record the following number pattern on the activity-sheet transparency: 3, 13, 23, 33, 32, 42, 52, 51)
- What does a downward arrow represent? (add 10)
- What does a horizontal arrow represent? (add or subtract 1)

▶

Divide the class into pairs, and give each pair a copy of Activity sheet A (4.3.2) and several bingo chips. Make sure each student still has a copy of the hundred chart.

In each pair, have partner *A* use bingo chips to create a number path on one of the hundred charts, without letting partner *B* see it. Then, ask partner *A* to use arrows to represent the path on the activity sheet. Have partner *A* tell partner *B* what the starting number is for the number path. Tell partner *B* to use the arrow path and more bingo chips to recreate the number path on the other hundred chart. When partners confirm they have made the same number path on their hundred charts, have partner *A* record the path in numbers under the arrow path on the activity sheet. Then, tell partners to reverse roles, with partner *B* using bingo chips to create a number path for partner *A* to recreate.

Activity Sheet A

Directions to students:

Have partner *A* use bingo chips to create a number path on one of the hundred charts, without letting partner *B* see it. Then, have partner *A* use arrows to represent the path on the activity sheet. Have partner *A* tell partner *B* what the starting number is for the number path. Have partner *B* use the arrow path and more bingo chips to recreate the number path on the other hundred chart. When you confirm that you have both made the same number path on your hundred charts, have partner *A* record the path in numbers under the arrow path on the activity sheet. Reverse roles, and have partner *B* use bingo chips to create a number path for partner *A* to recreate (4.3.2).

Activity: Part Two

Distribute 1-300 number charts (4.3.3) and additional copies of Activity Sheet A (4.3.2), and have students repeat the number-path activity from Activity: Part One.

Note: Photocopy the 1-300 number chart onto 11" x 17" paper for students.

Activity: Part Three

Distribute various other number charts (included, 4.3.5-4.3.23) and additional copies of Activity Sheet A (4.3.2), and have students repeat the number-path activity from Activity: Part One.

Activity: Part Four

Explain that students will now use blank number charts to create number-sequence puzzles. Place the overhead copy of Activity Sheet B (4.3.4) on the overhead, and ask:

- How many spaces are there on this grid?
- How do you know?
- How many numbers could be represented on this grid?

Record the number 764 somewhere near the centre of the grid, and have students help you fill in the rest of the numbers in a logical way. Then, ask:

- What number is at the beginning of the grid?
- How many more is the number at the end of the grid than the number at the beginning of the grid?
- Is that what you expected?

Distribute Activity Sheet B (4.3.4), and have students record a number greater than 200 somewhere near the centre of the grid.

Then, divide the class into pairs of students, and tell partners to exchange activity sheets with each other. Have students fill in the rest of the numbers on their partners' number charts and then exchange activity sheets again. Once students have checked the filled-in numbers on their own number charts for accuracy, distribute scissors, and tell students to cut along the grid lines of their charts to create several puzzle pieces. Have students store their puzzle pieces in envelopes. Tell students to label the outside of their envelopes with the number sequence of their puzzle (for example, 200-299).

Activity Sheet B

Directions to students:

Record a number greater than 200 somewhere near the centre of the grid. Exchange activity sheets with your partner, fill in the rest of the numbers on your partners' number chart, and exchange activity sheets again. Check the numbers on your own number chart for accuracy, and then cut along the grid lines of your chart to create several puzzle pieces. Store your puzzle pieces in an envelope. Label the outside of your envelope with the number sequence of your puzzle (4.3.4).

Activity Centre

At a centre, have copies of the various number charts students used throughout the lesson as well as scissors and envelopes. Tell students to cut apart the number charts to create different number-sequence puzzles to share with their classmates and families.

Note: To avoid getting the pieces of two or more puzzles mixed up, tell students to work on only one puzzle at a time and to put the puzzle pieces into a labelled envelope before beginning a new one.

Assessment Suggestion

Observe students as they participate in the lesson's activities, focusing on each student's ability to manipulate and recognize numbers on the various number charts. Use the Anecdotal Record sheet, found on page 15, to record observations.

1-100 Hundred Chart

1	2	3	4	5	6	7	8	9	10
11	12	13	14	15	16	17	18	19	20
21	22	23	24	25	26	27	28	29	30
31	32	33	34	35	36	37	38	39	40
41	42	43	44	45	46	47	48	49	50
51	52	53	54	55	56	57	58	59	60
61	62	63	64	65	66	67	68	69	70
71	72	73	74	75	76	77	78	79	80
81	82	83	84	85	86	87	88	89	90
91	92	93	94	95	96	97	98	99	100

Date: ____________ Name: ____________

Number Paths

Arrow path

Number path

Arrow path

Number path

Arrow path

Number path

Arrow path

Number path

1-300 Number Chart

1	2	3	4	5	6	7	8	9	10
11	12	13	14	15	16	17	18	19	20
21	22	23	24	25	26	27	28	29	30
31	32	33	34	35	36	37	38	39	40
41	42	43	44	45	46	47	48	49	50
51	52	53	54	55	56	57	58	59	60
61	62	63	64	65	66	67	68	69	70
71	72	73	74	75	76	77	78	79	80
81	82	83	84	85	86	87	88	89	90
91	92	93	94	95	96	97	98	99	100
101	102	103	104	105	106	107	108	109	110
111	112	113	114	115	116	117	118	119	120
121	122	123	124	125	126	127	128	129	130
131	132	133	134	135	136	137	138	139	140
141	142	143	144	145	146	147	148	149	150
151	152	153	154	155	156	157	158	159	160
161	162	163	164	165	166	167	168	169	170
171	172	173	174	175	176	177	178	179	180
181	182	183	184	185	186	187	188	189	190
191	192	193	194	195	196	197	198	199	200
201	202	203	204	205	206	207	208	209	210
211	212	213	214	215	216	217	218	219	220
221	222	223	224	225	226	227	228	229	230
231	232	233	234	235	236	237	238	239	240
241	242	243	244	245	246	247	248	249	250
251	252	253	254	255	256	257	258	259	260
261	262	263	264	265	266	267	268	269	270
271	272	273	274	275	276	277	278	279	280
281	282	283	284	285	286	287	288	289	290
291	292	293	294	295	296	297	298	299	300

Date: ____________________ **Name:** ________________________________

My Number-Sequence Puzzle

0-99 Number Chart

0	1	2	3	4	5	6	7	8	9
10	11	12	13	14	15	16	17	18	19
20	21	22	23	24	25	26	27	28	29
30	31	32	33	34	35	36	37	38	39
40	41	42	43	44	45	46	47	48	49
50	51	52	53	54	55	56	57	58	59
60	61	62	63	64	65	66	67	68	69
70	71	72	73	74	75	76	77	78	79
80	81	82	83	84	85	86	87	88	89
90	91	92	93	94	95	96	97	98	99

100-199 Number Chart

100	101	102	103	104	105	106	107	108	109
110	111	112	113	114	115	116	117	118	119
120	121	122	123	124	125	126	127	128	129
130	131	132	133	134	135	136	137	138	139
140	141	142	143	144	145	146	147	148	149
150	151	152	153	154	155	156	157	158	159
160	161	162	163	164	165	166	167	168	169
170	171	172	173	174	175	176	177	178	179
180	181	182	183	184	185	186	187	188	189
190	191	192	193	194	195	196	197	198	199

101-200 Number Chart

101	102	103	104	105	106	107	108	109	110
111	112	113	114	115	116	117	118	119	120
121	122	123	124	125	126	127	128	129	130
131	132	133	134	135	136	137	138	139	140
141	142	143	144	145	146	147	148	149	150
151	152	153	154	155	156	157	158	159	160
161	162	163	164	165	166	167	168	169	170
171	172	173	174	175	176	177	178	179	180
181	182	183	184	185	186	187	188	189	190
191	192	193	194	195	196	197	198	199	200

200-299 Number Chart

200	201	202	203	204	205	206	207	208	209
210	211	212	213	214	215	216	217	218	219
220	221	222	223	224	225	226	227	228	229
230	231	232	233	234	235	236	237	238	239
240	241	242	243	244	245	246	247	248	249
250	251	252	253	254	255	256	257	258	259
260	261	262	263	264	265	266	267	268	269
270	271	272	273	274	275	276	277	278	279
280	281	282	283	284	285	286	287	288	289
290	291	292	293	294	295	296	297	298	299

201-300 Number Chart

201	202	203	204	205	206	207	208	209	210
211	212	213	214	215	216	217	218	219	220
221	222	223	224	225	226	227	228	229	230
231	232	233	234	235	236	237	238	239	240
241	242	243	244	245	246	247	248	249	250
251	252	253	254	255	256	257	258	259	260
261	262	263	264	265	266	267	268	269	270
271	272	273	274	275	276	277	278	279	280
281	282	283	284	285	286	287	288	289	290
291	292	293	294	295	296	297	298	299	300

300-399 Number Chart

300	301	302	303	304	305	306	307	308	309
310	311	312	313	314	315	316	317	318	319
320	321	322	323	324	325	326	327	328	329
330	331	332	333	334	335	336	337	338	339
340	341	342	343	344	345	346	347	348	349
350	351	352	353	354	355	356	357	358	359
360	361	362	363	364	365	366	367	368	369
370	371	372	373	374	375	376	377	378	379
380	381	382	383	384	385	386	387	388	389
390	391	392	393	394	395	396	397	398	399

301-400 Number Chart

301	302	303	304	305	306	307	308	309	310
311	312	313	314	315	316	317	318	319	320
321	322	323	324	325	326	327	328	329	330
331	332	333	334	335	336	337	338	339	340
341	342	343	344	345	346	347	348	349	350
351	352	353	354	355	356	357	358	359	360
361	362	363	364	365	366	367	368	369	370
371	372	373	374	375	376	377	378	379	380
381	382	383	384	385	386	387	388	389	390
391	392	393	394	395	396	397	398	399	400

400-499 Number Chart

400	401	402	403	404	405	406	407	408	409
410	411	412	413	414	415	416	417	418	419
420	421	422	423	424	425	426	427	428	429
430	431	432	433	434	435	436	437	438	439
440	441	442	443	444	445	446	447	448	449
450	451	452	453	454	455	456	457	458	459
460	461	462	463	464	465	466	467	468	469
470	471	472	473	474	475	476	477	478	479
480	481	482	483	484	485	486	487	488	489
490	491	492	493	494	495	496	497	498	499

401-500 Number Chart

401	402	403	404	405	406	407	408	409	410
411	412	413	414	415	416	417	418	419	420
421	422	423	424	425	426	427	428	429	430
431	432	433	434	435	436	437	438	439	440
441	442	443	444	445	446	447	448	449	450
451	452	453	454	455	456	457	458	459	460
461	462	463	464	465	466	467	468	469	470
471	472	473	474	475	476	477	478	479	480
481	482	483	484	485	486	487	488	489	490
491	492	493	494	495	496	497	498	499	500

500-599 Number Chart

500	501	502	503	504	505	506	507	508	509
510	511	512	513	514	515	516	517	518	519
520	521	522	523	524	525	526	527	528	529
530	531	532	533	534	535	536	537	538	539
540	541	542	543	544	545	546	547	548	549
550	551	552	553	554	555	556	557	558	559
560	561	562	563	564	565	566	567	568	569
570	571	572	573	574	575	576	577	578	579
580	581	582	583	584	585	586	587	588	589
590	591	592	593	594	595	596	597	598	599

501-600 Number Chart

501	502	503	504	505	506	507	508	509	510
511	512	513	514	515	516	517	518	519	520
521	522	523	524	525	526	527	528	529	530
531	532	533	534	535	536	537	538	539	540
541	542	543	544	545	546	547	548	549	550
551	552	553	554	555	556	557	558	559	560
561	562	563	564	565	566	567	568	569	570
571	572	573	574	575	576	577	578	579	580
581	582	583	584	585	586	587	588	589	590
591	592	593	594	595	596	597	598	599	600

600-699 Number Chart

600	601	602	603	604	605	606	607	608	609
610	611	612	613	614	615	616	617	618	619
620	621	622	623	624	625	626	627	628	629
630	631	632	633	634	635	636	637	638	639
640	641	642	643	644	645	646	647	648	649
650	651	652	653	654	655	656	657	658	659
660	661	662	663	664	665	666	667	668	669
670	671	672	673	674	675	676	677	678	679
680	681	682	683	684	685	686	687	688	689
690	691	692	693	694	695	696	697	698	699

601-700 Number Chart

601	602	603	604	605	606	607	608	609	610
611	612	613	614	615	616	617	618	619	620
621	622	623	624	625	626	627	628	629	630
631	632	633	634	635	636	637	638	639	640
641	642	643	644	645	646	647	648	649	650
651	652	653	654	655	656	657	658	659	660
661	662	663	664	665	666	667	668	669	670
671	672	673	674	675	676	677	678	679	680
681	682	683	684	685	686	687	688	689	690
691	692	693	694	695	696	697	698	699	700

700-799 Number Chart

700	701	702	703	704	705	706	707	708	709
710	711	712	713	714	715	716	717	718	719
720	721	722	723	724	725	726	727	728	729
730	731	732	733	734	735	736	737	738	739
740	741	742	743	744	745	746	747	748	749
750	751	752	753	754	755	756	757	758	759
760	761	762	763	764	765	766	767	768	769
770	771	772	773	774	775	776	777	778	779
780	781	782	783	784	785	786	787	788	789
790	791	792	793	794	795	796	797	798	799

701-800 Number Chart

701	702	703	704	705	706	707	708	709	710
711	712	713	714	715	716	717	718	719	720
721	722	723	724	725	726	727	728	729	730
731	732	733	734	735	736	737	738	739	740
741	742	743	744	745	746	747	748	749	750
751	752	753	754	755	756	757	758	759	760
761	762	763	764	765	766	767	768	769	770
771	772	773	774	775	776	777	778	779	780
781	782	783	784	785	786	787	788	789	790
791	792	793	794	795	796	797	798	799	800

800-899 Number Chart

800	801	802	803	804	805	806	807	808	809
810	811	812	813	814	815	816	817	818	819
820	821	822	823	824	825	826	827	828	829
830	831	832	833	834	835	836	837	838	839
840	841	842	843	844	845	846	847	848	849
850	851	852	853	854	855	856	857	858	859
860	861	862	863	864	865	866	867	868	869
870	871	872	873	874	875	876	877	878	879
880	881	882	883	884	885	886	887	888	889
890	891	892	893	894	895	896	897	898	899

801-900 Number Chart

801	802	803	804	805	806	807	808	809	810
811	812	813	814	815	816	817	818	819	820
821	822	823	824	825	826	827	828	829	830
831	832	833	834	835	836	837	838	839	840
841	842	843	844	845	846	847	848	849	850
851	852	853	854	855	856	857	858	859	860
861	862	863	864	865	866	867	868	869	870
871	872	873	874	875	876	877	878	879	880
881	882	883	884	885	886	887	888	889	890
891	892	893	894	895	896	897	898	899	900

900-999 Number Chart

900	901	902	903	904	905	906	907	908	909
910	911	912	913	914	915	916	917	918	919
920	921	922	923	924	925	926	927	928	929
930	931	932	933	934	935	936	937	938	939
940	941	942	943	944	945	946	947	948	949
950	951	952	953	954	955	956	957	958	959
960	961	962	963	964	965	966	967	968	969
970	971	972	973	974	975	976	977	978	979
980	981	982	983	984	985	986	987	988	989
990	991	992	993	994	995	996	997	998	999

901-1000 Number Chart

901	902	903	904	905	906	907	908	909	910
911	912	913	914	915	916	917	918	919	920
921	922	923	924	925	926	927	928	929	930
931	932	933	934	935	936	937	938	939	940
941	942	943	944	945	946	947	948	949	950
951	952	953	954	955	956	957	958	959	960
961	962	963	964	965	966	967	968	969	970
971	972	973	974	975	976	977	978	979	980
981	982	983	984	985	986	987	988	989	990
991	992	993	994	995	996	997	998	999	1000

4 Skip Counting

Materials

- 1-100 hundred chart (included with lesson 3. Make a photocopy for each student as well as an overhead transparency.) (4.3.1)
- bingo chips
- 1-300 number chart (included with lesson 3. Make an overhead copy as well as a photocopy for each student.) (4.3.3)
- overhead projector
- 10-1000 number chart (included. Make a photocopy for each student.) (4.4.1)
- various other number charts (included with lesson 3. Make a photocopy of each number chart for each student.) (4.3.5-4.3.23)
- nonpermanent overhead markers

Activity: Part One

Explain that students will now try to recognize number patterns their classmates have created. To begin, display the 1-100 hundred chart on the overhead. Use a bingo chip to cover the number 26. Without revealing your skip counting pattern, continue using bingo chips to cover every second number on the chart. When you reach 40, stop, and ask students:

- Can you describe my number pattern? (forward skip counting by 2s, or every second number)
- Can you count out the number pattern? (26, 28, 30…)
- What is the skip counting pattern? (forward by 2s)
- How could we represent the pattern numerically? (26, 28, 30…)

Repeat this process to demonstrate skip counting patterns by 5s and 10s.

Distribute 1-100 hundred charts (4.3.1) and bingo chips, and have students use the chips to create their own forward skip counting patterns (by 2s, 5s, or 10s) on their charts. Then, divide the class into pairs or small groups, and ask students to take turns sharing their patterns with each other. Have the partners (or the other members of the group) determine what the student's number pattern is.

Distribute Activity Sheet A (4.4.2), and ask students to record their number patterns numerically. Have students repeat the activity until they have completed their activity sheets.

Activity Sheet A

Directions to students:

Use bingo chips to create a number pattern on your 1-100 hundred chart that shows forward skip counting by 2s, 5s, or 10s. Share your pattern with your partner (or with the rest of your group), and have your partner (or the other members of your group) determine what your number pattern is. Record your number pattern numerically on the activity sheet. Repeat the activity until you have completed the activity sheet (4.4.2).

Activity: Part Two

Display the overhead copy of the 1-300 number chart (4.3.3). Use bingo chips to demonstrate backward skip counting patterns by 2s, 5s, and 10s.

Now, distribute copies of the 1-300 number chart, and have students use bingo chips to create their own backward skip counting patterns (by 2s, 5s, or 10s) on their charts. Divide the class into pairs or small groups, and ask students to take turns sharing their patterns with each other. Have the partners (or other members of the group) determine what the student's number pattern is.

Distribute Activity Sheet B (4.4.3), and tell students to record their number patterns numerically, repeating the activity until they have completed their activity sheets.

Activity Sheet B

Directions to students:

Use bingo chips to create a number pattern on your 1-300 number chart that shows backward skip counting by 2s, 5s, or 10s (4.4.3).

Activity: Part Three

Distribute to students bingo chips and copies of the 10-1000 chart (4.4.1). Suggest a random number from which students should start (for example, 310), and have students use their bingo chips to show the number patterns created when they:

- skip count forward by 100s
- skip count backward by 100s

Activity: Part Four

Expose students to skip counting using various number charts by repeating the previous activities with some of the other number charts (4.3.5-4.3.23).

Ensure that students practice the following skip counting patterns:

- forward and backward by 2s, 3s, and 4s using starting points that are multiples of 2, 3, and 4 respectively
- forward and backward by 5s, 10s, and 100s from random starting points

Activity: Part Five

Provide students with more opportunities to use number lines to practice skip counting by 2s, 3s, 4s, and 5s. Then, distribute Activity Sheet C (4.4.4) Activity Sheet D (4.4.5), Activity Sheet E (4.4.6), and Activity Sheet F (4.4.7), and have students follow the directions and record a skip counting pattern on each number line provided.

Activity Sheet C

Directions to students

Follow the directions, and record a skip counting pattern on each number line provided (4.4.4).

Activity Sheet D

Directions to students

Follow the directions, and record a skip counting pattern on each number line provided (4.4.5).

Activity Sheet E

Directions to students

Follow the directions, and record a skip counting pattern on each number line provided (4.4.6).

Activity Sheet F

Directions to students

Follow the directions, and record a skip counting pattern on each number line provided (4.4.7).

Problem Solving

- Beginning at 237, skip count by 5s six times. What number do you get?
- Beginning at 492, skip count by 2s thirteen times. What number do you get?
- If you began at 386 and skip counted by 5s, would you say the number 416? Explain how you know.

Note: Reproducible masters for these problems can be found on page 494.

10-1 000 Number Chart

10	20	30	40	50	60	70	80	90	100
110	120	130	140	150	160	170	180	190	200
210	220	230	240	250	260	270	280	290	300
310	320	330	340	350	360	370	380	390	400
410	420	430	440	450	460	470	480	490	500
510	520	530	540	550	560	570	580	590	600
610	620	630	640	650	660	670	680	690	700
710	720	730	740	750	760	770	780	790	800
810	820	830	840	850	860	870	880	890	900
910	920	930	940	950	960	970	980	990	1000

Date: ________________ Name: ____________________________

Hundred-Chart Patterns

1. This pattern shows forward skip counting by ________s:

________, ________, ________, ________, ________, ________,

________, ________, ________, ________, ________, ________...

2. This pattern shows forward skip counting by ________s:

________, ________, ________, ________, ________, ________,

________, ________, ________, ________, ________, ________...

3. This pattern shows forward skip counting by ________s:

________, ________, ________, ________, ________, ________,

________, ________, ________, ________, ________, ________...

4. This pattern shows forward skip counting by ________s:

________, ________, ________, ________, ________, ________,

________, ________, ________, ________, ________, ________...

5. This pattern shows forward skip counting by ________s:

________, ________, ________, ________, ________, ________,

________, ________, ________, ________, ________, ________...

Date: ________________ Name: ____________________________

1-300 Number-Chart Patterns

1. This pattern shows backward skip counting by _______s:

_________, _________, _________, _________, _________, _________,

_________, _________, _________, _________, _________, _________...

2. This pattern shows backward skip counting by _______s:

_________, _________, _________, _________, _________, _________,

_________, _________, _________, _________, _________, _________...

3. This pattern shows backward skip counting by _______s:

_________, _________, _________, _________, _________, _________,

_________, _________, _________, _________, _________, _________...

4. This pattern shows backward skip counting by _______s:

_________, _________, _________, _________, _________, _________,

_________, _________, _________, _________, _________, _________...

5. This pattern shows backward skip counting by _______s:

_________, _________, _________, _________, _________, _________,

_________, _________, _________, _________, _________, _________...

Date: ______________________ Name: ______________________

Using Number Lines for Skip Counting by 2s

On the number line below, skip count forward by 2s from 100 to 150.

100 101 102 103 104 105 106 107 108 109 110 111 112 113 114 115 116 117 118 119 120 121 122 123 124 125 126 127 128 129 130 131 132 133 134 135 136 137 138 139 140 141 142 143 144 145 146 147 148 149 150

On the number line below, skip count backward by 2s from 296 to 246.

246 247 248 249 250 251 252 253 254 255 256 257 258 259 260 261 262 263 264 265 266 267 268 269 270 271 272 273 274 275 276 277 278 279 280 281 282 283 284 285 286 287 288 289 290 291 292 293 294 295 296

On the number line below, skip count forward by 2s from 634 to 684.

634 635 636 637 638 639 640 641 642 643 644 645 646 647 648 649 650 651 652 653 654 655 656 657 658 659 660 661 662 663 664 665 666 667 668 669 670 671 672 673 674 675 676 677 678 679 680 681 682 683 684

Date: ______________________ Name: ______________________

Skip Counting by 5s on a Number Line

On the number line below, skip count forward by 5s from 850 to 900.

850 851 852 853 854 855 856 857 858 859 860 861 862 863 864 865 866 867 868 869 870 871 872 873 874 875 876 877 878 879 880 881 882 883 884 885 886 887 888 889 890 891 892 893 894 895 896 897 898 899 900

On the number line below, skip count backward by 5s from 275 to 225.

225 226 227 228 229 230 231 232 233 234 235 236 237 238 239 240 241 242 243 244 245 246 247 248 249 250 251 252 253 254 255 256 257 258 259 260 261 262 263 264 265 266 267 268 269 270 271 272 273 274 275

On the number line below, skip count forward by 5s from 605 to 655.

605 606 607 608 609 610 611 612 613 614 615 616 617 618 619 620 621 622 623 624 625 626 627 628 629 630 631 632 633 634 635 636 637 638 639 640 641 642 643 644 645 646 647 648 649 650 651 652 653 654 655

Date: ______________________ Name: ______________________

Skip Counting by 3s on a Number Line

On the number line below, skip count forward by 3s from 0 to 48.

0 1 2 3 4 5 6 7 8 9 10 11 12 13 14 15 16 17 18 19 20 21 22 23 24 25 26 27 28 29 30 31 32 33 34 35 36 37 38 39 40 41 42 43 44 45 46 47 48

On the number line below, skip count backward by 3s from 99 to 51.

51 52 53 54 55 56 57 58 59 60 61 62 63 64 65 66 67 68 69 70 71 72 73 74 75 76 77 78 79 80 81 82 83 84 85 86 87 88 89 90 91 92 93 94 95 96 97 98 99

On the number line below, skip count forward by 3s from 333 to 381.

333 334 335 336 337 338 339 340 341 342 343 344 345 346 347 348 349 350 351 352 353 354 355 356 357 358 359 360 361 362 363 364 365 366 367 368 369 370 371 372 373 374 375 376 377 378 379 380 381

Date: ______________________ Name: ______________________

Skip Counting by 4s on a Number Line

On the number line below, skip count forward by 4s from 0 to 48.

0 1 2 3 4 5 6 7 8 9 10 11 12 13 14 15 16 17 18 19 20 21 22 23 24 25 26 27 28 29 30 31 32 33 34 35 36 37 38 39 40 41 42 43 44 45 46 47 48

On the number line below, skip count backward by 4s from 80 to 32.

32 33 34 35 36 37 38 39 40 41 42 43 44 45 46 47 48 49 50 51 52 53 54 55 56 57 58 59 60 61 62 63 64 65 66 67 68 69 70 71 72 73 74 75 76 77 78 79 80

On the number line below, skip count forward by 4s from 444 to 492.

444 445 446 447 448 449 450 451 452 453 454 455 456 457 458 459 460 461 462 463 464 465 466 467 468 469 470 471 472 473 474 475 476 477 478 479 480 481 482 483 484 485 486 487 488 489 490 491 492

5 Skip Counting by 25s

Materials

- large, floor hundred chart (Use an inexpensive vinyl tablecloth, or purchase some vinyl material from a fabric store. Use a permanent marker to create a 10 x 10 grid. Fill in the grid with the numbers 1 to 100.)
- hundred charts (included with lesson 3. Make one photocopy for each student.) (4.3.1)
- chart paper
- markers
- number line, 0-100 (Use adding machine or cash register tape, available at office supply stores. On the tape, record calibrations and numbers from 0 to 100. Number lines are also available for purchase at teacher supply stores.)
- tape
- metre stick or pointer
- calculators (one for each student)
- 1-metre lengths of string (two for each student. Tie a knot at one end of each piece of string.)
- beads with large holes (two colours. You will need at least fifty beads of each colour for each student.)
- quarters

Activity: Part One: Skip Counting by 25s

Use the following activities to introduce students to skip counting by 25s:

- Use quarters to give students a real-life example of counting by 25s to 100 ($1). Students should become familiar with the values of one, two, three, and four quarters. Create problems for students such as the following:
    - Stacie earned one quarter doing chores. How much money does she have?
    - How much money will Stacie have if she earns one more quarter? Another quarter? Even one more?
- Have students count by 1s, slowly and in unison, to 100. Ask students to stand up briefly when they reach each multiple of 25.
- Have students repeat the previous activity using the backward number sequence. Beginning at 100, ask students to count backward and stand up briefly when they reach each multiple of 25.
- Have students take turns counting aloud by 25s as they walk through the counting sequence on a large, floor hundred chart. Encourage the rest of the class to quietly recite the number sequence as each student does his/her counting walk.
- Have students walk through the backward number sequence, beginning at 100 and counting backward by 25s, while the rest of the students quietly recite the numbers.
- Have students use hundred charts to count by 25s by "finger walking," counting both forward and backward.
- Display a 0-100 number line by taping it to a wall. Have students use the number line to practice skip counting by 25s, both forward and backward, to 100. Select individual students to use a metre stick to point to the numbers as the rest of the class says them.
- Show students how to use the constant feature on their calculators to show patterns of skip counting by 25s.

Note: Different calculators activate the constant feature in different ways. A common way to skip count by 25s using the constant key is to press "+25" and then press the "=" sign repeatedly. Before doing this activity with students, experiment with the calculators they will be using.

Activity: Part Two: Skip Counting by 25s with Beads

Note: For this activity, students will be stringing beads. Tie a knot at one end of each piece of string before distributing them to students.

Provide each student with a 1-metre piece of string and at least 100 beads in two different colours – at least fifty of each colour. Have students create bead patterns that show skip counting by 25s. Once they have completed their patterns, help students tie knots at the tops of their pieces of string. Be sure there is enough room on the string to move the beads up and down slightly.

Now, have students use their bead strings to practice skip counting by 25s, both forward and backward. Ask them to move the beads up and down, counting and pointing as they say the number sequences.

Activity: Part Three: Using an Empty Number Line to Skip Count by 25s

Use an empty number line to skip count by 25s. Draw a horizontal line on chart paper, and record a 0 at the far, left end. Then, select one student to draw a "jump" for each number as the rest of the students skip count aloud by 25s to 100. Once students have completed the skip counting number sequence, have them help you determine the numbers that should go below the number line, and record them, as in the following example:

0 25 50 75 100

Continue to use empty number lines to practice with students both forward and backward skip counting by 25s to 100.

Distribute Activity Sheet A (4.5.1), and have students fill in the missing numbers and then skip count by 25s, drawing a triangle around each number they say.

Activity Sheet A

Directions to students:

Fill in the missing numbers. Count by 25s. Draw a triangle around each number that you say (4.5.1).

Problem Solving

Use a hundred chart to help you answer this question:

- How many numbers do you say when you count from 1 to 100 by 25s?

Note: A reproducible master for this problem can be found on page 494.

Date: ____________ Name: ____________________

Skip Counting by 25s

	2	3	4		6	7			
11		13	14		16	17		19	
21	22	23		25		27	28	29	
31		33	34		36	37	38		40
	42	43	44				48	49	50
	52	53		55	56	57	58		
61		63	64	65			68	69	70
71		73		75	76	77		79	
81	82	83		85	86	87	88	89	
91	92	93	94	95	96	97	98	99	

6 How Much Is 1 000?

Materials

- *How Much, How Many, How Far, How Heavy, How Long, How Tall Is 1000?*, a book by Helen Nolan
- container filled with popcorn kernels (make sure there are more than 1 000 kernels in the container)
- popcorn air popper
- popcorn bowl
- sticky notes
- chalkboard
- chalk
- long piece of rope
- index cards
- place-value mat (included. Photocopy onto an 8½" x 11" sheet of tagboard for each student.) (4.6.1)
- stapler
- place-value cards (included. Photocopy one set onto tagboard for each student.) (4.6.2)
- scissors
- scrap paper
- bingo chips
- place-value number tents (included. Photocopy one set onto tagboard for each student. Cut apart the number tents on the solid lines, and fold along the dotted lines.) (4.6.3)

Activity: Part One

Read with students the book *How Much, How Many, How Far, How Heavy, How Long, How Tall Is 1000?* Discuss how 1 000 objects/items can sometimes fit into a small container (for example, 1 000 grains of rice), while other times, a large parking lot would be required (for example, 1 000 cars). Ask students to suggest different examples of 1 000 objects/items.

Have students sit in a circle, and show them the container of popcorn kernels. Tell students to count out 1 000 kernels of popcorn. Have students look at the size of the collection, and ask:

- What size of container would these popcorn kernels fill? (small)

Use the air popper to pop the kernels into popcorn, and ask:

- What is the size of the collection now?
- What size of container does the collection require now? (medium or large)
- Did you expect 1 000 kernels to look like more or less kernels than it actually does?
- Did you expect 1 000 pieces of popcorn to look like more or less popcorn than it actually does?

Have students explain their thinking about collections of 1 000 objects/items in their math journals. Share the popcorn with students as they write.

Activity: Part Two

Note: Before beginning this activity, record, on sticky notes, random three-digit numbers between 100 and 999. You will need one sticky-note number for each student.

Distribute a sticky-note number to each student. Draw a horizontal line on the chalkboard, and record 0 at one end of the line and 1 000 at the other end. Have students come up to the chalkboard, one at a time, and stick their numbers where they think they belong on the number line. As each student approaches the number line, ask:

- Where do you think your number goes on the number line?
- What clues do you have from the other numbers on the number line?

Now, lay a long piece of rope in a straight line on the floor. Ask a group of students to stand on the rope. Record random three-digit numbers between 100 and 999 on index cards, and give one card to each student. Have students work cooperatively to put themselves in order along the number-line rope from the lowest number to the highest number. The challenge is that as they are organizing themselves, students must keep one body part on the rope at all times!

Note: For this activity, only order is important; proper spacing does not matter. For example, the space between students with consecutive numbers 100 and 233 does not have to be larger than the space between students with consecutive numbers 233 and 240.

Activity: Part Three

Provide each student with a place-value mat (4.6.1), a set of place-value cards (4.6.2), and a pair of scissors. Have students cut out their place-value mats (outer frame only) as well as each place-value card. Show students how to fold and staple their place-value mats by folding the top line backward, the bottom line forward, and stapling along the edge of the "Hundreds" and the "Ones" spaces (help students with the stapling). Demonstrate how to slip the place-value cards into the pocket of the place-value mat, as below:

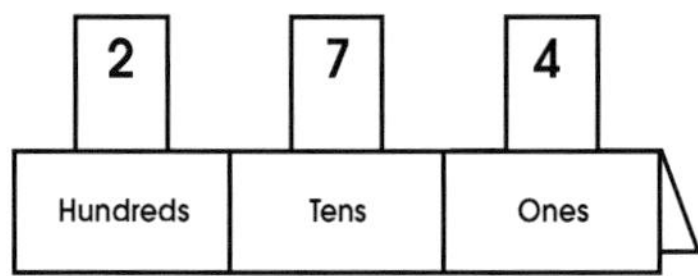

Record a three-digit number on a piece of scrap paper, but do not show your number to students. Give students clues that will help them build your number with their place-value cards on their place-value mats. Each clue should help students get closer to the actual answer.

For example:

- My number is between 300 and 500. (students build their own numbers in response)
- My number is an odd number. (students *may* change their numbers in response)
- My number is less than 350. (students *may* change their numbers in response)
- My number has 34 groups of ten in it. (students *may* change their numbers in response)
- The number of units in the ones place of my number is equal to the number of days in a week. (students *may* change their numbers in response)
- The number is 347.

Circulate through the classroom as students build their numbers. Discuss the clues to assist students who are having difficulty and to ensure that all students understand the significance of the clue.

Activity: Part Four

Distribute sets of place-value number tents (4.6.3) to students. Repeat the procedure from Activity: Part Three, but have students use the number tents to build their numbers rather than the place-value cards on place-value mats. To build numbers, have students place down their hundreds tents first, their tens tents overtop of the hundreds, and their ones tents overtop of the tens, as in the following diagram:

6

Problem Solving

Give students two random numbers between 1 and 1 000, and have them use the empty-number-line approach to determine the difference between the two numbers.

Note: A reproducible variation of this problem can be found on page 495. Remember that it is not necessary for students to be faithful to scale on their number lines.

Activity Centre

At an activity centre, place three number cubes, three sets of place-value cards, bingo chips, scrap paper, and a pencil. Have students play the In Between Game in groups of three.

Tell students that they will each roll three number cubes and use the numbers rolled to create a three-digit number. Ask player *A* to roll the number cubes first and use a set of place-value cards to create a three-digit number from the numbers rolled. For example, player *A* rolls a 6, a 4, and a 3, and then uses place-value cards to build the number 436.

Before players *B* and *C* create their three-digit numbers, have player *A* predict whether his/her three-digit number will be the highest, the lowest, or the in-between number of the 3 three-digit numbers. Ask player *A* to record his/her prediction on a piece of scrap paper without letting players *B* and *C* see it. Then, have each of players *B* and *C* roll the three number cubes and use a different set of place-value cards to create their three-digit numbers. If player *A*'s prediction is correct, he/she takes a bingo chip.

Ask players to repeat the entire process again: This time, player *B* rolls the number cube first and predicts whether his/her three-digit number will be the highest, the lowest, or the in-between number of the 3 three-digit numbers. Have players continue in this way; the first player to get five bingo chips wins the game.

Extensions

- Divide the class into pairs. Have students in each pair take turns choosing a three-digit number and recording clues that lead their partner to their number.
- Encourage students to take home their place-value mats, place-value cards, and place-value number tents to share with their families. Or, have students share the activity with students from another class.

Place-Value Mat

Hundreds	Tens	Ones

FOLD BACK

FOLD BACK

FOLD FORWARD

FOLD FORWARD

Place-Value Cards

9	8	7	6	5
0	1	2	3	4

Place-Value Number Tents

FOLD	FOLD	FOLD	FOLD	FOLD	FOLD	FOLD	FOLD	FOLD
1	2	3	4	5	6	7	8	10

FOLD	FOLD	FOLD	FOLD	FOLD
20	30	40	50	60

Place-Value Number Tents

FOLD	FOLD	FOLD	FOLD	FOLD
9	70	80	90	100

FOLD	FOLD	FOLD
200	300	400

Place-Value Number Tents

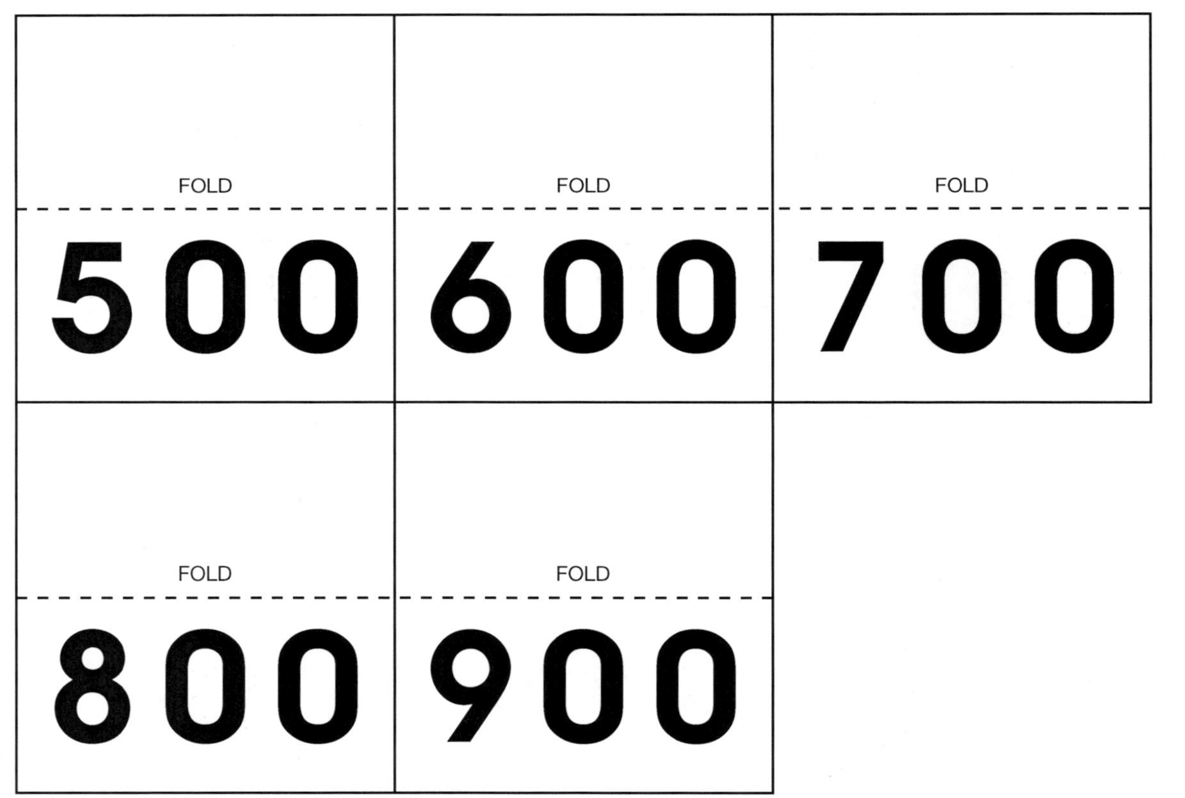

7 Walk to 1000

Materials

- pedometers (check with your school's physical education department, purchase cheap ones at sporting-goods stores, or borrow them from students, friends, and family members who have collected them from cereal boxes and/or fast-food giveaways. You will need as many as possible; ideally, enough for all students.)
- *Miz Berlin Walks*, a book by Jane Yolen
- chart paper
- markers
- blank paper
- pencils
- calculators (one for each student)

Activity: Part One

Read the book *Miz Berlin Walks* with students. Discuss "Miz" Berlin's stories and why Mary Louise enjoyed them so much. Ask:

- How many steps do you think Miz Berlin took each day?
- How many steps do you think Mary Louise took to the end of the block?
- How many steps do you think it would take *you* to get to the end of the block on which our school is located?
- How could we find out? (count steps while walking to the end of the block)

Take students outside, and distribute pedometers to several students (all students, if possible). Show students how to use their pedometers, and walk with them to the end of the block. Tell students to take regular strides as they walk.

Return to the classroom, and record, on a piece of chart paper, how many steps each student took. Then, put the number of steps in order from lowest to highest.

Ask students:

- Why did it take different students a different number of steps to get to the end of the block?
- Do you think it would take an adult a different number of steps to get to the end of the block than it would take a child?

Distribute blank paper and pencils, and ask students how many times they think they would have to walk up and down the block to get to 1000 steps. Have students explain their reasoning through pictures, numbers, and words.

Activity: Part Two

Explain that students will now conduct an experiment to see how many steps they take during the course of a regular school day. Give each student a copy of Activity Sheet A (4.7.1), and have students estimate how many steps they will take over the course of a day. As a reference, remind the class how many steps students took walking to the end of the block. Ask students to record their estimates on their activity sheets.

Distribute pedometers to students, and have them wear the pedometers for a regular school day. Tell students to take pedometer readings at the times specified on the activity sheet, and record their results on the chart. At the end of the day, have students determine the total number of steps taken.

Note: Have students remove their pedometers during lunchtime and recess. If you do not have enough pedometers for the whole class, divide the class into groups the size of the number of pedometers you do have, and have each group do the experiment on a different day.

▶

Once students have completed their charts, graph each student's total number of steps on a large chart-paper graph. Discuss students' findings. Ask:

- Did most students take about the same number of steps over the course of the day?
- What was the highest number of steps taken?
- What was the lowest number of steps taken?
- What could explain these differences?

Have students use the class chart to complete the rest of their activity sheet.

Activity Sheet A

Note: This is a two-page activity sheet.

Directions to students:

Estimate how many steps you will take over the course of the day, and record your estimate on the activity sheet. Wear the pedometer for a regular school day (remove it during lunch and recess), and take readings at the times specified on the activity sheet. Record your results on the chart, and determine the total number of steps you took over the course of the day. Use the class chart to complete the rest of the activity sheet (4.7.1).

Distribute calculators, and have students determine the total number of steps the entire class took over the course of the day. Finally, have students write about their learning in their math journals. Encourage students to reflect on any surprises they may have encountered in the activity.

Problem Solving

Jay walks 850 steps both to and from school each day. He walks home for lunch as well. How many steps does Jay take between home and school each day? Over three days?

Note: A reproducible master for this question can be found on page 495.

Activity Centre

Have students use the Internet and/or the library to do some research about healthy living (including the benefits of exercise). Tell students to write their own healthy-living plans.

Extensions

- Have students challenge the school custodian or principal to wear a pedometer during a regular school day. Compare the total number of steps he/she takes to the total numbers of steps taken by individual students.

- Use the data collected to estimate the total number of steps the average student, the school custodian, or the principal might take over the course of a regular school week.

Date: ________________ Name: ____________________________

Steps in a Day

I estimate that I will take ____________ steps today.

I made this estimate because ________________________________

____.

My Pedometer Readings

Before Morning Recess	At Lunch	Before Afternoon Recess	End of School Day

In total, I walked ____________ steps today.

The actual number of steps I took was ____________ more/less (circle one) than my estimate.

Use the pedometer readings on your chart to determine how many steps you took during each portion of the day:

From school start to morning recess ____________

From morning recess to lunch ____________

From lunch to afternoon recess ____________

From afternoon recess to end of school day ____________

I took the most steps during this portion of the day: ____________.

Date: ________________ **Name:** ____________________________

On the chart below, record the total number of steps each of four of your classmates took over the course of the day. Also, record your name and total number of steps on the chart.

Name	Total Number of Steps

Put the number of steps totals (from the previous chart) in order from lowest to highest.

____________, ____________, ____________, ____________,

____________.

Together, all five students took ____________ steps over the course of the day.

8 One Hundred Pennies

Materials

- *The Hundred Penny Box*, a book by Sharon Bell Mathis
- collection of pennies (you will need several pennies for in-class demonstrations. Also, each student will need a penny dated for each year of his/her life as well as a penny dated for the year of his/her birth.)
- overhead transparency of Activity Sheet A (4.8.1)
- penny book-cover template (included. Make one photocopy for each student.) (4.8.2)
- penny book-page template (included. Each student will need one penny-book page for each year of his/her age, plus one.) (4.8.3)
- scissors
- glue
- stapler

Activity: Part One

Read the book *The Hundred Penny Box* with students. Then, have students sit in a circle, and display your collection of pennies. Ask:

- How can we tell which year this penny was minted (made)?
- How can we determine the age of the penny?
- How old is this penny? (point to a specific penny)
- What year will it be when this penny is 100 years old?
- What is the word we sometimes use for "100 years"?
- What year will it be when you are one century old?

Display the overhead transparency of Activity Sheet A (4.8.1). Tell students that they must record, in the boxes on their activity sheets, the year of their first birthday, the years that will occur between their first birthday and their 100th birthday, and the year of their 100th birthday.

Point to the first empty box on the grid, and ask:

- What number (year) will go here?
- How many years will fit into each row?

Allow students time to fill in their grids (hundred charts). Circulate through the classroom to assess each student's ability to recognize changes as numbers pass over decades and centuries. Then, have students use their hundred charts to complete the questions that follow it.

Activity Sheet A

Note: This is a two-page activity sheet.

Directions to students:

On the blank hundred chart, record the year of your first birthday, the years that will occur between your first birthday and your 100th birthday, and the year of your 100th birthday. Then, use your hundred chart to complete the questions that follow it (4.8.1).

Activity: Part Two

Note: Before beginning this activity, encourage students to look at home for pennies dated for each year of their lives as well as a penny dated for the year of their birth.

Explain to students that they will each gather their own penny collection, just like great-great-aunt Dew from the book *The Hundred Penny Box*. Students will create books to hold their pennies and the memories they have from each year. In their books, students may include events that happened in their lives, events that happened in their communities, and events that happened around the world.

Distribute to each student one penny book cover (4.8.2), one penny book page (4.8.3) for each year of his/her age plus one more, scissors, and glue. Tell students to cut out each page of their penny book as well as the cover.

Tell students to glue one penny to each page of their penny books, beginning with the penny dated for the year of their birth. Then, for each page (year), have students record any memories they have of that year about their families, their communities, and/or the world. Brainstorm with students about things they could include in their books. For example:

- 1998: the new community centre was built
- 1999: I learned how to walk
- 2000: new millenium

...and so on.

Note: Students may also want to consult their families for help with items to include in their penny books, particularly for years in the earlier parts of their lives.

Help students staple their penny books together.

Problem Solving

- The summer Olympic games are held every four years. If there was a summer Olympic games in 2004, when will the next five summer Olympic games occur?
- The winter Olympic games are also held every four years. If there was a 2002 winter Olympic games, in which years were the five winter Olympics previous to 2002 held?

Note: Reproducible masters for these problems can be found on page 495.

Activity Centre

Place a selection of coins at a centre along with pencils and paper. Have students do rubbings of each coin and then determine the age of each coin.

Extensions

- Have students visit the "Learning Centre" link of the Currency Museum website at http://www.currencymuseum.ca/eng/learning/learnAndPlay.php. Through interactive games and activities, students will learn more about Canadian currency, its history, and its role in society.
- Have each student interview a senior citizen to learn more about the history of his/her family or community.

Assessment Suggestion

Meet with students individually, and have them describe, and answer questions about, the 100th birthday number charts they created. Use the Individual Student Observations sheet, found on page 16, to record your results.

Date: ____________________ Name: ________________________________

My 100th Birthday Number Chart

Date: ____________________ **Name:** ________________________________

1. On what year does your number chart begin? ____________________

2. What year will it be when you are one century old? _______________

3. What year will it be when you are fifty years old? _________________

4. What year will it be when you turn twenty-five? ____________________

5. What year will it be when you turn eighty? ____________________

6. What patterns do you notice on your completed number chart?

____

____

____

____

Penny-Book-Cover Template

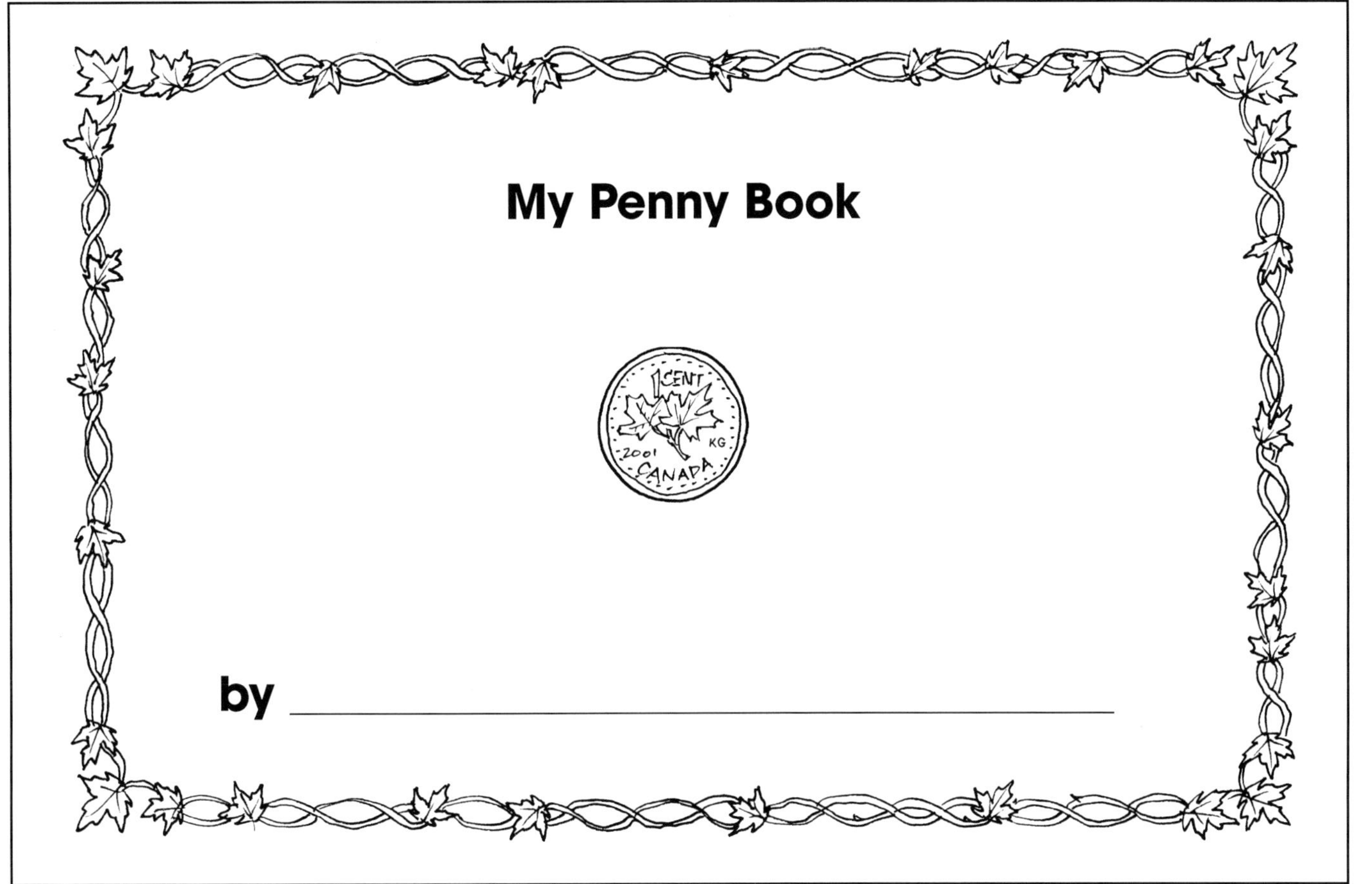

Coin designs © courtesy of the Royal Canadian Mint

Image des pieces © courtoisie de la Monnaie royale canadienne

Penny-Book-Page Template

9 $1000 Budget

Materials

- *The Berenstain Bears' Trouble with Money*, a book by Stan Berenstain and Jan Berenstain
- Digi-Blocks or base-ten blocks (for example, Dienes blocks)
- store catalogues and flyers
- chart paper
- markers
- scissors
- glue
- calculators (one for each student)

Activity: Part One

Present the following problem to students:

Bruce won $1 000 in a hockey raffle. His parents said he could buy one special treat, and the rest would go into a bank account towards his post-secondary education. Bruce has chosen a stereo that costs $395. How much money will go into his bank account?

Discuss with students some different strategies they could use to solve this problem. For example, a horizontal algorithm, mental math strategies (splitting or rounding).

Point out that students could also use Digi-Blocks or base-ten blocks to help them determine the answer. Show students the 1 000 block of a set of Digi-Blocks or base-ten blocks. Remove 395 blocks. Together with students, count the remaining blocks to determine the answer. Ask:

- How many groups of 100 did we remove? (3)
- How many groups of 10 did we remove (39)
- How many single Digi-Blocks did we remove? (395 all together, but five are not packed)
- How many groups of 100 remain in the box? (6)
- How many groups of ten remain? (60, but they are all packed into groups of 100, leaving no tens loose)
- How many single Digi-Blocks remain? (5)

Find a purchasable item in a flyer, and round the price of the item to the nearest dollar. For example, $645. On chart paper, record:

$1 000 – $645 =________

Have students use the Digi-Blocks (or base-ten blocks) to help you find the solution.

Give students a similar problem to solve in their math journals. Tell students to pretend they have each won a $1 000 prize. They each get to choose one item to buy and must put the rest of the money into a bank account.

Distribute scissors, glue, and store catalogues or flyers, and have each student find something to purchase. Ask students to cut out the pictures of their purchases and glue them into their math journals. Also, tell students to record the prices of their items under the pictures. Then, have students use Digi-Blocks to determine how much money they will deposit into their bank accounts once they have made their purchases. Tell students to draw pictures of their Digi-Blocks in their journals and explain their solutions. When students have completed their problems, have them take turns sharing their results and their thinking.

Activity: Part Two

Have students sit in a circle on the floor, and explain that they each have an imaginary budget of $1 000 to buy gifts for their entire family. Each student must purchase one gift for each person living in his/her home and may also purchase a gift for him/herself (students' gifts for themselves must not cost more than $100.) Distribute copies of Activity Sheet A (4.9.1), store catalogues and flyers, scissors, glue, Digiblocks,

and calculators. Tell students to find all their gift choices in the catalogues and flyers, cut them out, and glue each gift onto the chart (or onto the back of their activity sheet if more space is required). Then, have students use the rest of the chart to help keep track of their budgets. Tell students they may use either calculators or Digiblocks to help them make their calculations.

Activity Sheet A

Directions to students:

Cut out all the gifts you choose, and glue each gift onto the chart (or the back of your activity sheet). Use the rest of the chart to help you keep track of your budget. You may use either a calculator or Digiblocks to help you make your calculations (4.9.1).

Problem Solving

Use Activity Sheet A (4.9.1) to develop equations for students to solve. Have students use empty number lines to solve the problems. For example, say:

- Once you have purchased the gift for your mother (or father, or sister), how much money do you have left?

If a student purchased a ring worth $295 for his/her mother, the equation ($295 + ______= $1000) could be solved using one of the following number lines:

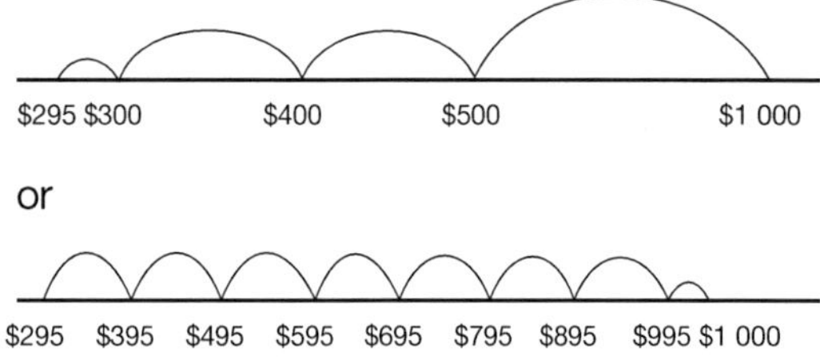

Note: Although efforts have been taken to achieve accurate scale on number lines in *Hands-On Mathematics Grade 3*, scale is not exact, both in terms of jump size as well as between numbers along the number line. Also note that it is not necessary for students to be faithful to scale on their own created number lines. The number line is a strategy to support students' thinking and to help them solve problems, and while correct number order is significant, accurate scale is not.

Activity Centre

Set up a mock store in your classroom. Use sticky notes to price various classroom items to $1 000 each, and have students use play money to purchase items and make change.

Note: Be sure to price all items in dollar amounts only, not in dollars and cents.

Extension

Have students visit the "at School" link of the Practical Money Skills website at http://www.practicalmoneyskills.com for quizzes and games that will help them learn more about money and budgeting.

Date: ____________________ **Name:** ________________________________

$1000 Gift Budget

Gift	Price	Amount of Money Left

10 Doubling

Material

- calculators
- Digi-Blocks or base-ten blocks
- paper
- pencils

Activity: Part One

Present students with the following problem:

Janessa and José are going to work for their parents over the holidays, and their parents will pay them in jellybeans. Both kids will work for 10 days, but each one has asked for a different rate of pay. Janessa asked to receive 100 jellybeans on the first day and 50 jellybeans on each of the following nine days. José asked to receive only 1 jellybean on the first day. For each remaining day, he will receive double the number of jellybeans he received the day before. Who made the better deal, Janessa or José? Why?

Ask students to record their predictions in their math journals, challenging them also to explain their reasoning. Next, have students take turns sharing their predictions and their reasoning. Finally, distribute Activity Sheet A (4.10.1), and have students use the chart to work through the computations and determine the answer. Distribute calculators to students who need help with the addition.

Activity Sheet A

Directions to students:

Determine how many jellybeans Janessa and José will each receive on each day, and how many jellybeans each will receive after 10 days (4.10.1).

Activity: Part Two

Divide the class into groups of five to ten students, and have students in each group sit in a circle. Give each group a block of 1 000 Digi-Blocks (or base-ten blocks) as well as a piece of paper and a pencil. Have the first student in each group take one Digi-Block. Then, moving in a clockwise direction, tell each student in the group to take a new set of blocks that is double the number of blocks the previous student took. Have one student in each group record the number of blocks each student takes.

Distribute copies of Activity Sheet B (4.10.2), and have students double each consecutive number on the grid and then answer the questions that follows the grid.

Note: The number at the beginning of a new row on the grid should be double the number at the end of the previous row.

Activity Sheet B

Directions to students:

Double each consecutive number on the grid. Use your calculations to answer the questions that follows the grid (4.10.2).

Problem Solving

Begin with the number 88. Double the number three times. What number do you end up with? How many times can you double the number before you reach 1 000?

Note: A reproducible master for this problem can be found on page 495.

10

Activity Centre

At an activity centre, place the following books: *Sea Squares*, by Joy Hulme; *The Rajah's Rice: A Mathematical Folktale from India*, by David Barry; *Anno's Magic Seeds*, by Mitsumasa Anno; and *One Grain of Rice: A Mathematical Folktale*, by Demi. Also, have ready-made, blank booklets (fold together several pieces of white paper, and staple) at the centre. Ask students to read each of the books, all of which deal with doubling and multiplication patterns. Then, have students use blank booklets to create their own doubling books.

Extension

Distribute the extension activity sheet called "Tripling Numbers." Have students triple each consecutive number on the grid and then answer the questions that follow the grid.

Date: ______________ Name: ______________________

How Many Jellybeans?

Day	Janessa	José
1		
2		
3		
4		
5		
6		
7		
8		
9		
10		
Total Jellybeans Earned		

After 10 days, Janessa earned ____________ jellybeans while José earned ____________ jellybeans.

Janessa/José made the better deal.
(circle one)

Date: ____________ Name: ____________________

Doubling Numbers

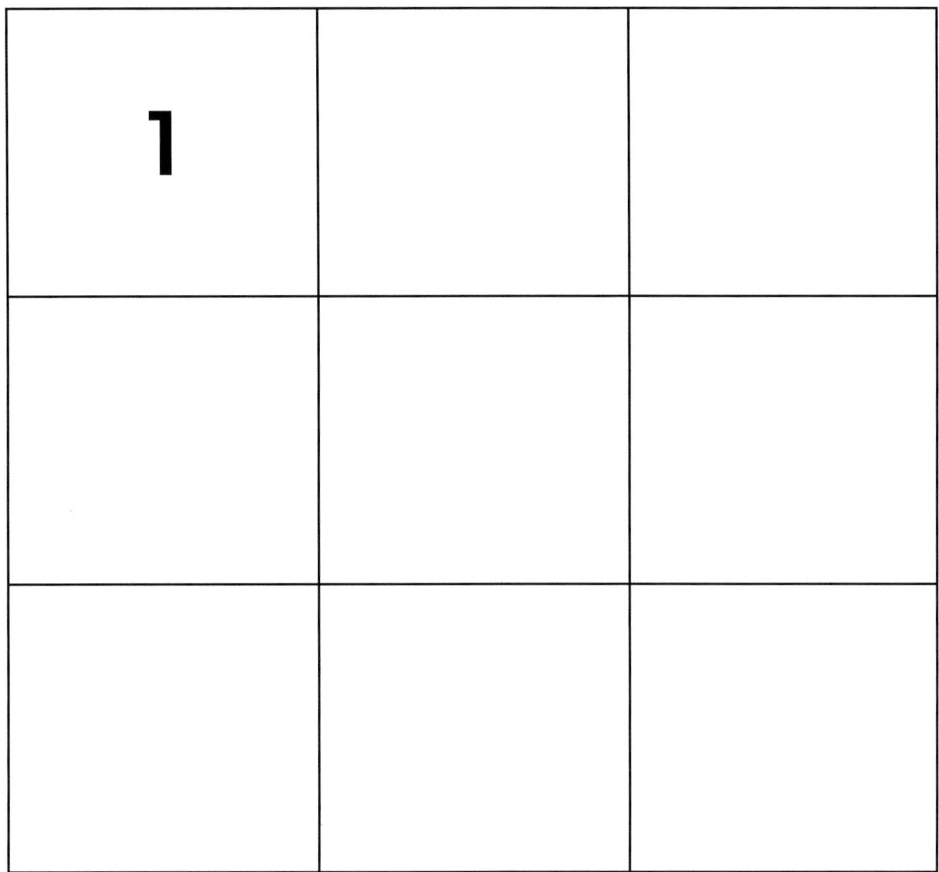

1		

Can you divide the numbers in the grid evenly by 2? How do you know?

___

___

___

Date: ____________________ **Name:** ________________________________

Tripling Numbers

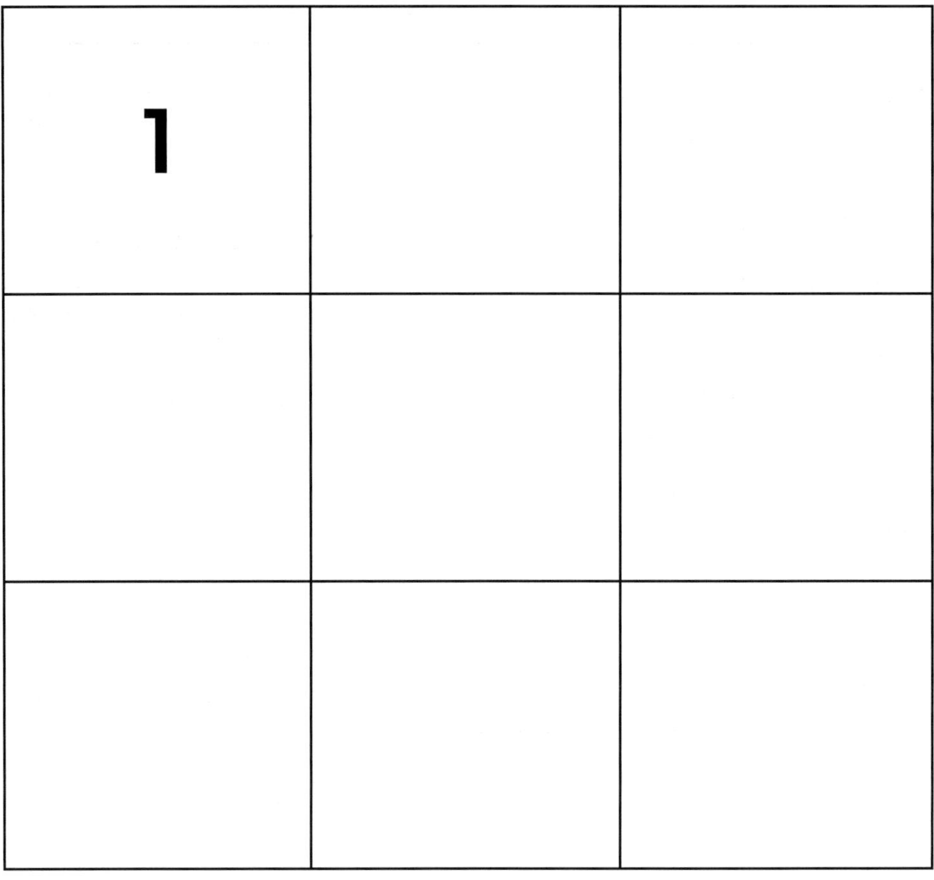

Are the numbers in the grid odd or even? ____________________

Can you divide the numbers in the grid evenly by 2? How do you know?

____

____

____

Extension

11 Numeral and Number-Word Chains

Materials

- large commercial classroom number line (0-100)
- place-value manipulatives (for example, Dienes blocks)
- coloured pencils
- numeral-chain cards (included. Photocopy, mount onto sturdy tagboard, laminate, and cut out cards.) (4.11.1)
- number-word chain cards (included. Photocopy, mount onto sturdy tagboard, laminate, and cut out cards.) (4.11.2)
- Memory-Game cards (included. Photocopy one set for each student.) (4.11.3)
- scissors

Activity: Part One

Explain that students will now play a game that requires them to read numerals and react quickly to statements or questions their classmates make or ask. Shuffle the numeral chain cards (4.11.1), and distribute one to each student. Keep the "start" card for yourself.

Note: For the numeral chain to work, it is essential that all cards are used. If necessary, distribute more than one card to some students.

Read the "start" card aloud, and work through the chain slowly with students. Have students use the classroom number line to help them locate numbers and solve each problem. Students may also find use of place-value manipulatives (such as Dienes blocks) to be helpful for this activity. As students' confidence increases, shuffle, and redistribute the cards, and increase the speed of the numeral-chain activity.

Activity: Part Two

Explain that students will now play a game that requires them to read number words and again react quickly to statements or questions their classmates make or ask. Shuffle the number-word chain cards (4.11.2), and distribute one to each student. Again, keep the "start" card for yourself.

Note: As with the numeral chain, for the number-word chain to work, it is essential that all cards are used. Distribute more than one card to some students if necessary.

As before, work through the chain slowly with students. As students' confidence increases, shuffle, and redistribute the cards, and increase the speed of the number-word chain activity.

Activity: Part Three

Distribute to each student one set (both sheets) of Memory-Game cards (4.11.3) and a pair of scissors. Have students cut out all their cards and then play the Memory Game alone or in pairs. Students can also take the game home to play with family members.

To play, tell students to shuffle their cards and then lay them, facedown, in four rows of six cards. Have students turn over two cards at a time, looking for matches between number words and numerals (for example, forty-seven and 47). If the two cards match, the player keeps the cards. If they do not match, the cards are turned over again. If playing in pairs, the player with the most matches at the end of the game wins.

Distribute Activity Sheet A (4.11.4) and coloured pencils, and have students use the number lines to help them solve each problem.

Activity Sheet A

Note: Enlarge Activity Sheet A onto 11" x 17" paper for students.

Directions to students:

Use the number lines to help you solve each problem (4.11.4).

Problem Solving

Have each student record a three-digit number in his/her math journal. Then, tell students to use the empty-number-line approach to determine different paths they could take from 0 to their chosen number. Have students show the expanded notation number sentence for each path as well.

For example, to get from 0 to 410, one could skip count by 4 hundreds and 1 ten, as below:

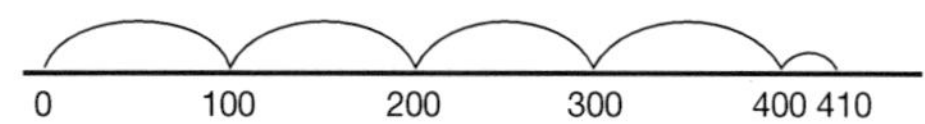

410 = 100 + 100 + 100 + 100 + 10

Note: Although efforts have been taken to achieve accurate scale on number lines in *Hands-On Mathematics Grade 3*, scale is not exact, both in terms of jump size as well as between numbers along the number line. Also note that it is not necessary for students to be faithful to scale on their own created number lines. The number line is a strategy to support students' thinking and to help them solve problems, and while correct number order is significant, accurate scale is not.

Or, one could skip count by 41 tens, as below:

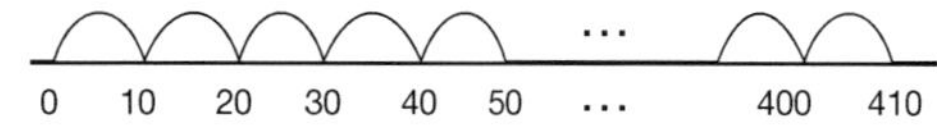

410 = 10 + 10 + 10...

Or, one could skip count by 40 tens and 11 ones, as below:

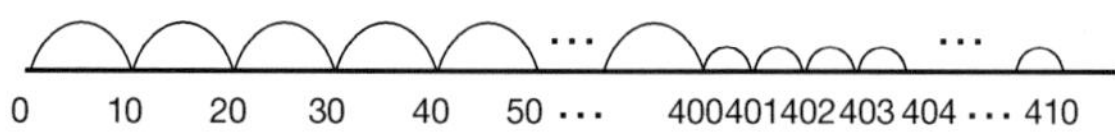

410 = 10 + 10 + 10...+ 1 + 1 + 1...

Note: A reproducible variation of this problem can be found on page 495.

Activity Centre

Have students cut out numerals and number words from newspapers and magazines to create letters for each other, their teachers, parents, principals, and so on.

Extensions

- Ask students to look through magazines, newspapers, and catalogues to find examples of numerals and number words. Then, have students work individually or in small groups to create collages from the numerals and number words.
- As a class or in small groups, create your own numeral chain(s).

Numeral-Chain Cards

START I have **175.** Who has 415 plus 1?	I have **416.** Who has 727 minus 10?	I have **717.** Who has 999 plus 1?
I have **1 000.** Who has 63 plus 11?	I have **74.** Who has ten groups of 10?	I have **100.** Who has 300 more than me?
I have **400.** Who has 400 plus 25?	I have **425.** Who has 600 minus 2?	I have **598.** Who has 598 plus 200?
I have **798.** Who has 1 000 minus 500?	I have **500.** Who has 200 minus 10?	I have **190.** Who has 10 more than 800?

Numeral-Chain Cards

I have **810.** Who has 101 more than 810?	I have **911.** Who has 200 less than 911?	I have **711.** Who has 300 more than 8?
I have **308.** Who has 40 more than 308?	I have **348.** Who has 20 groups of 10?	I have **200.** Who has 150 less than 200?
I have **50.** Who has 50 plus 25?	I have **75.** Who has 75 plus 400?	I have **475.** Who has 475 plus 200?
I have **675.** Who has 8 more than100?	I have **108.** Who has 200 plus 50?	I have **250.** Who has 10 more than 165?

Number-Word Chain Cards

START I have **fifty.** Who has five more than fifty?	I have **fifty-five.** Who has one hundred minus eight?	I have **ninety-two.** Who has forty less than ninety-two?
I have **fifty-two.** Who has ten more than fifty-two?	I have **sixty-two.** Who has ten groups of ten?	I have **one hundred.** Who has twenty less than one hundred?
I have **eighty.** Who has eighty plus four?	I have **eighty-four.** Who has three less than twenty?	I have **seventeen.** Who has seventeen plus thirty?
I have **forty-seven.** Who has nine more than seventy?	I have **seventy-nine.** Who has ten less than seventy-nine?	I have **sixty-nine.** Who has fourteen more than ten?

Number-Word Chain Cards

I have **twenty-four.** Who has ten less than twenty-four?	I have **fourteen.** Who has twenty-six plus ten?	I have **thirty-six.** Who has thirty-six plus forty?
I have **seventy-six.** Who has one more than eleven?	I have **twelve.** Who has seven groups of ten?	I have **seventy.** Who has thirty less than seventy?
I have **forty.** Who has forty plus twenty-five?	I have **sixty-five.** Who has eight more than ten?	I have **eighteen.** Who has eighteen plus twenty?
I have **thirty-eight.** Who has twenty minus one?	I have **nineteen.** Who has ten more than nineteen?	I have **twenty-nine.** Who has fifty less than one hundred?

Memory-Game Cards

47	63	98
72	19	67
44	32	11
29	84	99

Memory-Game Cards

forty-seven	sixty-three	ninety-eight
seventy-two	nineteen	sixty-seven
forty-four	thirty-two	eleven
twenty-nine	eighty-four	ninety-nine

Date: ______________________ Name: ______________________

Number Line Problems

0 1 2 3 4 5 6 7 8 9 10 11 12 13 14 15 16 17 18 19 20 21 22 23 24 25 26 27 28 29 30 31 32 33 34 35 36 37 38 39 40 41 42 43 44 45 46 47 48 49 50

I am 13 more than 28. Draw a blue square around me on the number line above.

I am 27 less than 50. Draw a red circle around me on the number line above.

I am 3 times 12. Draw a purple line under me on the number line above.

I am 2 less than 50. Draw a green triangle around me on the number line above.

0 51 52 53 54 55 56 57 58 59 60 61 62 63 64 65 66 67 68 69 70 71 72 73 74 75 76 77 78 79 80 81 82 83 84 85 86 87 88 89 90 91 92 93 94 95 96 97 98 99 100

I am 10 less than 30. Draw an orange square around me on the number line above.

I am 47 less than 96. Draw a green circle around me on the number line above.

I am 3 times 25. Draw a black line under me on the number line above.

I am 78 more than 22. Draw a yellow triangle around me on the number line above.

12 Fractions

Background Information for Teachers

A *fraction* expresses a part of a set, a ratio, or the relationship between a part and a whole. At the grade-one level, the focus is on fractions as part of a whole. Introducing students to part/whole relationships facilitates their understanding of money, time, and measurement. In this lesson, students demonstrate, and explain orally, an understanding of halves as part of a shape or solid.

Materials

- variety of snacks that can be cut in half, such as apples, oranges, pears, cheese slices, muffins (Have enough for just half the class, so that each item has to be shared.)

Safety Note: Be sure to consider any student allergies when selecting snack foods.

- knife, for teacher use only
- paper plates
- collection of greeting cards (collect cards that use a half fold only)
- construction paper
- scissors
- glue
- coloured paper
- crayons, pencil crayons, or markers

Activity: Part One

Display a variety of snack foods. Tell students that these treats are for a class snack. Ask:

- How many students are in our class?
- How many apples/muffins/cheese slices do we have?
- Do we have enough for all the students?
- What could we do to make sure that everyone gets some of each snack?
- How can we be sure that we share the snacks fairly?

Focus on the equal sharing of each snack with students. They will likely suggest cutting the snacks to make enough for everyone. Ask:

- How could I cut each item to make two equal parts?

Cut each food item in half, discussing and comparing the two equal parts. Share the snacks with students.

Activity: Part Two

Display a variety of greeting cards. Ask:

- What characteristic of a greeting card allows us to open and close it? (It is folded.)
- What shape was the paper before it was made into a card?

Open one of the cards to show the rectangular shape of the flat sheet. Ask:

- How was the sheet folded to make a card?

Explain that the sheet was folded in half. Open one of the cards, and show the fold line. Pass around the collection of greeting cards for students to examine.

Now, provide each student with a sheet of construction paper. Explain that they are going to make their own greeting cards. Challenge them to fold their sheets in half to make cards.

Note: Students can fold the sheets either widthwise or lengthwise, as long as they fold the sheets in half.

▶

12

After students have had time to experiment with folding their sheets of construction paper, have them share their solutions with the rest of the class.

Discuss the meaning of the term *one half*. Using one of the greeting cards, explain that the sheet is folded into two parts, and each part is equal in size. With the card closed, show how the two halves are the same size. Each part of the sheet is one half of the whole sheet.

Now, have students use their folded sheets to create greeting cards for classmates, family members, or friends.

Next, distribute Activity Sheet A (4.12.1). Have students cut out each shape, fold it in half, and then cut along the fold. Once they have made sure the two halves are equal, they can glue them onto a sheet of paper and then colour one of the halves.

Activity Sheet A

Directions to students:

Cut out one shape, and fold it into two, equal parts. Cut the shape in half along the fold line. Place one half on top of the other to make sure they are equal. Glue the halves onto a sheet of blank paper. Colour one half of the shape. Do the same for each of the four shapes (4.12.1).

Problem Solving

Present to students the following problems:

- Mark made a kite. He put blue paper on one half of the kite. He put white paper on the other half of the kite. Draw and colour what Mark's kite looks like.
- Michelle helped her mom bake an apple pie. They ate one half of the pie for supper. Draw a picture to show how much of the pie is left.
- Isabelle has a granola bar. She wants to share it with her brother, Sam. Draw a picture to show how the bar can be cut into 2 equal halves.

Note: Reproducible masters for the previous three problems can be found on page 496.

Extension

Add the term *one half* and the symbol *1/2* to the Math Word Wall.

Activity Centre

For this centre, you need play dough, simple cookie cutters, and plastic knives. Have students flatten the play dough, use the cookie cutters to cut out simple shapes, then cut the shapes in half. Students can check to see if the halves are equal by placing one on top of the other.

Assessment Suggestion

Have students complete the Student Self-Assessment sheet, found on page 21, to reflect on their learning about fractions.

Date: ____________ Name: ____________________

Show One Half

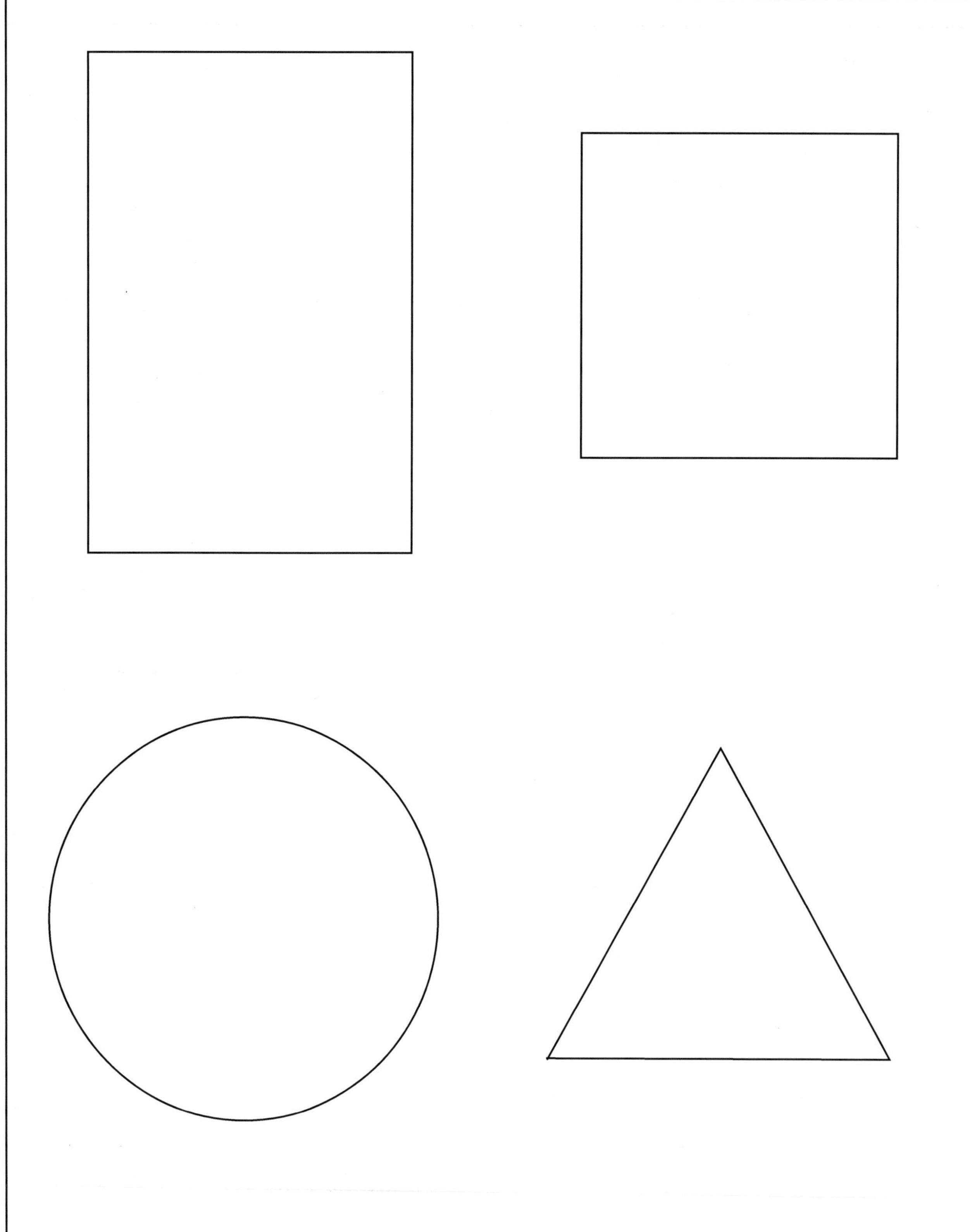

13 More Fractions: Halves

Background Information for Teachers

Provide many opportunities for students to use the language of fractions in natural settings, such as while they are measuring and sharing, while you are passing out materials, and so on. Be sure to focus on both:

- the fractional part of a whole, such as parts of an object. For example: half of the pizza
- the fractional part of a set, such as components of a group of objects. For example: half of the dozen eggs

Materials

- *Give me Half!* a book by Stuart Murphy
- fraction cards *A* (included. Make one photocopy for each student.) (4.13.1)
- crayons (five crayons for each student including one orange, one yellow, one green, one brown, and one red)
- envelopes
- scissors
- 10-centimetre squares of construction paper, in two colours (one square for each student. Have half as many squares in one colour as there are students in your class, and half as many squares in the other colour as there are students in your class.)

Activity: Part One

Provide each student with a copy of fraction cards *A* (4.13.1), which shows shapes or pictures divided into either two equal parts or two unequal parts. Have students cut apart their cards and then examine the shape or picture on each card. Ask:

- Into how many parts is each shape divided?
- Are all of the shapes divided into two *equal* parts?

Challenge students to sort the pictures into two groups: equal and not equal. Check their sorting, then have students put aside their unequal cards.

Together as a class, discuss the shapes that are divided equally into two parts. Explain to students that each of these cards shows a shape or picture divided into *halves*.

Now, distribute crayons to students, and provide them with the following instructions:

- Find your picture of the Popsicle. Colour one half of the Popsicle orange.
- Find your picture of the cracker. Colour one half of the cracker yellow.
- Find your oval shape. Colour one half of the oval green.
- Find your picture of the cookie. Colour one half of the cookie brown.
- Find your heart shape. Colour one half of the heart red.

Distribute envelopes, and have students store their fraction cards *A* (both the "halves" cards and the unequal cards) in the envelopes.

Activity: Part Two

Read the book, *Give Me Half!* Now, show students the one-half symbol ($\frac{1}{2}$). Have students retrieve their set of fraction cards *A* from their envelopes. Have students again sort the pictures into two groups: equal and not equal. On each "equal" card, ask students to record the one-half symbol on the uncoloured half of the shape/picture.

Problem Solving

Distribute to each student a pair of scissors and a 10-centimetre square of construction paper in one of two colours. Half of the class should have squares in one colour, and half of the class should have squares in the other colour.

13

Have students fold their squares diagonally in half, from corner to corner, and then cut along the folded lines to make two halves. Ask students:

- How many different ways can you put the triangles together so that the edges that are touching are the same length?

Have students work independently to solve this problem.

Now, pair up students so that each pair has two triangles in each colour.

Note: If you have an odd number of students in the class, work with the remaining student for this activity.

Tell the pairs of students to combine their triangle halves (each pair should have four halves, two halves in one colour and two halves in a second colour). Pose a second challenge for the pairs to solve by asking:

- How many different ways can you put four triangles together so that the edges that are touching are the same length?

Note: Students should be putting all four triangle halves together to form one new shape, in as many different ways as possible.

When the pairs of students have solved this problem, have them use their scissors to cut each of their triangles in half again. Each pair should now have eight triangles, four in one colour and four in the other colour. Ask:

- How many different ways can you put eight triangles together so that the edges that are touching are the same length?

Activity Centre

Divide the class into groups of two to four players. Provide each group with copies of "The Hexagon Race" game board (one copy for each player), a number cube, yellow hexagon pattern blocks, and red trapezoid pattern blocks (each player will need ten yellow hexagons and twenty red trapezoids).

Have players take turns rolling the number cube and taking as many red trapezoids as the number rolled. At the end of their turns, players may also trade any two red trapezoids (halves) for one yellow hexagon (whole). The first player to fill his/her board with yellow hexagons is the winner (4.13.2).

Extension

Add the terms *half/halves, equal,* and *unequal* to your classroom Math Word Wall.

Fraction Cards A

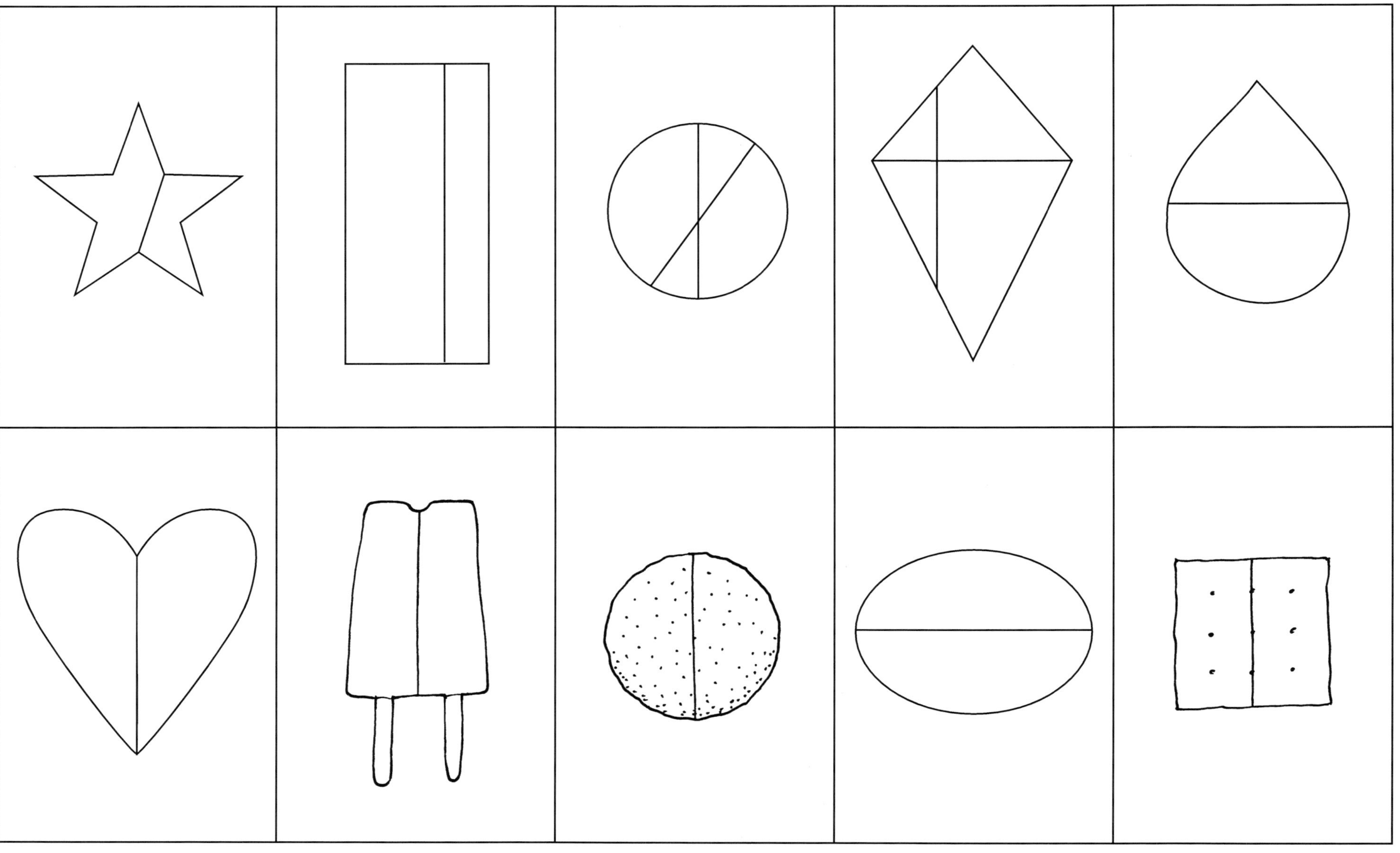

The Hexagon Race Game Board

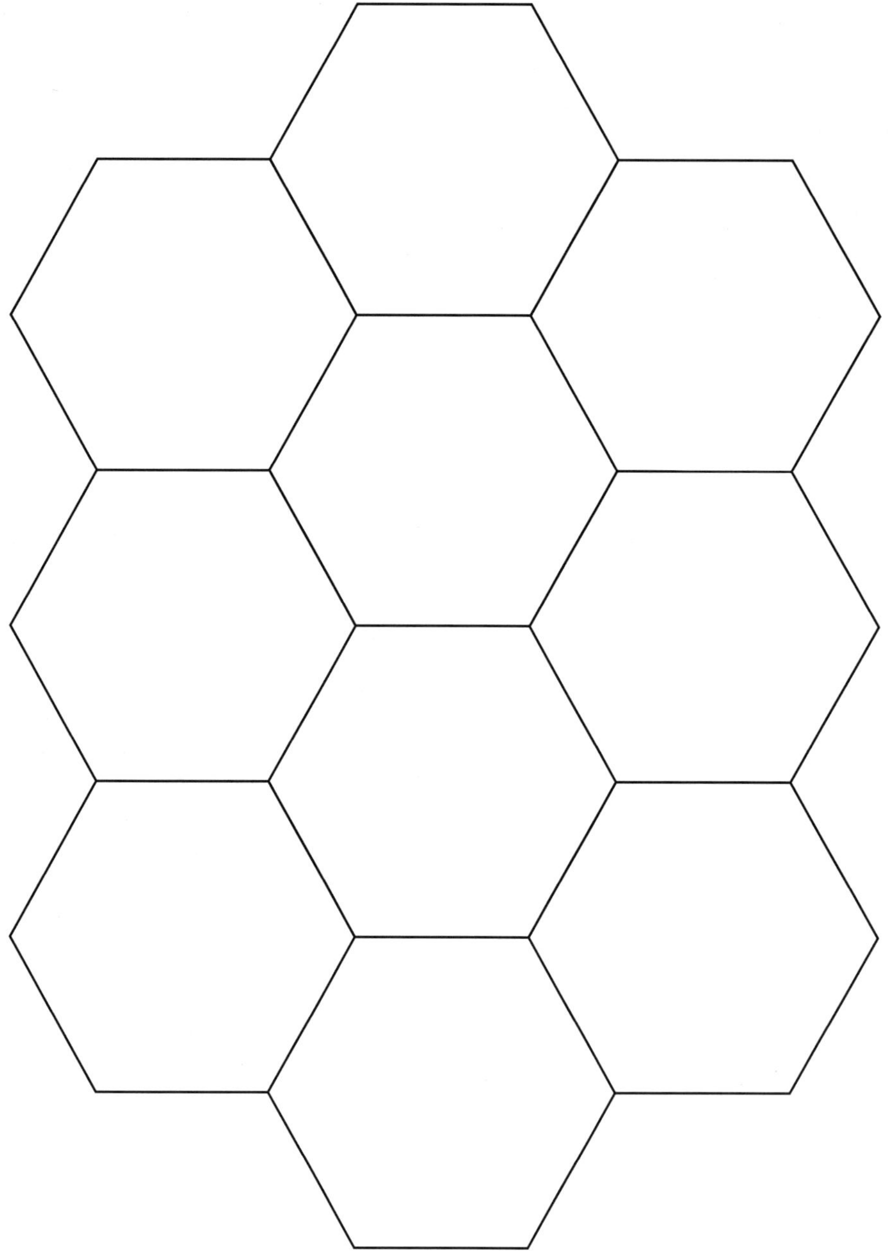

14 More Fractions: Fourths

Materials

- envelopes with fraction cards *A* (from lesson 17) (4.13.1)
- fraction cards *B* (included. Make a photocopy for each student) (4.14.1)
- envelopes
- chart paper
- markers
- crayons
- geoboards (one for each student)
- elastic bands (four for each student)

Activity: Part One

Have students sort their sets of fraction cards *A* into groups of halves and not halves. Review with students that a half is one of two *equal* parts of a divided whole. Have students put aside the cards that do not show halves. Collect these cards.

Provide each student with a set of fraction cards *B* (4.14.1) and a pair of scissors. Have students cut apart the cards. Ask:

- What can you tell me about how the shapes/pictures on these cards are divided?
- Is each shape divided into the same number of parts?
- Into how many parts are the shapes divided?

Have students sort their set of fraction cards *B* into shapes that are divided into fourths and shapes that are not. Ask students to put aside the shapes that are not divided into fourths and to focus on the shapes that are divided into fourths. Draw a circle on chart paper. Ask:

- What would one fourth of the circle look like?

Have students share their ideas. Then, divide the circle into fourths, and shade one fourth of the circle. Record the $\frac{1}{4}$ symbol on (or near) each quarter, as in the following diagram:

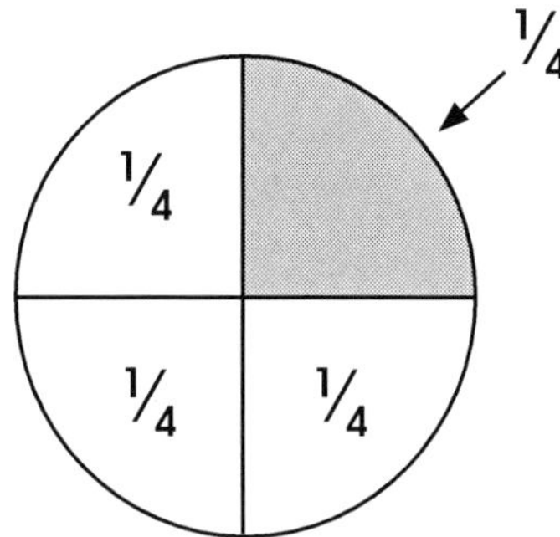

Have students colour in one fourth of each of their "fourths" fraction cards and record the $\frac{1}{4}$ symbol on (or near) each fourth.

Note: Have each student store all of his/her fraction cards (halves, thirds, and fourths) in an envelope.

Problem Solving

Use four elastic bands to find as many ways as you can to divide a geoboard into fourths. Be sure that you create four equal parts.

Note: A reproducible master for this problem can be found on page 496.

Extension

Add the terms *fourth(s)* and *quarters* to your classroom Math Word Wall.

Fraction Cards B

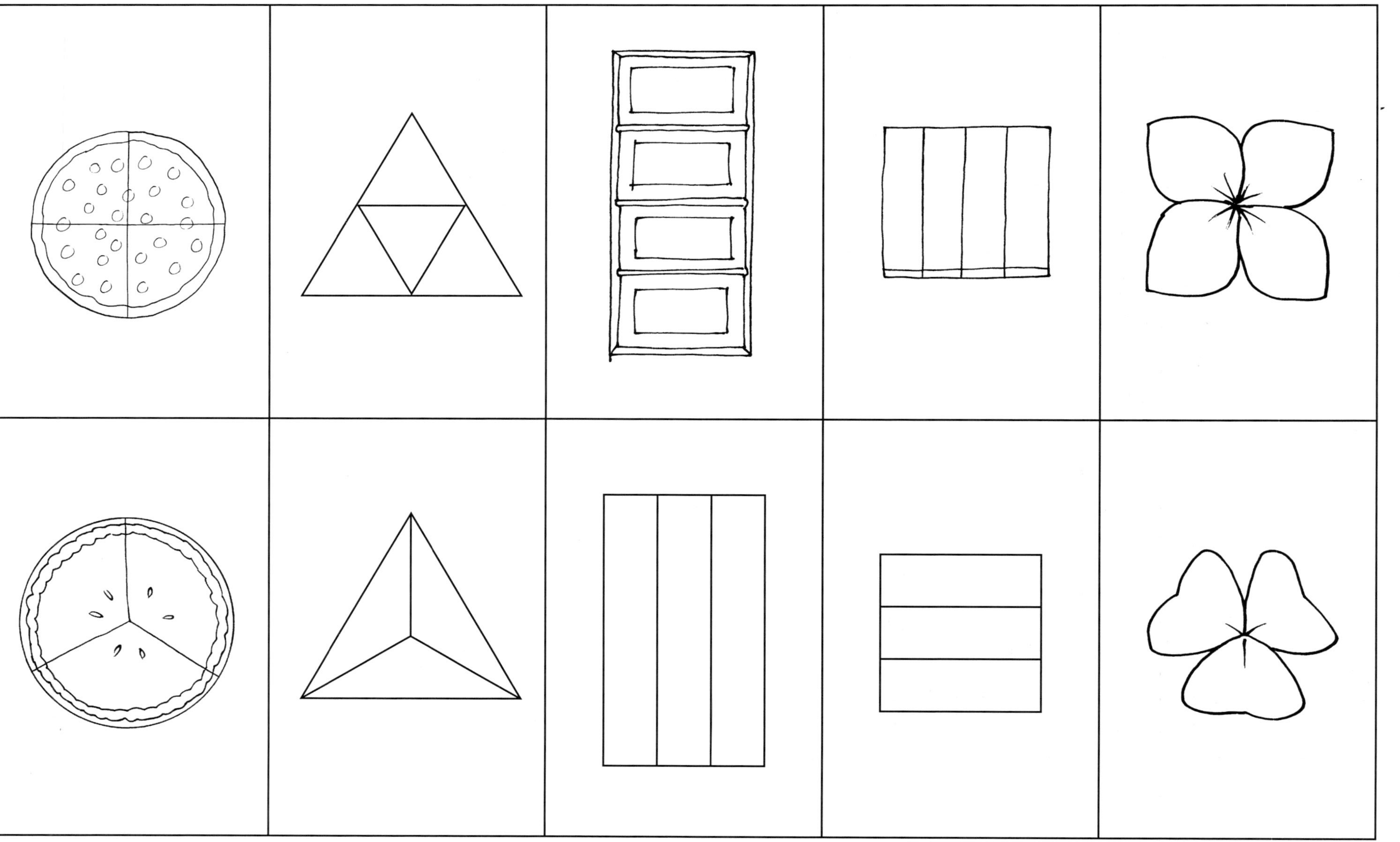

15 More Fractions: Thirds

Materials

- fraction cards (both sets *A* and *B*, one set for each student, in envelopes, from lessons 13 and 14)
- chart paper
- markers
- crayons
- geoboards (one for each student)
- elastic bands

Activity

Distribute envelopes of fraction cards (*A* and *B*) to students. Have students examine and sort their fraction cards into groups. Then, ask students:

- How did you sort your cards?
- How are the cards in each of your groups different from the cards in your other groups?

Discuss the different ways students sorted their cards. Ask students who did not already sort their cards by fractions to do so now. Ask students:

- Can you point to the cards that show halves?
- Can you point to the cards that show fourths or quarters?
- What does the third group of cards show?

Have students focus on the shapes/pictures divided into thirds. Draw a square on chart paper. Ask students:

- Can you show me one third of the square?

Have students share their ideas. Then, divide the square into thirds, and shade one third of the square. Record the $^1/_3$ symbol on (or near) each third of the square.

Have students use crayons to colour in one third of each of their "thirds" fraction cards and record the $^1/_3$ symbol on each part.

Note: Have students store all of their fraction cards in envelopes.

Problem Solving

Use three elastic bands to find as many ways as you can to divide a geoboard into thirds. Be sure that you create three equal parts.

Note: A reproducible master for this problem can be found on page 496.

Extension

Add the term *third(s)* to your classroom Math Word Wall.

16 Still More Fractions

Materials

- fraction pieces template (included. Make four photocopies of the sheet for each student, as well as four overhead transparencies of the sheet for demonstration.) (4.16.1)
- large envelopes
- overhead projector
- permanent overhead markers (four different colours)
- chart paper
- markers
- crayons (four different colours for each student)
- scissors
- scrap paper
- construction paper (one sheet for each student)
- small chalkboards or whiteboards
- chalk or whiteboard markers
- bingo chips (thirty-six for each group of five students)
- paper clips (two for each group of five students)
- sharp pencils (two for each group of five students)

Activity: Part One

Before beginning this activity, cut out the overhead-transparency circles from the fraction pieces templates (4.16.1), but do not cut out the individual fraction pieces. You will need one whole circle, two circles showing halves, three circles showing thirds, and four circles showing fourths.

Create a set of overhead fraction pieces (including $1/2$, $2/2$, $1/3$, $2/3$, $3/3$, $1/4$, $2/4$, $3/4$, and $4/4$, as well as one whole circle) by using different coloured permanent overhead markers to colour in different fraction pieces. For example, on a circle showing fourths, colour one quarter of the circle red. On a second circle showing fourths, colour one quarter of the circle red and a second quarter green. On a third circle showing fourths, colour one quarter of the circle red, a second quarter green, and a third circle blue, and so on.

Provide each student with a pair of scissors and four copies of the fraction pieces template (4.16.1). Have students cut out all the fraction-pieces circles (but not the individual fraction pieces).

Display the transparency of the whole circle on the overhead. Ask students:

- Is this circle divided into parts? (no)

Explain that this circle shows one whole. Now, display the circle that shows $1/2$. Ask:

- Is this circle divided into parts?
- Are the parts equal?
- How many parts are shown?
- How many parts are coloured in?

Have each student select a circle showing halves from his/her own set and use a crayon to colour in one half of the circle.

Display the overhead circle that shows $1/3$. Ask students:

- Is this circle divided into parts?
- Are the parts equal?
- How many parts are shown?
- How many parts are coloured in?

Have each student select a circle showing thirds from his/her set and use a crayon to colour in $1/3$ of the circle.

Now, display the overhead circle showing $2/3$. Ask:

- Is this circle divided into parts?
- Are the parts equal?
- How many parts are shown?
- How many parts are coloured in?

Have each student select a circle showing thirds from his/her set and use two different colours of crayons to colour in $^2/_3$ of the circle (a different colour for each third).

Repeat until each student has created a set of fraction pieces that includes circles showing $^1/_2$, $^2/_2$, $^1/_3$, $^2/_3$, $^3/_3$, $^1/_4$, $^2/_4$, $^3/_4$, and $^4/_4$, as well as one whole circle.

Note: Have students store their fraction pieces in envelopes when not in use.

Activity: Part Two

Provide each student with a sheet of construction paper to use as a work mat. Now, call out a fraction, and record it on chart paper. Have students show the same fraction by finding it among their own fraction pieces and displaying it on their work mats. For example, say:

- Show me one whole. (record on chart paper)
- Show me one fourth.
- Show me two fourths.
- Show me one third.

Repeat the activity, this time having students record the fractions you say on chalkboards or whiteboards.

Distribute Activity Sheet A (4.16.2) and divide students into groups of five to play "Fraction Bingo." Also provide each group with thirty-six bingo chips, two paper clips, two pencils, a pair of scissors, and scrap paper. Have students cut out their fraction bingo cards and spinner templates. Show students how make spinners with the paper clips, pencils and spinner templates. Ask groups to choose one player to be their caller. Have the caller distribute a fraction bingo card and nine bingo chips to each of the other four players. Explain the rules of the game to students.

Activity Sheet A

Note: This is a two-page activity sheet.

Directions to students:

Cut out the four fraction bingo cards. Choose one player to be the caller. Have the caller distribute a fraction bingo card and nine bingo chips to each of the other four players. Cut out the spinner templates. Use paper clips and pencils with the spinner templates to make spinners.

Have the caller spin both the shape spinner and the fraction spinner, one at a time. Then, have the caller call out the fraction and shape he/she spun. For example: "circle, $^1/_3$." Tell the caller to record the shape/fraction spun on scrap paper. Have players check their fraction bingo cards for shapes with the same fractions shaded. If a player has the correct shape/fraction, have him/her cover it with a bingo chip. Continue until one player fills his/her fraction bingo card and calls out, "Bingo!" Check that player's bingo card against the caller's recorded spins to make sure no errors have been made (4.16.2).

Distribute Activity Sheet B (4.16.3), and have students complete their Carroll diagrams by drawing, dividing, and correctly shading each shape.

Activity Sheet B

Directions to students:

Complete the Carroll diagram: Draw the correct shape in each box. Divide and colour each shape according to the fraction above it (4.16.3).

16

Problem Solving

- Draw several squares. Find all the different ways you can divide a square into fourths (four equal parts).
- Draw a triangle. Find a way to divide the triangle into thirds (three equal parts).
- Draw a triangle. Find a way to divide the triangle into fourths (four equal parts).

Note: Reproducible masters for these problems can be found on pages 496 and 497.

Fraction Pieces Template

Fraction Bingo

Fraction Bingo Cards

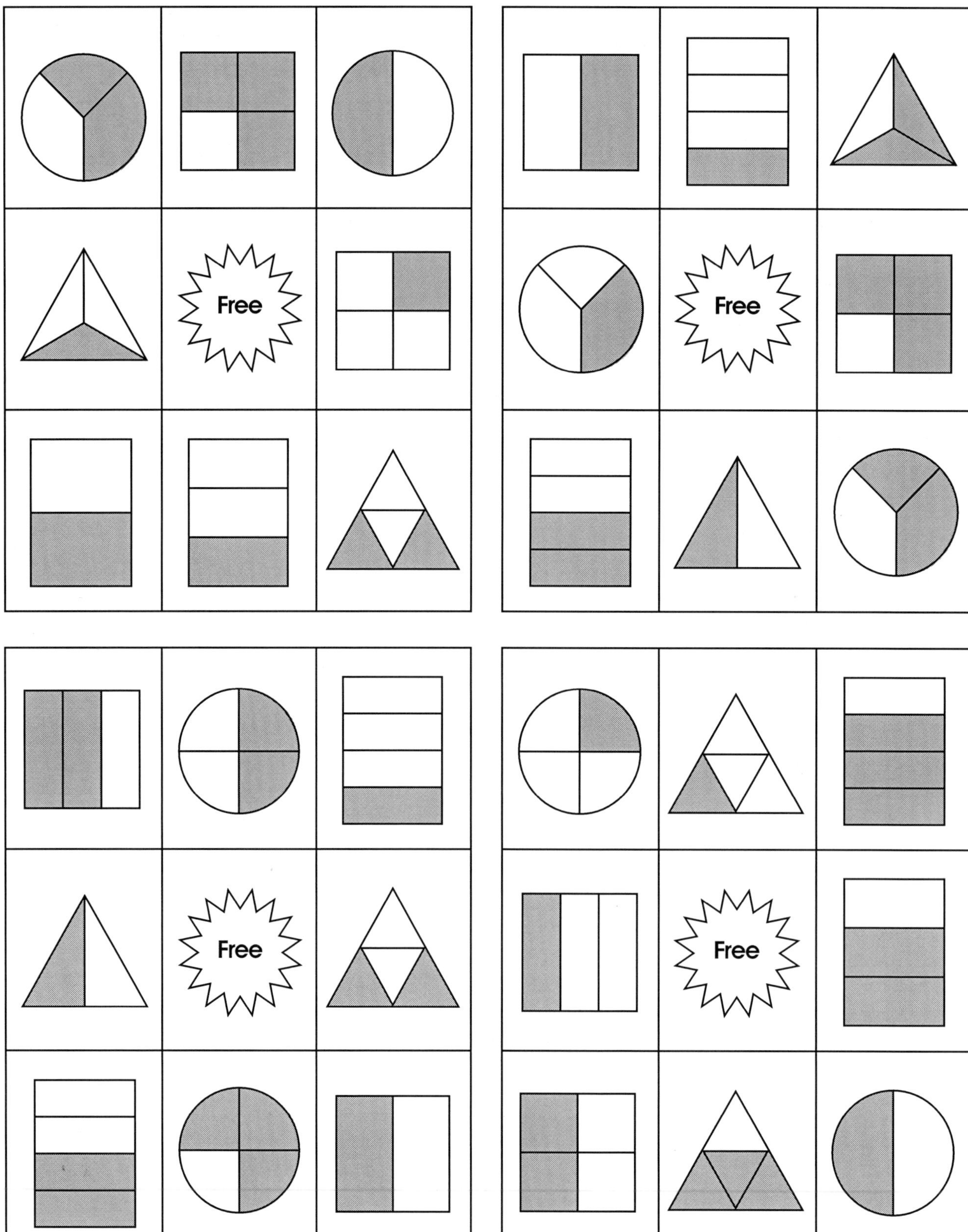

Spinner Templates

Shape Spinner

Fraction Spinner

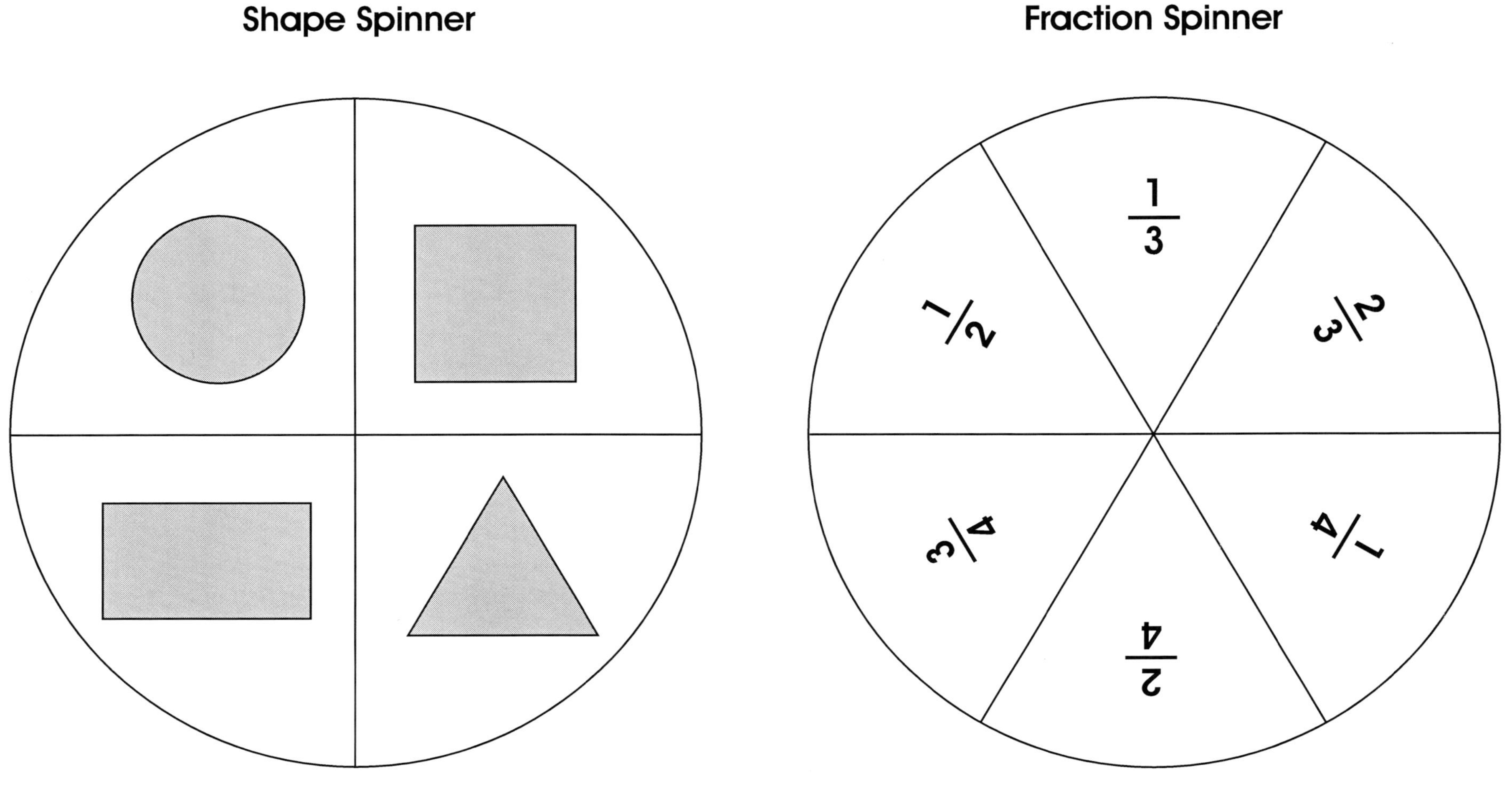

Date: ______________________ Name: ______________________

Shape Fractions

	$\frac{1}{4}$	$\frac{1}{3}$	$\frac{1}{2}$	$\frac{2}{4}$	$\frac{2}{3}$	$\frac{3}{4}$

17 Comparing Fractions

Materials

- pattern blocks (you will need a large quantity)
- chart paper
- markers (colours to match pattern block pieces)
- fraction pieces (made by students in previous lesson 16) (4.16.1)
- overhead transparencies of fraction pieces (from lesson 16) (4.16.1)
- overhead projector
- paper clips (one for each student)
- pencils (one for each student)

Activity: Part One

Have students sit in a circle. Place a large quantity of pattern blocks in the centre, and ask each student to take one hexagon. Ask:

- How could you cover half of your hexagon?
- Which block could you use to do this?
- Can you think of another way to cover half of the hexagon?

Allow students time to explore ways to cover half of their hexagons. Have students share their solutions, and record their ideas by drawing the shapes on chart paper. For example, draw a yellow hexagon and then draw the red trapezoid inside half of the hexagon. Or, draw the yellow hexagon and then draw three green triangles inside half of the hexagon.

Discuss with students how the area covered by the trapezoid is equal to the area covered by the three triangles.

Now, have students focus on their hexagons again. Ask:

- How could you cover one third of the hexagon?
- Which block could you use to do this?
- Can you think of another way to cover one third of the hexagon?

Allow students time to explore ways to cover one third of their hexagons. Have students share their solutions, and record their ideas by drawing the shapes on chart paper. For example, draw a yellow hexagon and then draw a blue rhombus inside one third of the hexagon.

Note: Ensure that the rhombus you draw is the same shape as the *blue*-rhombus pattern block, not the tan-rhombus pattern block.

Or, draw the yellow hexagon, and then draw two green triangles inside one third of the hexagon.

Discuss with students how the area covered by the trapezoid is equal to the area covered by the three triangles.

Activity: Part Two

Use the overhead fraction pieces (4.16.1) to compare fractions for students. For example, display the circles showing $\frac{1}{2}$ and $\frac{2}{4}$. Say:

- Look carefully at the coloured parts of these two circles. How are these circles different?
- How are these circles the same?
- Is the coloured area on both circles equal?

Overlap one circle on top of the other to show that the coloured areas are equal.

Now, have students use their fraction pieces to compare fractions. Ask students to spread out all of their fraction pieces in front of them. Ask questions such as:

- Can you display the fraction piece that shows $\frac{1}{3}$?
- Can you display the fraction piece that shows $\frac{1}{4}$?
- Which is the larger fraction?

Check for understanding by having students hold up their selected fraction pieces. Display the overhead fraction pieces showing $^1/_3$ and $^1/_4$. Overlap one circle on top of the other to show that the shaded area of the $^1/_3$ fraction piece is larger than the shaded area of the $^1/_4$ fraction piece.

Repeat this activity by comparing different fraction pieces.

Distribute Activity Sheet A (4.17.1) and scissors, and have students cut out their game boards, spinner templates, and fraction game pieces. Also, ask students to cut apart their fraction game pieces along the dotted lines.

Have students play "The Fraction Race" game in pairs. Distribute paper clips and pencils to students, and show them how to use them with their spinner templates to make spinners. Explain the rules of the game to students.

Activity Sheet A

Note: This is a two-page activity sheet.

Directions to students:

Cut out the game board, the spinner template, and the fraction game pieces. Cut apart the fraction game pieces along the dotted lines. Use a paper clip and a pencil with the spinner templates to make a spinner.

Play "The Fraction Race Game" with a partner. Take turns spinning your spinners, finding fraction game pieces to match the fractions spun, and placing the game pieces in circles on your game boards. The first player to fill in all the circles on his/her game board wins the game (4.17.1).

Problem Solving

You have half a pizza. How would you share it with 2 friends? With 3 friends? Four friends? Show your work.

Note: A reproducible master for this problem can be found on page 497.

Extension

Have students play "The Fraction Race Game" again, this time adding $^1/_8$ game pieces and a $^1/_8$ space to the spinner ($^1/_8$ game pieces and new spinner included). If a player lands on the "Free" space on the new spinner, he/she selects the fraction piece of his/her choice to place on his/her game board (4.17.2).

Assessment Suggestion

Use the Student Self-Assessment sheet, found on page 21, to have students reflect on their learning about fractions.

The Fraction Race Game

Game Board

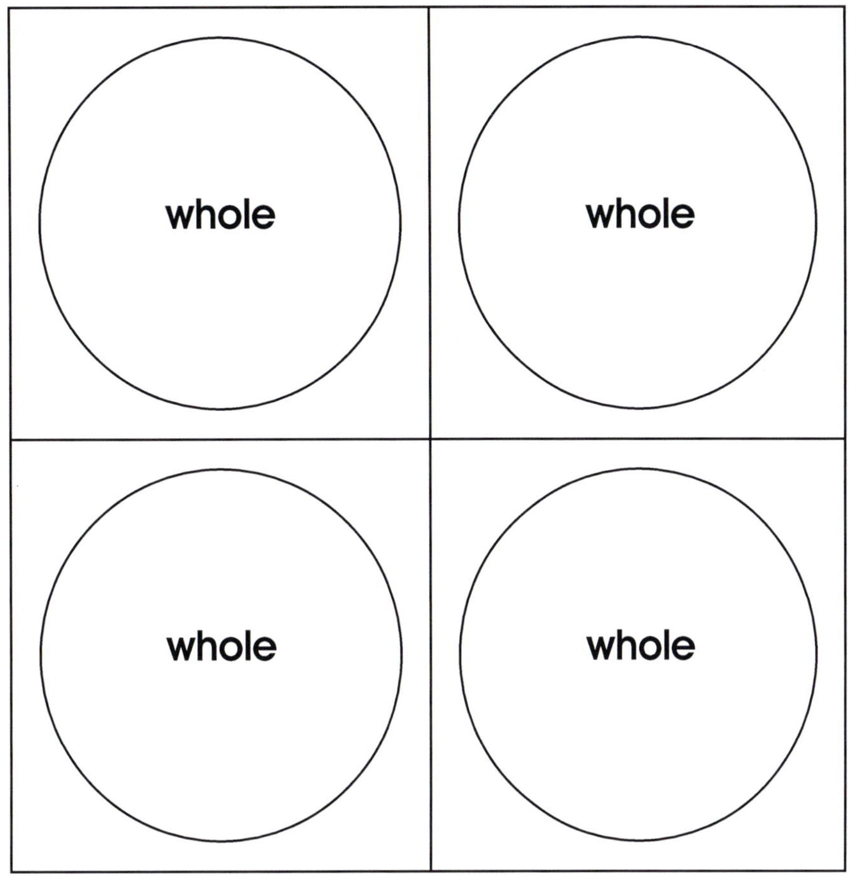

Spinner Template

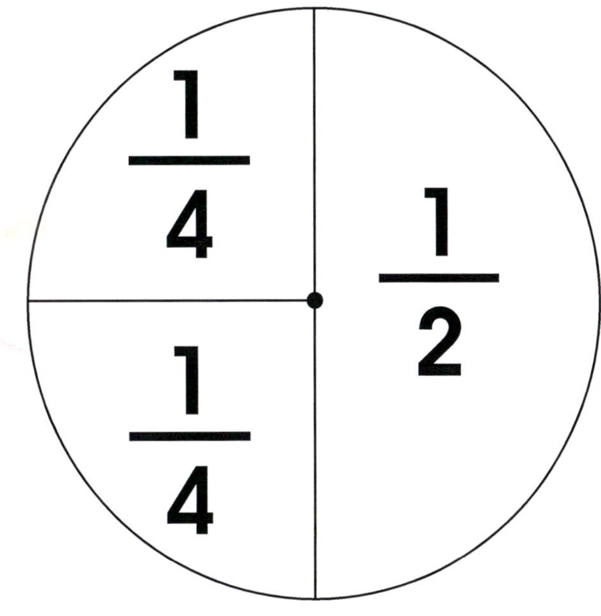

Fraction Game Pieces

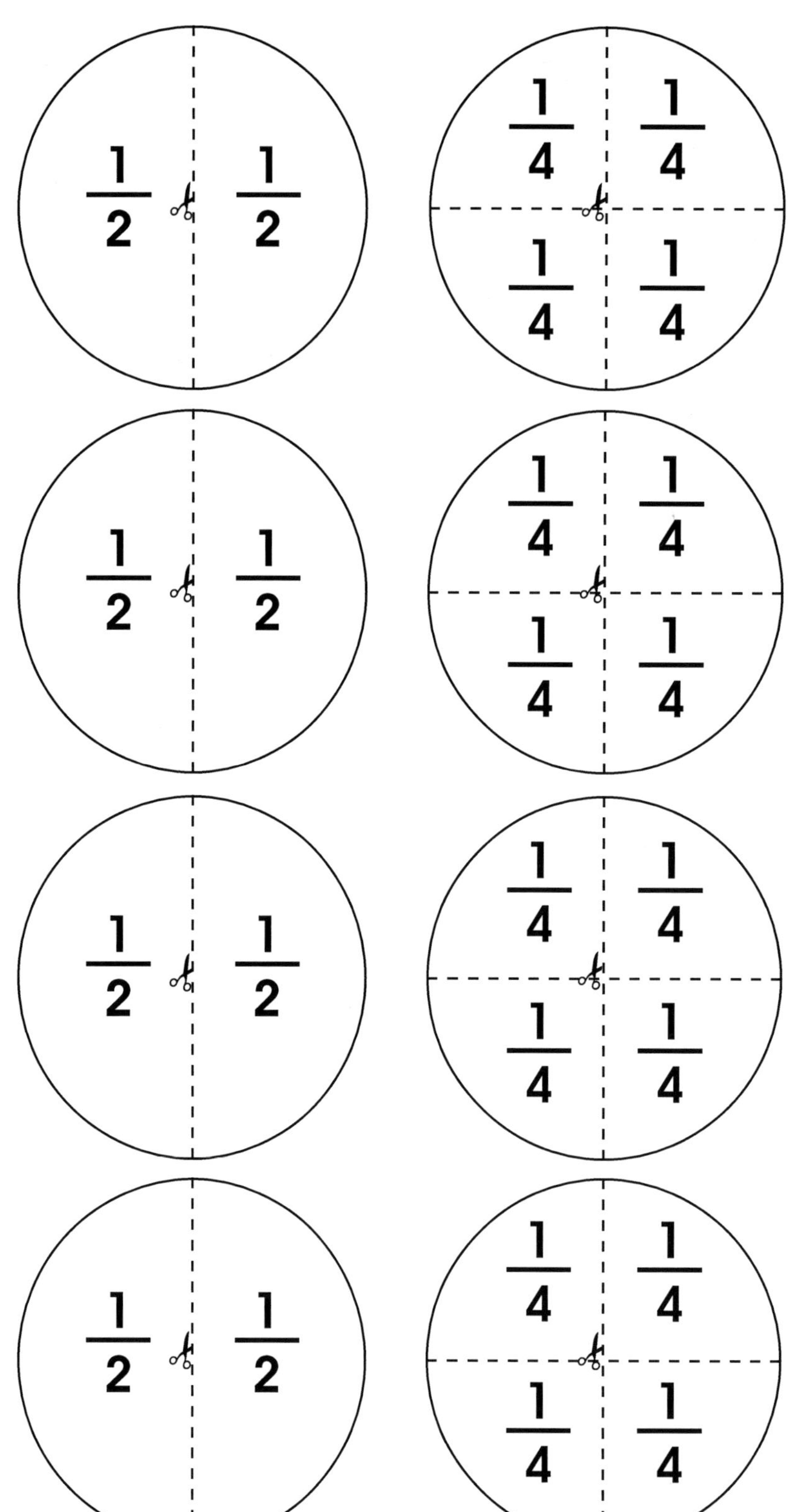

Extension Game Pieces and Spinner

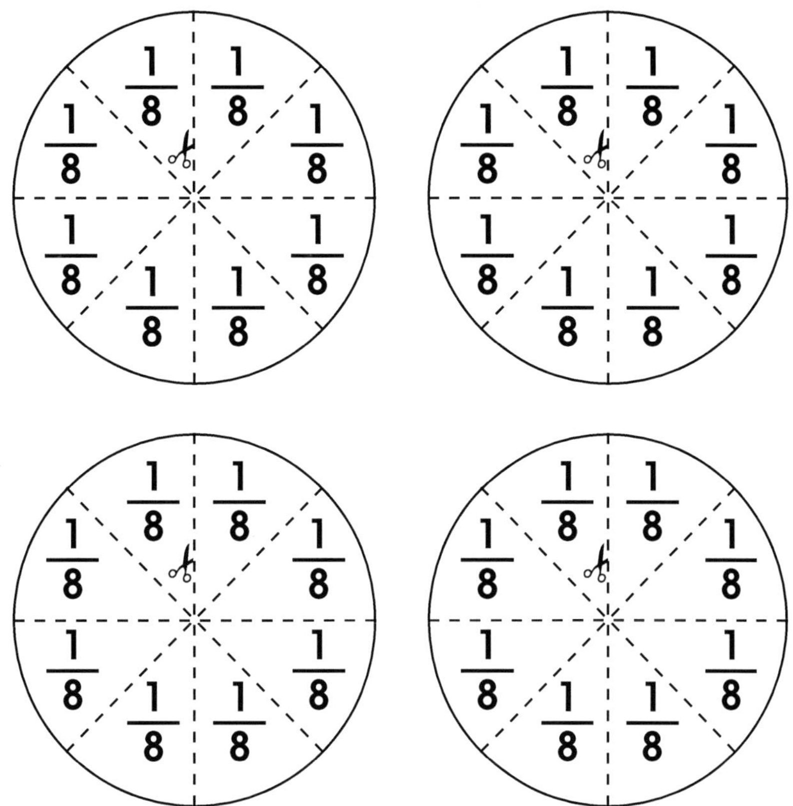

Spinner Templates

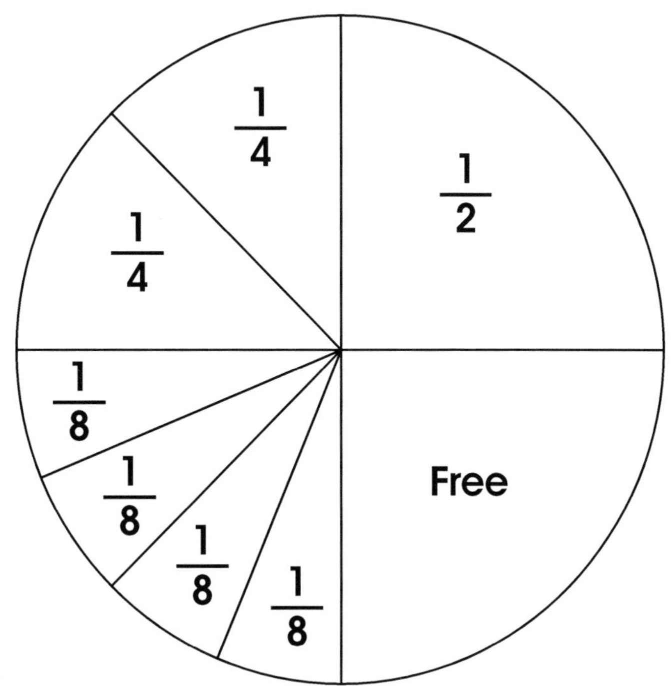

Problem-Solving Black Line Master: Number Concepts

Copy the following 4 sheets onto overhead transparencies to present to students as daily problem-solving activities. Or, photocopy the pages, and cut them apart for students, problem by problem. Have students paste the problems into their math journals or agendas for completion independently.

✂ -

Calculate the sum of all the digits in your telephone number. Then, calculate the sum of all the digits in your street address. Which sum is less? What is the difference between the sum of the digits in your telephone number and the sum of the digits in your street address?

Module 4, lesson 1

✂ -

Beginning at 237, skip count by 5s six times. What number do you get?

From module 4, lesson 4, page 426

✂ -

Beginning at 492, skip count by 2s thirteen times. What number do you get?

From module 4, lesson 4, page 426

✂ -

If you began at 386 and skip counted by 5s, would you say the number 416? Explain how you know.

From module 4, lesson 4, page 426

✂ -

Use a hundred chart to help you answer this question:

- How many numbers do you say when you count from 1 to 100 by 25s?

From module 4, lesson 5, page 435

▶

Choose two numbers between 1 and 1 000. Use the empty-number-line approach to determine the difference between the two numbers.

From module 4, lesson 6, page 439

Jay walks 850 steps both to and from school each day. He walks home for lunch as well. How many steps does Jay take between home and school each day? Over three days?

From module 4, lesson 7, page 446

The summer Olympic games are held every four years. If there was a summer Olympic games in 2004, when will the next five summer Olympics games occur?

From module 4, lesson 8, page 450

The winter Olympic games are also held every four years. If there was a 2002 winter Olympic games, in which years were the five winter Olympics previous to 2002 held?

From module 4, lesson 8, page 450

Begin with the number 88. Double the number three times. What number do you end up with? How many times can you double the number before you reach 1 000?

From module 4, lesson 10, page 458

Record a three-digit number. Draw an empty number line, and use it to show a path you could take from 0 to your number. Draw another empty number line, and show a different path you could take from 0 to your number.

Adapted from module 4, lesson 11, page 464

Mark made a kite. He put blue paper on one half of the kite. He put white paper on the other half of the kite. Draw and colour what Mark's kite looks like.

From module 4, lesson 12, page 473

Michelle helped her mom bake an apple pie. They ate one half of the pie for supper. Draw a picture to show how much of the pie is left.

From module 4, lesson 12, page 473

Isabelle has a granola bar. She wants to share it with her brother, Sam. Draw a picture to show how the bar can be cut into 2 equal halves.

From module 4, lesson 12, page 473

Use four elastic bands to find as many ways as you can to divide a geoboard into fourths. Be sure that you create four equal parts.

From module 4, lesson 14, page 479

Use three elastic bands to find as many ways as you can to divide a geoboard into thirds. Be sure that you create three equal parts.

From module 4, lesson 15, page 481

Draw several squares. Find all the different ways you can divide a square into fourths (four equal parts).

From module 4, lesson 16, page 484

Draw a triangle. Find a way to divide the triangle into thirds (three equal parts).

From module 4, lesson 16, page 484

Draw a triangle. Find a way to divide the triangle into fourths (four equal parts).

From module 4, lesson 16, page 484

You have half a pizza. How would you share it with 2 friends? With 3 friends? Four friends? Show your work.

From module 4, lesson 17, page 490

References for Teachers

Burns, Marilyn, and Robyn Silbey. *So You Have to Teach Math? Sound Advice for K-6 Teachers*. Sausalito, CA: Math Solutions Publications, 2000.

Fennell, Francis, et al. *Connect to NCTM Standards 2000: Making the Standards Work at Grade 3*. Chicago, IL: Creative Publications, 2000.

Ronfeldt, Suzy. *Third Grade Math: A Month to Month Guide*. Sausalito, CA: Math Solutions Publications, 2003.

Skinner, Penny. *It All Adds Up! Engaging 8-12-Year-Olds in Math Investigations*. Sausalito, CA: Math Solutions Publications, 1998.

Weinberg, Amy Shulman, et al. *Up and Down the Number Line: Changes (Investigations in Number, Data, and Space)*. Lebanon, IN: Dale Seymour Publications, 1994.

Van de Walle, John A. *Elementary and Middle School Mathematics*. Don Mills, ON: Addison Wesley Longman, 2001.

Module 5

Number Operations

Books for Children

Anno, Mitsumasa. *Anno's Magic Seeds*. New York, NY: Philomel Books, 1995.

______. *Anno's Math Games*. New York, NY: Philomel Books, 1987.

Anno, Mitsumasa, and Masaichiro Anno. *Anno's Mysterious Multiplying Jar.* New York, NY: Philomel Books, 1983.

Axelrod, Amy. *Pigs Will Be Pigs: Fun with Math and Money*. New York, NY: Simon & Schuster, 1994.

Boynton, Sandra. *Hippos Go Berserk!* New York, NY: Simon & Schuster, 1996.

Buckless, Andrea. *Too Many Cooks!* New York, NY: Scholastic, 2000.

Chorao, Kay. *Number One Number Fun*. New York, NY: Halliday House, 1995.

Chwast, Seymour. *The Twelve Circus Rings.* San Deigo, CA: Harcourt Brace Jovanovich, 1993.

Day, Nancy Raines. *Double Those Wheels*. New York, NY: Dutton Children's Books, 2003.

Edens, Cooper. *How Many Bears?* Toronto, ON: Maxwell Macmillan, 1994.

Friedman, Aileen. *The King's Commissioners*. New York, NY: Scholastic, 1994.

Garland, Sherry. *The Lotus Seed.* San Diego, CA: Harcourt Brace Jovanovich, 1993.

Giganti, Paul, Jr. *Each Orange Had Eight Slices: A Counting Book*. New York, NY: Greenwillow Books, 1992.

Hong, Lily Toy. *Two of Everything: A Chinese Folktale.* Morton Grove, IL: Albert Whitman, 1993.

Hulme, Joy N. *Counting by Kangaroos*. New York, NY: Scientific American Books for Young Readers, 1995.

______. *Sea Squares*. New York, NY: Hyperion Books for Children, 1991.

Hutchins, Pat. *The Doorbell Rang*. New York, NY: Greenwillow Books, 1986.

LoPresti, Angeline Sparagna. *A Place for Zero: A Math Adventure*. Watertown, MA: Charlesbridge, 2003.

Losi, Carol A. *The 512 Ants on Sullivan Street*. New York, NY: Scholastic, 1997.

Moore, Inga. *Six-Dinner Sid*. New York, NY: Simon & Schuster 1991.

Murphy, Stuart J. *Shark Swimathon*. New York, NY: HarperCollins, 2001.

______. *Betcha!* New York, NY: HarperCollins, 1997.

______. *Divide and Ride*. New York, NY: HarperCollins, 1997.

______. *Too Many Kangaroo Things to Do!* New York, NY: HarperCollins, 1996.

Neuschwander, Cindy. *Amanda Bean's Amazing Dream*. New York, NY: Scholastic, 1998.

Pinczes, Elinor J. *A Remainder of One*. New York, NY: Houghton Mifflin, 1995.

______. *One Hundred Hungry Ants*. New York, NY: Houghton Mifflin, 1993.

Rylant, Cynthia. *The Relatives Came.* Toronto, ON: Maxwell Macmillan, 1993.

Stamper, Judith. *Breakfast at Danny's Diner*. New York, NY: Grosset & Dunlap, 2003.

Tang, Greg. *The Grapes of Math*. New York, NY: Scholastic, 2001.

Viorst, Judith. *Alexander, Who Used to Be Rich Last Sunday*. New York, NY: Aladdin Books, 1988.

Introduction

The goal of the number operations module is to enhance students' computational fluency with addition, subtraction, multiplication, and division. In keeping with this goal, the activities in this module promote the use of various methods of computing.

The activities involving addition and subtraction focus on recalling basic number facts for these operations and on computing with three-digit numbers. They also highlight student-created algorithms, the development of estimation and mental-math skills, and the appropriate use of calculators. Of particular significance is the emphasis on student-created algorithms. Unlike traditional algorithms, student-generated algorithms give students additional insight into place-value concepts and the relationships between numbers.

It is important to note that number-operation questions are primarily presented in a horizontal format, which encourages the use of mental math and student-created algorithms. A vertical format implies the use of the standard algorithm, which inhibits students' number-sense abilities and flexible-thinking strategies.

The activities involving multiplication and division focus on basic number facts for these operations. They also include the development of operational properties such as the relationship between multiplication and division. These properties extend students' understanding of the operations and provide them with important strategies for learning the basic facts.

Many of the activities in this module involve a problem-solving approach to the teaching of mathematics, which encourages students to explore new ideas and to make sense of mathematical concepts in ways that are meaningful to them. It also encourages students to share their findings and justify their conclusions. It is a powerful technique that helps students develop their abilities to solve problems, to communicate, and to reason mathematically.

Some lessons in this module include a section called "Next Steps," which guides teachers through a subsequent sequence of activities to carry out with students, following developmentally from the main activities. For example, in the problem solving section of lesson 7, students are asked to use the strategy of their choice to solve addition story problems involving addition with three-digit numbers. Once students have mastered this, the next step is for them to create their own addition story problems for their classmates to solve.

Mathematics Vocabulary

Continue to use your classroom mathematics word wall to display new vocabulary as it is introduced. Throughout this module, teachers should use, and encourage students to use, vocabulary such as: *bridge to ten, compatible number, difference, sum, product, factor, times, multiply, divide,* and *digit*. Use, and encourage students to use, this vocabulary, both orally and in writing, and continue to review all vocabulary previously introduced.

Depending on your students' writing skills, also consider having them begin mathematics logbooks for recording:

- new math vocabulary
- mental-math strategies
- problem-solving strategies
- graphic organizers

1 Addition and Subtraction Facts to 18

Materials

- marvelous math machine (included. Photocopy sheet onto an overhead transparency.) (5.1.1)
- overhead projector
- nonpermanent overhead markers
- paper

Activity

Place the marvelous-math-machine transparency on the overhead. Explain to students that this machine does something to any number we put into it and then spits the number back out again.

Direct students' attention to the input/output table under the machine. Record a 1 in the first column of the first row and a 3 in the second column of the first row. Tell students that if you put a 2 into the machine, a 4 would come out. Record the 2 and the 4. Continue to describe the process, and record numbers in this manner: when a 3 goes into the machine, a 5 comes out; when a 4 goes into the machine, a 6 comes out, and so on, as in the following diagram:

In	Out
1	3
2	4
3	5
4	6

Ask students:

- What pattern do you see in the numbers on the chart?
- If we put a 5 into the machine, what number would come out?
- If an 8 came out of the machine, what number would we have put in?
- What rule is the marvelous math machine using to change numbers before spitting them back out? (add 2)

Repeat the process with a more difficult series of input/output numbers, such as:

In	Out
5	9
9	13
14	18
1	5
7	
	7
	14
0	

Once you get to rows five through eight of the chart, have students help you fill in the missing numbers.

Repeat the process several more times, using rules such as:

- add the number to itself
- add 8
- subtract 3
- double the number plus 1

Distribute Activity Sheet A (5.1.2), and have students complete the input/output tables in part 1. For part 2, tell students to fill in the missing numbers in each table so that the sum of each number pair equals the number at the top of the chart.

1

Activity Sheet A

Directions to students:

Complete the input/output tables in part 1. For part 2, fill in the missing numbers in each table so that the sum of each number pair equals the number at the top of the chart (5.1.2).

Problem Solving

- Tony sold some newspapers on Monday, and he sold 8 newspapers on Tuesday. Altogether, he sold 17 newspapers. How many papers did Tony sell on Monday?
- Bruce and Robbie are playing cards. Robbie has 9 cards. Together, the two boys have 14 cards. How many cards does Bruce have?
- Gwen had 7 dimes. Nicky had 6 dimes and 3 pennies. Gwen's father gave her some more dimes. Now she has 13 dimes. How many dimes did Gwen's father give her?

Note: Reproducible masters for these problems can be found on page 609.

Activity Centre

Note: For this activity centre, each pair of students will need a deck of playing cards from which the face cards have been removed.

Distribute decks of cards to pairs of students. Tell students to shuffle their cards and place them, facedown, in a pile between them. Have player *A* in each pair pick up three cards from the deck (without showing them to player *B*), find the sum of the numbers on the cards, and tell player *B* what the sum is. Next, tell player *A* to choose one of the three cards, place it facedown between them, and show the remaining two cards to player *B*, as in the diagram below:

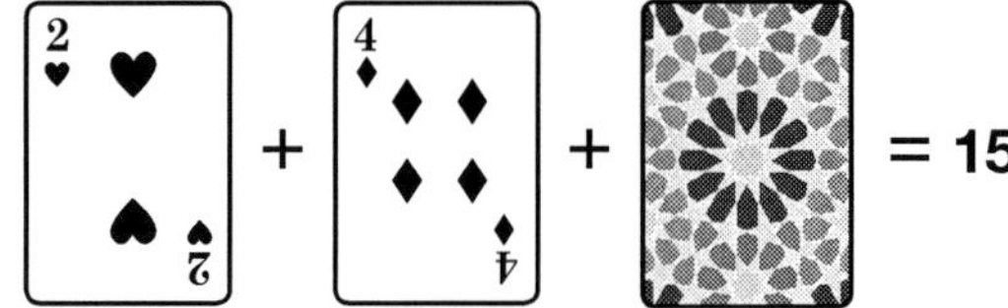

Have player *B* determine what the number on the facedown card is. Then, tell students to exchange roles and repeat the activity.

Marvelous Math Machine

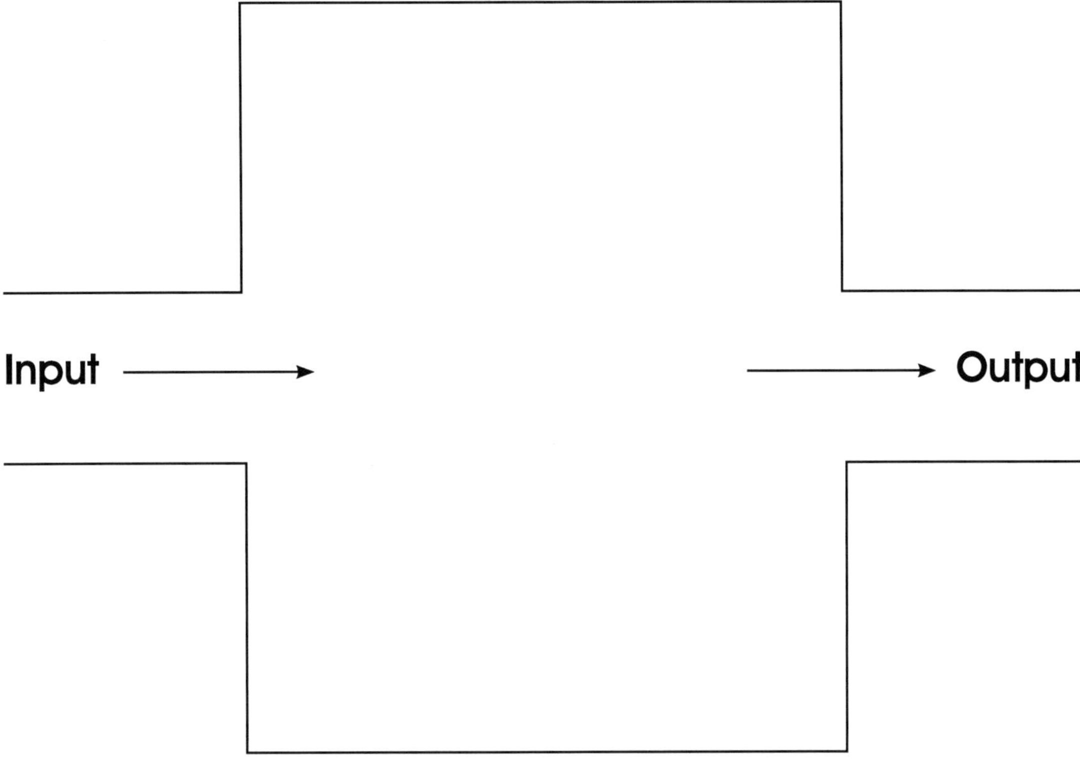

Input/Output Table

In	Out

Date: ____________________ Name: ________________________________

Input/Output Tables

Part 1

In	Out
6	16
2	12
	11
	18
	10

In	Out
12	6
18	12
15	9
	3
	11

Part 2

13	
6	
	8
9	

16	
8	
9	
	10

2 More Addition and Subtraction Facts

Materials

- two 6-sided number cubes (large or overhead number cubes work well for these activities)
- chart paper
- markers
- paper
- pencils
- Zero game cards (included. Photocopy one set of cards for each group of four students. Mount cards onto sturdy tagboard, and cut out.) (5.2.2)
- +, −, and = cards (included. Photocopy two sets of cards for each group of four students. Mount cards onto sturdy tagboard, and cut out.) (5.2.3)

Activity: Part One

Distribute paper and pencils to students. Roll the two number cubes, and record, on chart paper, the numbers you rolled. Challenge students to record, on their own paper, as many addition and subtraction number sentences as they can for which the answer equals the sum of the numbers you rolled.

For example, if the sum of the two numbers rolled is 7, students record number sentences for which 7 is the answer, such as the following:

- 12 − 5 = 7
- 3 + 4 = 7
- 15 − 9 + 1 = 7

Note: Students do not have to use the numbers rolled in their number sentences, just the sum of the two numbers rolled. Encourage students to consider number sentences that have more than two addends, such as the third example above.

Once students have had an opportunity to record their number sentences, ask students to share their sentences with the rest of the class. Below the two numbers recorded on chart paper, record the correct number sentences students share.

Next, challenge students to find the longest number sentence that has the same answer as the sum of the two numbers rolled. Repeat the activity several times.

Distribute Activity Sheet A (5.2.1). Tell students to make each number sentence in part 1 true by recording an addition or subtraction sign in the box and filling in one of the missing numbers from the list at the top of the sheet. For part 2, have students make each number sentence true by recording addition and/or subtraction signs in the boxes.

Activity Sheet A

Directions to students:

Make each number sentence in part 1 true by recording an addition or subtraction sign in the box and filling in one of the missing numbers from the list at the top of the sheet. For part 2, make each number sentence true by recording addition and/or subtraction signs in the boxes (5.2.1).

Activity: Part Two

Note: For this activity, each group of four students will need a set of Zero game cards (thirty-eight cards comprised of two times each of the numbers 0 through 18) (included, 6.2.2) and two sets of +, −, and = cards (eight "+" cards, eight "−" cards, and eight "=" cards) (included, 6.2.3). Photocopy, and cut out all cards ahead of time.

Organize students into groups of four, and have them play Zero. Give each group a set of Zero game cards and two sets of +, −, and = cards. Have player *A* in each group shuffle the Zero game (number) cards and deal four cards to each player. Tell player *A* to place the remaining cards, facedown, in the centre of the playing area. Also, have player *A* spread out the +, −,

2

and = cards, face up, so that they are available to all four players.

Tell players that their goal is to use all four of their number cards and any of the +, –, or = cards they need in order to make number sentences that equal 0. For example, with the cards 4, 8, 6, and 2, a player could make the sentence 6 – 2 + 4 – 8 = 0, as in the diagram below:

Have player *A* go first and draw a card from the facedown deck. If player *A* decides to keep the drawn card, he/she must discard one of his/her original four cards and place it, face up, into a discard pile. Tell player *B* to go next and draw the top card from either the facedown deck or the face-up discard pile. If player *B* keeps the drawn card, he/she must discard one of his/her original four cards. Have players continue to take turns with this process. Players may also decide to pass a turn. The first player who can use all four number cards in his/her hand together with any of the +, –, or = cards to build a number sentence that equals 0 wins the game.

Date: ____________________ Name: ________________________________

What Is Missing?

Missing Numbers:	7	6	10	8	4	9	15	2

Part 1

3 □ _______ = 11

11 □ 7 = _______

_______ □ 3 = 9

18 □ _______ = 11

7 □ _______ = 17

8 □ _______ = 17

□ _______ 8 = 7

_______ □ 1 □ 3 = 6

Part 2

6 □ 1 □ 5 = 10

5 □ 7 □ 9 = 3

1 □ 4 □ 1 □ 2 = 2

2 □ 3 □ 5 □ 2 = 8

510 – 5.2.2

Zero Game Cards

0	0	1	1
2	2	3	3
4	4	5	5

Zero Game Cards

6	6	7	7
8	8	9	9
10	10	11	11

Zero Game Cards

12	12	13	13
14	14	15	15
16	16	17	17

Zero Game Cards

18	18

+, −, and = Cards

+	+	+	+
−	−	−	−
=	=	=	=

3 One- and Two-Digit Addition and Subtraction

Materials

- blank ten frames (templates included. Photocopy at least five blank ten frames onto overhead transparencies.) (5.3.1)
- pennies
- overhead projector
- overhead transparencies
- overhead markers
- scrap paper
- pencils
- addition and subtraction cards (included. Photocopy one set of cards for each pair of students. Mount cards onto sturdy tagboard, and cut out.) (5.3.3)

Activity: Part One

Present the following problem to students.

Mark has 48¢ in his pocket. His sister gives him 5¢ more. How much money does Mark have now?

Tell students that you will now use ten frames to solve this problem. Ask:

- How can we use pennies with the ten frames to show 48¢?

Place five blank ten frames onto the overhead, and use pennies to show the 48¢ that Mark originally had in his pocket, as in the following diagram.

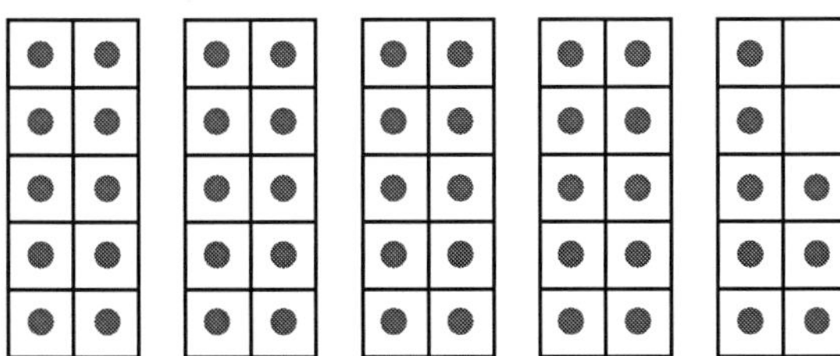

Now, have students determine how to use the ten frames to add the additional 5¢ Mark's sister gave to him. Place five more pennies onto the overhead, beside the ten frames. Then, point to the ten frame with only eight pennies, and ask students:

- How many more pennies do we need to add to the eight pennies to equal ten pennies and fill the frame?

Move two pennies from the group of five pennies beside the ten frames onto the ten frame with eight pennies, to fill the frame. Ask:

- What is 48 plus 2?
- How many pennies are left over from the group of five pennies that was beside the ten frames? (3)
- What is 50 plus 3?

Tell students that 48 + 5 = 53, since 48 + 2 = 50 and 3 more is 53. Explain that students found the sum of 48 + 5 by *bridging to ten*.

Repeat the procedure for new problems such as

- 28 + 6 = ____
- 7 + 8 = ____
- 49 + 7 = ____

Distribute Activity Sheet A (5.3.2), and have students make each problem easier to solve by bridging to ten. Then, have students find the sum for each problem.

Activity Sheet A

Directions to students:

Make each problem easier to solve by bridging to ten. Then, find the sum (5.3.2).

Activity: Part Two

Record the following two problems on the overhead:

27 + 8 = ____ 30 + 5 = ____

Distribute scrap paper and pencils, and have students find the answer to each problem.

▶

Ask:

- What strategy did you use to solve each problem?
- Did you find a way to simplify each problem?

Have students share the strategies they used to solve the problems. Stress that any strategy is valid if it enables you to answer a problem.

Using the two previous problems as examples, demonstrate, or have a student demonstrate, how to make a problem easier to solve by using the bridge-to-ten strategy. For example:

The problem 30 + 5 = _____ was fairly easy to solve because I simply added the ones (5) to the tens (30).

To solve the problem 27 + 8 = _____, I split up the 8 into 3 and 5 and bridged to 30. The problem then became 30 + 5 = 35.

Now, record the following sets of problems on the overhead:

56 + 7 = _____ 60 + 3 = _____

38 + 5 = _____ 40 + 3 = _____

76 + 6 = _____ 80 + 2 = _____

Have students find the answer(s) to each set of problems. Ask:

- What strategy did you use to solve each problem?
- Did you find a way to simplify any of the problems? Which problem(s), and how did you simplify it (them)?

Have students share the strategies they used to solve the problems.

Activity: Part Three

Divide the class into pairs of students, and give each pair a set of addition and subtraction cards (included, 5.3.3). Have students in each pair sort their cards into two sets: easier to solve and harder to solve.

When students finish sorting the cards, have them share their results and explain their reasoning.

Problem Solving

Note: Orally present the following story problems, and have students solve them mentally, encouraging them to use the bridge-to-ten strategy.

- Jake found 7 seashells on the beach. He took them home and added them to the 28 seashells he collected last week. How many seashells does Jake have now?
- There are 36 horses in the corral. Dario opened the gate and let in 8 more horses. How many horses are in the corral now?
- Sophie had 86¢. Her brother Ryan found 6¢, and he gave it to Sophie. How much money does Sophie have now?
- Forty-seven third-grade students go to summer camp. Nine fourth-grade students also go to camp. Altogether, how many third- and fourth-grade students go to summer camp?
- Mel is 18 years old. Her brother is 6 years older than she is. How old is Mel's brother?
- Bill is using centimetre blocks to build a tower. On Monday, the tower was 38-centimetres high. On Tuesday, he added another 5 centimetres to the height of his tower. What is the total height of Bill's tower now?

Note: Reproducible masters for these problems can be found on pages 609 and 610.

▶

3

Extensions

- Add the term *bridge to ten* to your classroom math word wall.
- Introduce students to the bridge-to-ten strategy for subtraction. For example, to find the difference between 38 and 44 (44 – 38 =):
  - think 38 + 2 = 40, and 4 more equals 44
  - 2 + 4 is 6
  - 44 – 38 = 6

Blank Ten Frames

Date: ____________ Name: ____________________

Bridge to Ten

Example: 26 + 8 =

26 + 4 = 30 and 4 more is 34.

Problem	Bridge-to-Ten Strategy
19 + 6 = ______	______ + ______ = ______ and ______ more is ☐
49 + 9 = ______	______ + ______ = ______ and ______ more is ☐
35 + 8 = ______	______ + ______ = ______ and ______ more is ☐
86 + 5 = ______	______ + ______ = ______ and ______ more is ☐
77 + 4 = ______	______ + ______ = ______ and ______ more is ☐
54 + 8 = ______	______ + ______ = ______ and ______ more is ☐
28 + 7 = ______	______ + ______ = ______ and ______ more is ☐
15 + 8 = ______	______ + ______ = ______ and ______ more is ☐
47 + 6 = ______	______ + ______ = ______ and ______ more is ☐
36 + 9 = ______	______ + ______ = ______ and ______ more is ☐

Addition and Subtraction Cards

29+5=	88+8=	50+8=	46+8=
38+6=	30+3=	40+2=	69+4=
70+5=	40+9=	75+8=	80+6=
87+7=	20+7=	10+9=	57+5=
60+4=	86+9=	90+1=	36+9=

4 Addition and Subtraction with a Calculator

Materials

- calculators (one for each student)
- overhead calculator (optional)
- overhead projector (optional)

Activity

Note: In this lesson, students use the constant feature on their calculators. Different calculators activate this feature in different ways. On some, you must press "+, 1, =" and then continue to press the "=". On others, pressing "=" twice will engage the feature. On others still, you must press "1, +, +" and then continue to press the "=" sign. Before beginning this lesson, be sure to experiment with the calculators students will be using.

Distribute calculators to students, and show them how to use the constant feature (use the overhead calculator if you have one). For example, to add 1 repeatedly to 5, "press 5 + 1," press "=", and then continue to press "=." Or, to add 7 repeatedly to 4, press "4 + 7," press "=," and then continue to press "=."

Show students several more examples. Then, have students use their calculators to repeatedly add 3 to 8 and then repeatedly add 6 to 4.

Divide the class into pairs of students, and distribute a calculator and a copy of Activity Sheet A (5.4.1) to each pair. Have one student in each pair act as the recorder while the other operates the calculator. Ask students to work together to complete the activity sheet.

Activity Sheet A

Directions to students:

Have one partner act as the recorder while the other operates the calculator. Work together to complete the activity sheet, recording your answers in the space provided (5.4.1).

When students have completed the activity sheet, have them share their answers with their classmates.

Problem Solving

Have students use calculators to solve each of the following problems:

- Using *only* the 3, the 5, the +, and the = keys, which numbers from 3 to 30 can you make?
- How can you make the calculator show 756 if the 7 key and the 5 key are broken? How many *different* ways can you make the calculator show 756? What are they? For example, press: "300 + 400 + 30 + 20 + 6."
- Make each of the following number sentences true by putting the correct addition and subtraction signs between the numbers:
  - 76 ☐ 13 ☐ 10 = 73
  - 82 ☐ 17 ☐ 19 ☐ 9 = 89
  - 34 ☐ 24 ☐ 25 ☐ 12 = 21

Note: Reproducible masters for these problems can be found on pages 610 and 611.

Extension

Have students use their calculators to explore number relationships and patterns that involve multiplication and division.

Date: ________________ Names: ____________________________

____

Using the Constant Feature

1. Press "5" on your calculator. Add 9 repeatedly, and record the numbers that you see:

____ ____ ____ ____ ____ ____ ____ ____ ____ ____

What patterns do you see? ____________________________

____

2. Press "5" on your calculator. Add 10 repeatedly, and record the numbers that you see:

____ ____ ____ ____ ____ ____ ____ ____ ____ ____

What patterns do you see? ____________________________

____

3. Press "5" on your calculator. Add 99 repeatedly, and record the numbers that you see:

____ ____ ____ ____ ____ ____ ____ ____ ____ ____

What patterns do you see? ____________________________

____

4. Press "5" on your calculator. Add 100 repeatedly, and record the numbers that you see:

____ ____ ____ ____ ____ ____ ____ ____ ____ ____

What patterns do you see? ____________________________

____

5. Look at your answers to questions 3 and 4. How can you add 99 + 99 without using a calculator or a paper and pencil?

____

____

5 Addition of Hundreds

Materials

- base-ten materials such as wooden craft sticks grouped into 10s and 100s, base-ten blocks (for example, Dienes blocks), or base-ten cards (included in the introduction to *Hands-On Mathematics Grade Three*, pages 93-104).
- place-value mat template (included. Photocopy, and laminate, one mat for each student.) (5.5.2)
- Got You! cards (included. Photocopy, one set of cards for each pair of students. Mount cards onto sturdy tagboard, and cut out.) (5.5.3)
- paper
- pencils

Activity: Part One

Distribute copies of Activity Sheet A (5.5.1), base-ten materials, and place-value mats (5.5.2), and have students use the base-ten materials and place-value mats to solve the problems on the activity sheet.

Activity Sheet A

Directions to students:

Solve each problem on the activity sheet any way you know how. Use base-ten materials and a place-value mat to help you, or solve the problems in your head (5.5.1).

Once students have completed their activity sheets, ask:

- What do you notice about the problems on the activity sheet?
- How are all the problems alike?
- How do they differ?
- What do you know about adding hundreds?

Activity: Part Two

Divide the class into pairs of students. Give each pair a set of Got You! Cards (5.5.3), and have students play Got You! Tell students to shuffle their cards and spread them out, facedown, between them. Have each player pick up a card at the same time. The player whose card has the greater sum keeps both cards. If the two cards have the same sum, both players pick up another card. The player whose card has the greater sum gets all four cards. Play continues until there are no cards left to pick up. The player with the most cards wins.

Activity Centre

Have pairs of students use the Got You! cards (5.5.3) to play the game Take Three. Ask students to lay their cards, facedown, between them. Have each player draw three cards at the same time and decide which card has the greatest sum. Ask both players to show their cards to their partner, point to the card with the greatest sum, and state the sum. The player who has the card with the greatest sum gets all six cards. Play continues until there are no cards left to pick up; the player with the most cards wins.

Next Steps

- Introduce students to the addition of hundreds to non-multiples of ten. For example, 342 + 200.
- Use similar activities to introduce students to subtraction of hundreds.
- Adapt the games Got You! and Take Three to give students practice with subtraction of hundreds.

Date: ____________ Name: ____________

Making Connections

7+1 = ______ 70+10 = ______ 700+100 = ______	2+1 = ______ 20+10 = ______ 200+100 = ______
4+1 = ______ 40+10 = ______ 400+100 = ______	9+1 = ______ 90+10 = ______ 900+100 = ______
6+3 = ______ 60+30 = ______ 600+300 = ______	5+2 = ______ 50+20 = ______ 500+200 = ______
4+4 = ______ 40+40 = ______ 400+400 = ______	3+5 = ______ 30+50 = ______ 300+500 = ______
4+3 = ______ 40+30 = ______ 400+300 = ______	1+6 = ______ 10+60 = ______ 100+600 = ______
2+7 = ______ 20+70 = ______ 200+700 = ______	3+2 = ______ 30+20 = ______ 300+200 = ______

Place-Value Mat Template

Thousands	Hundreds	Tens	Ones

Got You! Cards

100+200	100+900	200+800
400+200	500+400	100+100
200+100	300+100	400+300
500+500	100+300	200+200
300+200	400+400	600+100
100+400	200+300	300+300

Got You! Cards

400 + 500	600 + 200	100 + 500
200 + 400	300 + 400	400 + 600
600 + 300	100 + 600	200 + 500
300 + 500	500 + 100	600 + 400
100 + 700	200 + 600	300 + 600
500 + 200	700 + 100	100 + 800

Got You! Cards

200 + 700	400 + 100	500 + 300
700 + 200	700 + 300	800 + 100
800 + 200	900 + 100	

6 Compatible Numbers

Background Information for Teachers

This lesson focuses on *compatible numbers*: pairs of numbers that are simpler to work with than many other numbers because they can be added together more easily. Compatible numbers fit together almost naturally to make target numbers, and help to simplify mental computations. For example, compatible numbers for 10 include all pairs of addends whose sums equal ten, including 0 and 10, 1 and 9, 2 and 8, and so on.

Numbers that are multiples of 10 and 5 are also compatible numbers. For example:

- compatible numbers for 100 include 60 and 40; 75 and 25; and so on
- compatible numbers for 250 include 150 and 100; 225 and 25; and so on

Compatible numbers also include other addend combinations whose sum equals target benchmark numbers that are not necessarily multiples of 5 and 10. For example:

- compatible numbers for 100 include 23 and 77, 37 and 63, and so on

Materials

- numeral cards, 0-10 (included. Photocopy, and cut out.) (5.6.1)
- pocket chart
- dimes and nickels (use real or play coins)
- chart paper
- markers
- paper
- pencils
- beaded number line to 100 (Loosely string two colours of large beads onto a long piece of string in an *AB* pattern of ten beads: 10 red beads, 10 blue beads, to 100. Be sure there is enough room for beads to slide slightly along the string.)
- clothespin
- large craft sticks (one for each student)

Activity: Part One: Making Pairs to Ten

Note: Although making pairs to ten is considered to be review for grade-three students, it is included here to help introduce the concept of *compatible numbers*.

Display the numeral cards 0-10 (5.6.1) in the pocket chart. Ask students:

- Can you find a pair of numbers that together add up to 10?

As students identify pairs of numbers, put the numeral cards side-by-side in the pocket chart.

Activity: Part Two: Compatible Numbers for 100 Using Multiple-of-Five Addends

Note: If students know the compatible numbers for 10 and are comfortable with place value to 100, they will likely be able to bridge this understanding to compatible numbers for 100.

Explain that students will now work with the numbers they would say when counting by 5s and find compatible numbers for 100. First, have students begin at 5 and slowly skip count aloud by 5s, to 100. As students recite each number, record it on chart paper. Ask:

- From this list of numbers, can you find two numbers that you could add together to make 100?

▶

Have students offer their suggestions, and record, on chart paper, each correct set of compatible numbers for 100. Point to one set of compatible numbers (for example, 65 and 35), and say:

- Sixty-five and thirty-five are compatible numbers for the target number of 100.

Explain that the compatible numbers always add up to the target number (in this case, 100).

Divide the class into pairs of students, and provide each pair with ten dimes, two nickels, and copies of Activity Sheet A (5.6.2). Explain that students will work together and use the dimes and nickels to build compatible numbers for 100. Ask students:

- Can you use your dimes and nickels to make compatible numbers for 100?

Tell students to use their coins to make compatible numbers for 100. For example:

- three dimes and one nickel, six dimes and one nickel: 35 and 65
- four dimes, six dimes: 40 and 60
- one dime and one nickel, eight dimes and one nickel: 15 and 85

Have students work with their partners to complete the activity sheet. Encourage students to think out loud and discuss their ideas with each other as they explore compatible numbers.

Activity Sheet A

Directions to students:

Use the coins to find, and record, compatible numbers for 100 (5.6.2).

Once the pairs have completed their activity sheets, have students share their results. On chart paper, create an organized list of the compatible numbers for 100, beginning with compatible numbers that have 0 in the ones place and following with numbers that have 5 in the ones place.

Activity: Part Three: Breaking Apart Target Numbers into Compatible Numbers

Note: In this activity, students break apart target numbers into two compatible numbers that are multiples of 5. Have students use manipulatives if you are presenting the activity at an entry level; have students use pictures or words if you are presenting the activity at a higher level.

On chart paper, record the number 85. Ask students:

- How many compatible numbers can we find for this number?

Distribute dimes, nickels, paper, and pencils. Have students use the coins, the paper and pencils (for drawing and recording), or mental-math strategies to help them determine compatible numbers for 85. Then, have students take turns offering their suggestions, and record correct compatible numbers on chart paper.

Repeat the activity with several target numbers to 100, and then extend to numbers beyond 100. For example, record the number 350 on chart paper. Explain that this target number can be broken down into several different compatible numbers, including:

- 300 and 50
- 200 and 150
- 25 and 325

Record each of these compatible numbers on chart paper. Ask students:

- How many other compatible numbers can we find for 350?

Ask students to use the coins, paper, and pencils, or mental-math strategies to help them determine compatible numbers for 350.

Again, have students take turns offering their suggestions, and record correct compatible numbers on chart paper. Repeat the activity with several target numbers to 1000.

Distribute Activity Sheet B (5.6.3), and have students record two sets (pairs) of compatible numbers for each target number.

Activity Sheet B

Directions to students:

Record two sets (pairs) of compatible numbers for each target number (5.6.3).

Activity: Part Four: Compatible Numbers off the Multiple

Display the beaded 100 number line for students. Ask:

- How many beads are there on this string?

Have students count the first 10 beads and then predict how many beads there are on the number line.

Explain that students will now use the beaded number line to find compatible numbers for 100. This time, they are looking for *all* compatible numbers for 100, not just the numbers they say when counting by 5s. That is, they are looking for any two numbers whose sum equals 100.

Have students examine the beaded number line again. Attach a clothespin to the string right after the first bead. Ask students:

- What number goes with 1 to equal 100? (99)
- What other compatible numbers for 100 can we find using the beaded number line? (7 and 93, 24, and 76, and so on)

As students suggest compatible numbers for 100, record the numbers on chart paper.

Distribute Activity Sheet C (5.6.4), and have students use the diagram of the beaded number line to find, and record, ten sets (pairs) of compatible numbers for 100. Encourage students to find more than just the numbers they say when counting by 5s.

Activity Sheet C

Directions to students:

Use the diagram of the beaded number line to find, and record, ten sets (pairs) of compatible numbers for 100 (5.6.4).

Activity: Part Five: Finding Compatible Numbers

Before beginning this lesson, use a marker to record compatible numbers for 100 onto pairs of craft sticks. For example, record 37 on one stick, and record 63 on another. Make enough sets of compatible-number sticks so that there is one pair for every two students in the class.

Distribute a craft stick to each student, and point out that each stick has a number on it. Tell students that each student has one of a pair of compatible numbers for 100 recorded on his/her stick. Have students find classmates whose number is compatible to their own. Remind students that if the two numbers are compatible for 100, they will add up to 100. Allow time for students to circulate the classroom and find their compatible number partners.

Extensions

- Add the term *compatible numbers* to your classroom math word wall.
- Select a target number with which students can play a memory game. Divide the class into pairs of students, and distribute several blank index cards and a marker to each pair. Have students record, on the cards, compatible numbers for the target number (one number per card). Tell students to mix up their cards and place them, facedown, between them. Have partners take turns turning over two cards. If the cards are compatible numbers for the target number, the player keeps the cards. If not, the player returns the cards, facedown, to the play area. Play continues until all compatible numbers have been found. The player with the most cards at the end of the game wins.

Numeral Cards 0-10

0	1	2	3
4	5	6	7
8	9	10	

Date: ____________ Name: ____________________

Compatible Numbers for 100

Compatible Numbers for 100	

Date: ____________ Name: ____________________

Compatible Numbers

550	

675	

180	

300	

995	

210	

440	

725	

800	

705	

Date: ____________________ Name: ____________________

More Compatible Numbers for 100

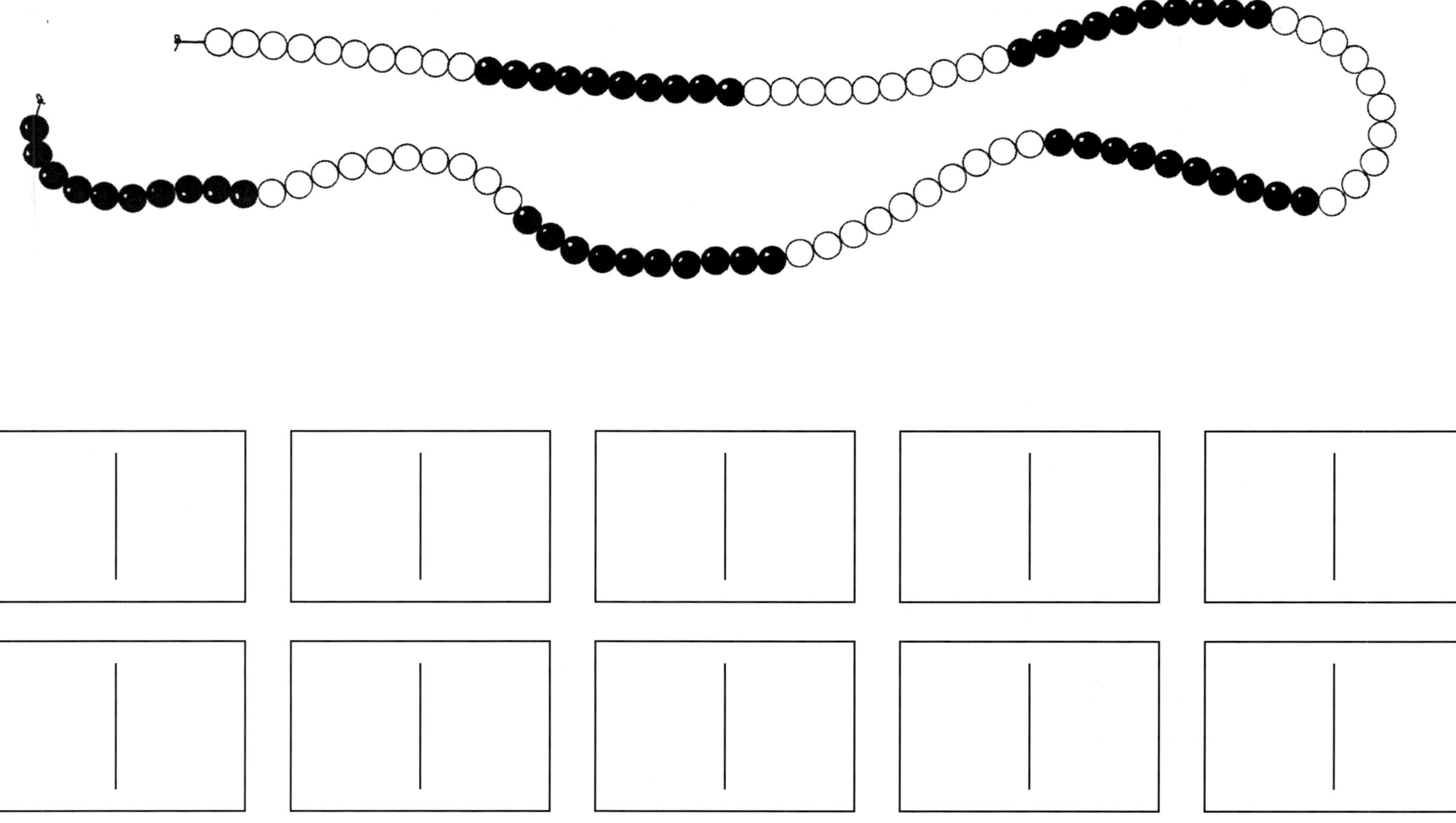

7 Addition with Three-Digit Numbers

Materials

- chart paper
- markers
- base-ten materials such as stir sticks (or wooden craft sticks) and stir-stick bundles, play money, abaci, or base-ten blocks (for example, Dienes blocks)
- place-value mats (template included with lesson 5. Photocopy one mat for each student.) (5.5.2)
- place-value number tents (included in module 4, lesson 6. Photocopy one set for each student, and one more set for demonstration. Cut apart tents on the solid lines, fold along the dotted lines, and store in Ziploc bags.) (4.6.3)

Activity: Part One

Present the following problem to students:

In the gym, 345 chairs have been set up for a concert. The school custodian adds 127 more chairs. How many chairs are in the gym now?

Have students use strategies and/or materials of their own choice (for example, base-ten materials and place-value mats, empty number lines) to solve the problem.

Ask students:

- What is the answer to the problem?
- What does the answer tell you? (how many chairs are in the gym after more have been added)
- Is your answer reasonable? How do you know?
- How did you solve the problem?
- What is another way to solve the problem?
- How can you prove that your answer is correct?

On chart paper, record students' explanations of how they solved the problem. For example:

345 + 127 = ________

345 = 300 + 40 + 5

127 = 100 + 20 + 7

300 + 100 = 400

40 + 20 = 60

5 + 7 = 12

400 + 60 + 12 = 472

First, I wrote both numbers in expanded notation. Then, I added 300 to 100 and got 400. Next, I added 40 to 20 and got 60. Then, I added 5 to 7 and got 12. Finally, I added 400 + 60 + 12 together and got a total of 472.

Or:

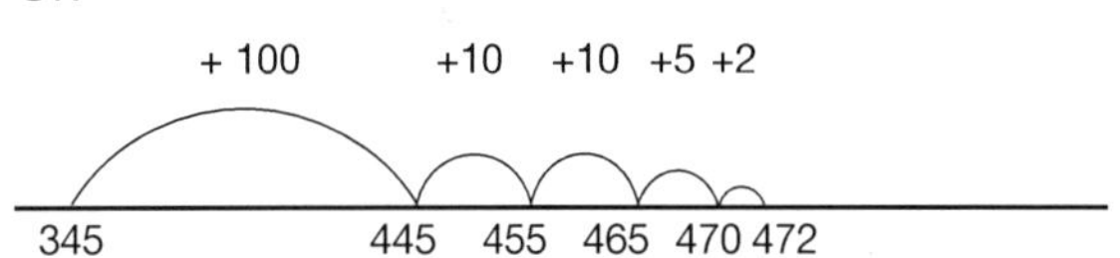

I used an empty number line.

Note: Although efforts have been taken to achieve accurate scale on number lines in *Hands-On Mathematics Grade 3*, scale is not exact, both in terms of jump size as well as between numbers along the number line. Also note that it is not necessary for students to be faithful to scale on their own created number lines. The number line is a strategy to support students' thinking and to help them solve problems, and while correct number order is significant, accurate scale is not.

Or: I changed 345 to 350 and I changed 127 to 125. Then, I added 350 and 125 to get 475. Then, I subtracted the extra 5 that I had added to the 345, and I got 470. Finally, I added the 2 that I had subtracted from the 127, and I got an answer of 472.

Or:

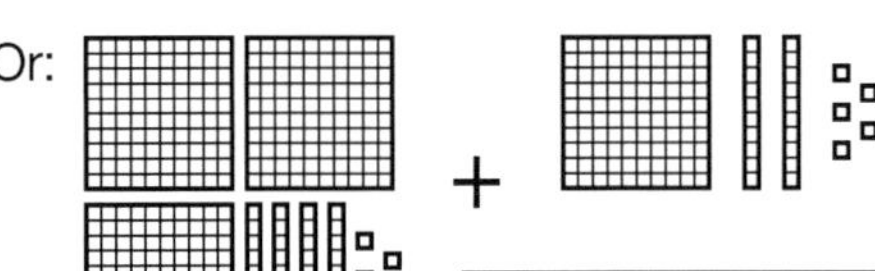

I used base-ten blocks.

Activity: Part Two

Gather students together into a semicircle, and introduce the place-value number tents (4.6.3). Show students how the tents can be stacked to make a number, as in the following diagram:

346 =

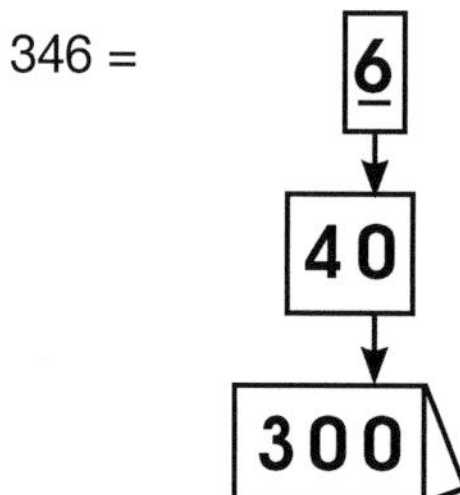

On chart paper, record the following problem:

243 + 356 = _______

Use tent cards to make both numbers. Have two students (students *A* and *B*) stand up, and give each student one of the numbers to hold. Then, ask four more students to stand up (students *C*, *D*, *E*, and *F*) and help separate the two numbers you built. Tell students *A* and *B* to continue holding the hundreds tents (200 and 300) while students *C* and *D* take the tens tents (40 and 50) and students *E* and *F* take the ones tents (3 and 6). The two original numbers should now be separated into their expanded forms (200, 40, 3 and 300, 50, 6).

Next, ask students to look at all six numbers and decide which ones belong together (combine like terms). Have the students holding the hundreds tents (students *A* and *B*) move together followed by the students holding the tens tents (students *C* and *D*) and then the students holding the ones tents (students *E* and *F*).

Now, ask students to find the sum of the two hundreds numbers. Exchange the two hundreds tents for the 500 tent. Do the same with the tens tents (exchange them for the 90 tent) and the ones tents (exchange them for the 9 tent). Finally, put the three new tents together to make the number 599. Record each step of the process on chart paper.

Model the process again, this time using a problem that requires regrouping. For example:

338 + 257 = _______

300 + 200 = 500 30 + 50 = 80 8 + 7 = 15

When it is time to find the sum of the ones tents (8 + 7), tell the two students holding them to exchange their tents for the 10 tent and the 5 tent. Combine the tents to create the number 15. Then, ask the two students to "pull apart" the number 15 into its expanded form (10 + 5). Have the student holding the 10 tent go, and stand with the student holding the 80 tent. Exchange these two tents for the 90 tent. Put the number tents together to create the sum: 595. Record each step of the process on chart paper.

Problem Solving

Present the following problems, and have students use the strategy of their choice to solve each one.

- Carl sold 128 tickets for the school play. Joseph sold 75 tickets. How many tickets did the two boys sell altogether?
- Fern wants to watch one movie that is 95 minutes long and another movie that is 153 minutes long. How long will it take Fern to watch both movies?
- Mr. Peters tagged 352 butterflies last week and 241 butterflies this week. How many butterflies did Mr. Peters tag altogether?

7

- William made 125 chocolate-chip cookies, 145 oatmeal cookies, 115 peanut-butter cookies, and 75 doughnuts for the school bake sale. How many cookies did William make?

Note: Reproducible masters for these problems can be found on page 611.

Once students have solved all four problems, discuss the strategies they used for each one.

Next Step

Have students create their own addition-story problems for their classmates to solve.

8 More Addition with Three-Digit Numbers

Materials

- base-ten blocks
- place-value mats (optional. Template included with lesson 5. Photocopy one mat for each pair of students.) (5.5.2)
- paper
- pencils
- chart paper
- markers
- Big-Sum score sheets (included. Photocopy one sheet for each student.) (5.8.2)
- Big-Sum numeral cards, 1-5 (included. Photocopy one sheet of numeral cards for each pair of students. Mount cards onto sturdy tagboard, and cut out. Each pair should have two of each number from 1 to 5.) (5.8.3)

Activity: Part One

Divide the class into pairs of students, and distribute to each pair a set of base-ten blocks, a place-value mat if necessary, some paper, and a pencil. On chart paper, record the following numbers: 143, 176, 231. Below the numbers, record the following problems:

1) Which two numbers have a sum that is greater than 390?
2) Which two numbers have a sum that is less than 350?
3) Which two numbers have a sum that is between 365 and 400?
4) What is the sum of all three numbers?

Have students use the base-ten blocks (and place-value mats, if necessary) to help them solve each problem. Ask students to record a number sentence for each problem.

Once students have solved all four problems, have them share their findings with the rest of the class and explain how they found their answers.

Activity: Part Two

Distribute base-ten blocks, place-value mats if necessary, and copies of Activity Sheet A (5.8.1), and have students use the blocks to help them solve the problems. Tell students to show their work and explain the strategy they used to solve each problem.

Activity Sheet A

Note: This is a two-page activity sheet.

Directions to students:

Use your base-ten blocks (and place-value mat) to help you solve the problems. Show your work, and explain the strategy you used to solve each problem (5.8.1).

Activity: Part Three

Divide the class into pairs of students, and have students play the game Big Sum. Give each pair two Big-Sum score sheets (5.8.2), one set of Big-Sum numeral cards, 1-5 (*two* of each number from 1 to 5) (5.8.3), and a set of base-ten blocks.

Tell students that the goal of Big Sum is to use the numeral cards to build the largest sum possible. Ask students to shuffle their cards and spread them out, facedown, between them. Have players take turns picking a card and placing it on one of the boxes of his/her score sheet. Once a card has been placed in a box, it cannot be moved. When both players have filled all the boxes on their score sheets, they can each use the base-ten blocks to help them find the sum of their two numbers. The player with the largest sum wins.

▶

8

Problem Solving

- Matthew accidentally tore a page out of his social studies book. He told his teacher that the sum of the page numbers (on the front and the back of the torn-out page) is 189. What are the page numbers on the page Matthew tore out?
- Francine has six boxes of pears to load into her truck. The first box has 118 pears in it. The other boxes have 117, 119, 116, 117, and 115 pears in them. Francine makes three trips to her truck. On each trip, she loads two boxes, with a total of 234 pears, into the truck. Which two boxes does Francine load on each trip?

Note: Reproducible masters for these problems can be found on page 612.

Assessment Suggestion

Meet with students one on one, and provide them with base-ten materials, paper, and pencils. First, tell students to estimate the sum of 437 and 182, and then have them find the actual sum of the two numbers using a strategy of their choice. Finally, ask students to explain how they solved the problem.

Note: Tell students to use the base-ten materials *only* if they need them.

Assess students' abilities to:

- make reasonable estimates of the sum
- determine the correct sum of the numbers
- solve the problem *without* use of base-ten materials
- give appropriate explanations of how they solved the problem

List these criteria on the Rubric sheet, found on page 18, and record your observations.

Date: ____________ Name: ____________________

Adding Three-Digit Numbers

463+529=________

175+250=________

325+ ________ =367

________+276=691

Date: ________________ Name: ____________________________

Use any two of the following numbers to complete each number sentence below:

117	128	129	137	143

_______ + _______ = 280

_______ + _______ = 245

_______ + _______ = 265

_______ + _______ = 271

Big-Sum Score Sheet

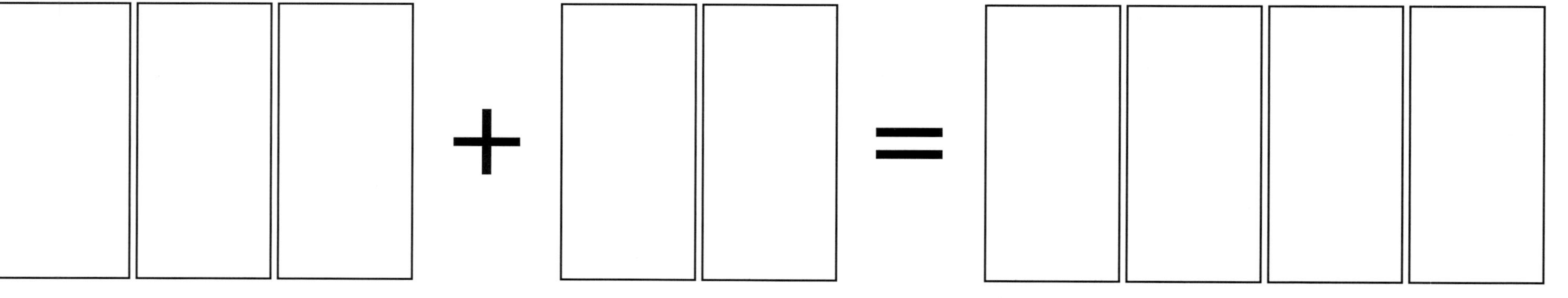

Big-Sum Numeral Cards

1	2	3	4	5
1	2	3	4	5

9 Solving Multiple-Step Problems

Background Information for Teachers

This lesson helps students learn how to analyze multiple-step problems. Problems presented in the lesson do not involve complex calculations, and so students will be able to spend more time talking about what they need to know to solve them and what they expect the answers to look like.

Materials

- manipulatives such as counters or bingo chips (optional)
- paper
- pencils

Activity

Present the following problem to students:

Jeffery made two batches of cookies. There were 24 cookies in the first batch and 13 cookies in the second batch. He ate 6 cookies. How many cookies does Jeffrey have now?

Have students discuss the problem. Ask:

- What is happening in this problem?
- What will the answer tell you?
- What do you need to know to solve the problem?
- What do you need to do to solve the problem?
- How many steps are there in the problem?
- What do you estimate the answer will be?

Have students record their estimates in their math journals. Then, if necessary, have various manipulatives available for students' use, and ask students to solve the problem and then compare their answers to their estimates. Tell students to state their answers in a sentence.

Repeat the same procedure to help students analyze and solve the following multi-step problems:

- Sarah found 15 shells at the beach. Andrew found 9 more shells than Sarah. Altogether, how many seashells did Sarah and Andrew find?
- Yale went to the store to buy some groceries. A package of cheese costs $4 and a bag of apples costs $5. Yale bought 2 bags of apples and 1 package of cheese. How much money did Yale spend on groceries?
- Peter put his hockey cards into three piles. There are 8 hockey cards in the first pile. The second pile has 6 more cards than the first pile. The third pile has 5 fewer cards than the second pile. How many hockey cards does Peter have?
- Natasha has 12 marbles. She lost $^1/_2$ of them, so she bought 12 more. How many marbles does Natasha have now?

Note: Reproducible masters for these problems can be found on page 612.

Next Step

Have students create their own multi-step story problems for their classmates to solve.

10 Subtraction with Three-Digit Numbers

Materials

- base-ten materials such as stir sticks (or wooden craft sticks) and stir-stick bundles, play money, abaci, or base-ten blocks
- place-value mats (optional. Template included with lesson 5. Photocopy one mat for each student.) (5.5.2)
- place-value number tents (included in module 4, lesson 6. Photocopy one set, cut apart tents on solid lines, and fold along dotted lines.) (4.6.3)
- chart paper
- markers

Activity: Part One

Present the following problem to students:

The school principal ordered 367 doughnuts for the school picnic. The grade twos and threes took 123 doughnuts. How many doughnuts are left for the remaining grades?

Have students solve the problem using base-ten materials of their choice (for example, stir sticks and stir-stick bundles, play money, abaci, or base-ten blocks). Ask:

- What is the answer to the problem? What does the answer tell you?
- Is your answer reasonable? How do you know?
- How did you solve the problem?
- What is another way to solve the problem?
- How can you prove that your answer is correct?

On chart paper, record students' explanations of how they solved the problem. For example:

367 – 123 = _____

300 – 100 = 200

60 – 20 = 40

7 – 3 = 4

200 + 40 + 4 = 244

First, I subtracted 100 from 300 and got 200. Next, I subtracted 20 from 60 and got 40. Then, I subtracted 3 from 7 and got 4. Finally, I added the three differences together and got 244.

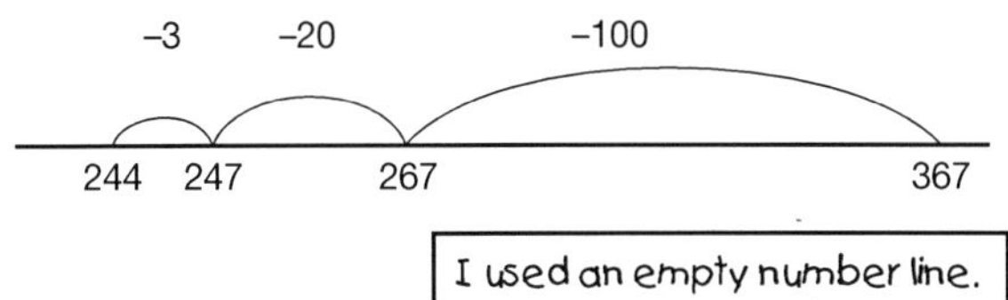

I used an empty number line.

Note: Although efforts have been taken to achieve accurate scale on number lines in *Hands-On Mathematics Grade 3*, scale is not exact, both in terms of jump size as well as between numbers along the number line. Also note that it is not necessary for students to be faithful to scale on their own created number lines. The number line is a strategy to support students' thinking and to help them solve problems, and while correct number order is significant, accurate scale is not.

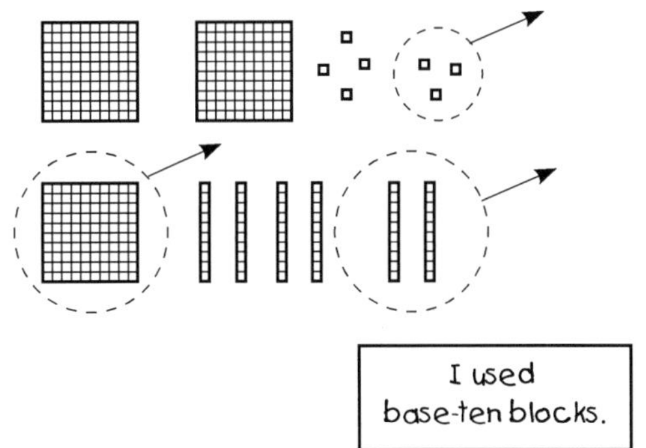

I used base-ten blocks.

Activity: Part Two

On chart paper, record the following problem:

298 – 57 = _____

Show students how to use place-value number tents to solve the problem. First, use tent cards to make the number 298. Then, break the number apart into its expanded form (200, 90, 8). Have students help you to subtract 50 from 90 by replacing the 90 tent with the 40 tent. Also, ask students to help you subtract 7 from 8 by replacing the 8 tent with the 1 tent. Reassemble the 200 tent with the two new tents to make the difference: 241.

Now, record, on chart paper, the following problem:

436 – 129 = ____

Use tent cards to make the number 436. Break it apart into its expanded form (400, 30, 6). Have students subtract 100 from 400 by replacing the 400 tent with the 300 tent. Then, tell students to subtract 20 from 30 by replacing the 30 tent with the 10 tent.

Point out for students that in order to subtract 9 from 6, they need to combine the 10 tent (from the previous step) with the 6 tent to make 16. Then, tell students to subtract 9 from the 16 tent. Replace the two tents with the 7 tent. Put the three tents together to make the difference: 307.

Problem Solving

Present the following problems, and have students use strategies of their choice to solve each one. Encourage students to use a different strategy for each problem:

- On Saturday, 187 children went to the circus. On Sunday, 74 children went to the circus. How many more children went to the circus on Saturday than on Sunday?
- Dana has 345 stamps in her collection. She gives away 129 stamps. How many stamps does Dana have in her collection now?
- Charles is saving his money for some new hockey equipment. He needs $209 to buy the skates, helmet, and jersey that he wants. He has $150 saved up already. How much more money does Charles need to save?
- Sarah's mom has 463 photos in her photo album. If Sarah is in 284 of these photos, how many of the photos is Sarah not in?
- Paul works at the ballpark refreshment stand, which sells hotdogs, hamburgers, and boxes of popcorn. At the last game, Paul sold 268 hotdogs, 143 hamburgers, and 75 boxes of popcorn. How many more hotdogs than hamburgers did Paul sell?

Note: Reproducible masters for these problems can be found on page 613.

Once students have solved all the problems, discuss the strategies they used. For each problem, ask several students:

- What strategy did you use to solve this problem?
- Why did you choose this strategy?

Next Step

Have students create their own subtraction-story problems for their classmates to solve.

11 More Subtraction with Three-Digit Numbers

Materials

- base-ten blocks
- other base-ten materials
- place-value mats (optional. Template included with lesson 5. Photocopy one mat for each student.) (5.5.2)
- spinners (templates included. Photocopy one spinner for each pair of students. Mount spinners onto sturdy tagboard, and cut out. Also, photocopy one spinner onto an overhead transparency, and cut out.) (5.11.1)
- paper clips (one for each pair of students and one for demonstration)
- pencils (one for each pair of students and one for demonstration)
- chart paper
- markers
- Big Dif subtraction cards (included. Photocopy one set for each pair of students. Mount cards onto sturdy tagboard, and cut out. Store cards in Ziploc bags.) (5.11.4)
- scrap paper

Activity: Part One

Divide the class into pairs of students, and provide each pair with a copy of Activity Sheet A (5.11.2), a set of base-ten blocks, and a place-value mat if necessary. Tell students that you will use a spinner to spin numbers, and they must use the numbers to build a subtraction problem on their activity sheets. Their goal is to create a subtraction problem that results in the largest difference possible.

Use a pencil and a paper clip with the overhead spinner to spin the first number.

Note: Use the pencil point to hold the paper clip in place at the centre point of the spinner. The paper clip will spin freely as the arrow of the spinner.

Tell each pair of students to record the number you spin in one of the six boxes in question 1 on their activity sheets. Spin a second number, and have students record it on their activity sheets. Repeat four more times. Now, ask students to solve their subtraction problems. Tell students they may use their base-ten blocks to help them find the solution.

Have students share their answers and explain how they found the difference between the two numbers. On chart paper, record students' explanations.

Distribute to each pair a spinner template (5.11.1), a paper clip, and a pencil, and show students how to put their spinners together. Have students complete their activity sheets by using their own spinners to build numbers for subtraction problems.

Variation: Have students create subtraction problems with the smallest difference possible.

Activity Sheet A

Directions to students:

Use your spinner to build numbers for subtraction problems. Create subtraction problems with the largest (or smallest) difference possible (5.11.2).

Distribute Activity Sheet B (5.11.3), and base-ten blocks. Have students use two different strategies to solve each problem. Ask students to show their work and describe each strategy they use. Tell students they may use the base-ten blocks to help them solve the problems.

▶

Activity Sheet B

Directions to students:

Use two different strategies to solve each problem. Show your work, and describe each strategy you use. You may use the base-ten blocks to help you solve the problems (5.11.3).

Activity: Part Two

Distribute Big Dif subtraction cards (5.11.4) to pairs of students, and have them play Big Dif. Tell students to shuffle their cards and spread them out, facedown, between them. Ask players to take turns turning over a card and using materials (base-ten materials, scrap paper and pencils, and so on) and strategies of their choice to solve the problem on the card. Have the partners then use materials and strategies of their choice to check that the answer is correct. If the answer is correct, tell the player who turned over the card to keep it. If the answer is not correct, ask players to move the card out of play (no one keeps the card). Play continues until there are no cards left. When all cards have been played, the player with the most cards wins the game.

Problem Solving

- There are 168 boys and 165 girls who attend Marshall Elementary School. On Monday, 109 students were away from school on a field trip. How many students went to school on Monday?
- Todd, Chris, and Paul all live east of Pattersville on Highway Road. Todd lives 178 kilometres from Pattersville. Chris lives 59 kilometres closer to Pattersville than Todd does. Paul lives 163 kilometres from Chris. How far does Paul live from Pattersville?

Note: Reproducible masters for these problems can be found on pages 613 and 614.

Assessment Suggestion

Meet with students individually, and provide them with base-ten blocks, paper, and pencils. Present students with the following problem:

Philip has $210 and his brother, Mike, has $160. Philip spends $38 on new CDs and another $95 on sports equipment. How much money does Philip have now?

Have students estimate the solution and then find the actual difference. Assess students' abilities to:

- make reasonable estimates of the difference
- recognize that the amount of money Mike has is irrelevant
- recognize that the solution to the problem involves two steps
- find the correct solution to the problem

List these criteria on the Rubric sheet, found on page 18, and record your observations.

Spinner Templates

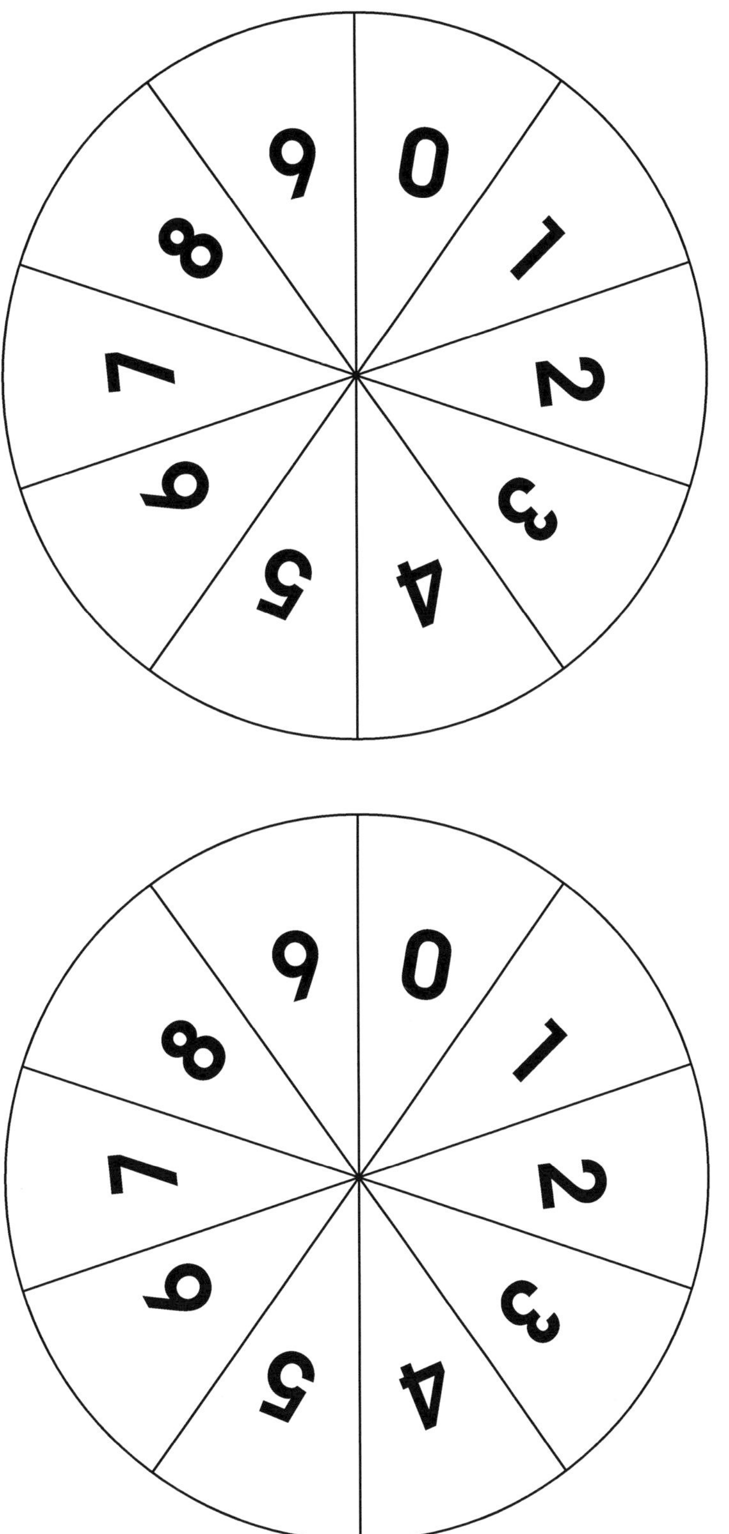

Date: ____________________ Name: ____________________

Building Subtraction Problems

1. ☐☐☐ – ☐☐☐ = ☐☐☐
2. ☐☐☐ – ☐☐☐ = ☐☐☐
3. ☐☐☐ – ☐☐☐ = ☐☐☐
4. ☐☐☐ – ☐☐☐ = ☐☐☐
5. ☐☐☐ – ☐☐☐ = ☐☐☐
6. ☐☐☐ – ☐☐☐ = ☐☐☐

Date: ____________ Name: ____________________

Solving Three-Digit Subtraction Problems

235 – 128 = ________

Strategy 1

Strategy 2

604 – 281 = ________

Strategy 1

Strategy 2

846 – 335 = ________

Strategy 1

Strategy 2

Date: ________________ Name: ____________________________

Use any two of the numbers in the box to make each subtraction problem below true:

218	164	134	337	643

_______ – _______ = 30

_______ – _______ = 425

_______ – _______ = 203

_______ – _______ = 479

_______ – _______ = 306

Find the missing digit for each subtraction problem below:

1. 38☐ – 1☐4 = ☐28

2. ☐26 – 1☐2 = 65☐

Big Dif Subtraction Cards

876–321=	904–587=	611–300=
588–311=	286–101=	777–268=
987–270=	323–192=	496–103=
398–189=		

12 Choosing a Method for Solving Problems

Materials

- calculators (one for each student)
- pencils and paper
- chart paper
- markers

Activity

Divide the class into two groups. Tell students they will all be solving the same addition and subtraction problems but students in group 1 will use calculators to solve the problems while students in group 2 will solve the problems in their heads.

Distribute calculators to students in group 1, and orally present the following problems to both groups, one problem at a time.

- 6 + 8 =
- 15 – 9 =
- 10 + 10 + 10 + 10 =
- 50 + 50 + 50 + 50 + 50 + 50 =
- $1 – $0.25 =
- 40 + 8 =
- 800 – 200 =
- 99 + 99 + 99 + 99 =
- 56 – 29 =
- 140 – 20 + 7 =

Have students in both groups solve one problem at a time. Before moving on to the next problem, discuss which group of students was able to correctly solve the problem the fastest.

Note: Since students *within* each group will also solve the problem at varying rates, consider having students raise their hands when they have completed the problem, and make a general judgment about when *most* students in each group have completed the problem.

Now, distribute a piece of chart paper and a marker to each group of students, and have each group make two lists of addition and subtraction problems. List *A* should include five addition and subtraction problems that would be most effectively solved using a calculator. List *B* should include five addition and subtraction problems that would be most effectively solved using mental math. Have students share their lists with each other and explain their reasoning.

Distribute calculators, pencils and paper, and copies of Activity Sheet A (5.12.1), and have students choose the method of computation that would be most effective for solving each problem. Then, ask students to use their chosen strategy to solve the problem.

Activity Sheet A

Note: This is a two-page activity sheet.

Directions to students:

Choose the method of computation that would be most effective for solving each problem. Explain why you chose each method. Finally, use your chosen strategy to solve the problem (5.12.1).

Extension

Help students identify situations (problems) where only an estimate is required. For example, present students with the following problem:

Kerry needs $100 to buy a new bike. In March, she earned $15. In April, she earned $35 and in May, she earned $70. Does Kerry have enough money to buy the bike?

Have students decide whether or not they need to know the exact amount of money Kerry earned.

Date: ____________________ Name: ____________________

Choosing the Best Method for Solving Problems

Problem	Method (check one)			Why?	Solution
	In Your Head	Calculator	Paper and Pencil		
150 + 100 + 300 =					
783 − 254 =					
695 + 721 + 835 =					
49 + 49 + 49 =					
267 + 564 =					
340 − 100 =					

Date: ______________________ **Name:** ______________________

Record a problem for which using a calculator would be the most effective way to find the solution.

Record a problem for which using mental math would be the most effective way to find the solution.

Record a problem for which using paper and a pencil would be the most effective way to find the solution.

---

13 Exploring Multiplication – Part One

Background Information for Teachers

Students' understanding of addition must be fully entrenched before they are introduced to multiplication. When they are ready for it, students will begin making their own multiplication connections through exposure to skip counting and repeated addition. Be sure to assess students' addition skills, including skip counting and repeated addition, before formally teaching multiplication.

As they do with addition and subtraction, students acquire an understanding of multiplication and division operations by solving story problems. These problems provide students with a purpose for computing. They also offer a context that helps students grasp the meaning of an operation and when it is used.

In this lesson, students use manipulatives, diagrams, and symbols to illustrate the process of multiplication. The multiplication symbol is not introduced at this point.

Materials

- counters
- paper
- pencils
- chart paper
- markers

Activity: Part One

Divide the class into small, working groups of students, and distribute counters, paper, and pencils to the groups. Ask each group to discuss, and solve, the following problem:

- Coach McIntyre is making sandwiches for the baseball team. There are 12 boys on the team. He will make 1 sandwich for each player. How many pieces of bread will Coach McIntyre need?

Allow each group to determine the strategy they will use to solve the problem. Some groups may decide to use counters to help find a solution. Others may use a more abstract strategy such as drawing a picture or using symbols to add 2 + 2 + 2 and so on. Have the groups share their solutions and explain their strategies and reasoning.

Activity: Part Two

Ask students to name things that come in 2s (for example, two eyes, two wheels on a bicycle), and record their suggestions on chart paper. Then, distribute paper and pencils, and have students work with partners to make lists of things that naturally come in groups. Beside its name, have students record the number of items found in each group. For example:

- Legs on a table – 4
- Eggs in a carton – 12
- Wheels on a tricycle – 3
- Toes on one foot – 5

Have students share their lists, and record them on chart paper.

Activity: Part Three

Explain to students that *multiplication* is a way of determining how many items there are altogether when there are equally-sized groups of items.

Have students solve multiplication problems involving some of the items that come in groups, which they identified earlier. For example:

- We set up 3 tables for the party. Each table has 4 legs. How many table legs are there altogether?
- Max has 2 feet. He has 5 toes on each foot. How many toes does Max have?

13

Invite students to share their solutions to the problems and to explain their reasoning. Centre the discussion on questions such as:

- How many groups are there? (3 groups of table legs, 2 groups of toes)
- How many items are there in each group? (4 table legs, 5 toes)
- How many items are there altogether? How do you know?
- What is another way of finding out how many items there are altogether?
- How do you know your answer is right?

Problem Solving

Five owls go hunting at night. Each owl catches 3 mice. How many mice do the owls catch in total?

Note: A reproducible master for this problem can be found on page 614.

14 Exploring Multiplication – Part Two

Background Information for Teachers

In this lesson, students use manipulatives, diagrams, and symbols to illustrate the process of multiplication. The multiplication symbol is still not introduced.

Materials

- counters (at least thirty-six for each pair of students)
- six-sided number cubes (one for each pair of students)
- paper cups (six for each pair of students)
- chart paper
- markers

Activity: Part One

Divide the class into pairs of students, and distribute counters, number cubes, and paper cups to each pair. Tell students they will be making groups of counters and putting each group into a paper cup. Ask the pairs to roll their number cubes twice. The first roll will determine how many groups (paper cups) of counters they should make. The second roll will determine how many counters they should put into each group. For example, if a pair of students rolls a 3 and then a 2, they should take 3 paper cups and put 2 counters into each cup.

Once students have made their groups of counters, have them determine the total number of counters they put into cups. Have each pair repeat the activity several times.

Activity: Part Two

Now, have students repeat the previous activity and record their results. Distribute Activity Sheet A (5.14.1), and demonstrate how to record the activity. Select a student to roll a number cube twice and report the numbers to the class. Draw sets on chart paper to match the numbers the student rolled. Write the corresponding number sentence below the sets, as in the following example:

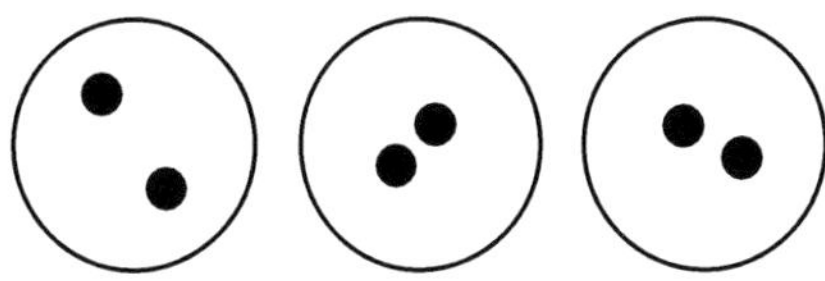

3 groups of 2 equals 6

Now, have students work with the same partners as in the previous activity to complete their activity sheets.

Activity Sheet A

Directions to students:

Roll the number cube. Draw as many groups (large circles) as the number you rolled. Roll the number cube again. In each group (circle), draw as many dots, stars, or *Xs* as the second number you rolled. Record a number sentence under your drawing. Record the number of groups, the number of pictures (dots, stars, or *Xs*) in each group, and the total number of pictures. Repeat four more times (5.14.1).

Next Step

Introduce the concept of multiplication as repeated addition. Review Activity Sheet A (5.14.1) with students. Then, use one student's completed activity sheet to create repeated-addition number sentences on chart paper. For example:

3 groups of 2 equals 6 or

2 + 2 + 2 = 6

Date: ____________ Name: ____________________

Partner: ____________________

Recording Sets of Counters

Sets	Number of Groups	Pictures in Each Group	Total
Example: (3 circles with 2 dots each) 3 groups of 2 equals 6	3	2	6

15 Exploring Multiplication – Part Three

Background Information for Teachers

This lesson introduces students to the array model for multiplication. An *array* is an arrangement of objects into equal-sized rows. Real-life examples of arrays include muffin tins, sheets of stamps, and egg cartons.

Materials

- coloured tiles (twenty-four for each student)
- chart paper
- markers
- coloured pencils

Activity: Part One

Divide the class into pairs of students, and give each pair twenty tiles. Present students with the following scenario:

> *Mrs. Diamond wants to rearrange the 8 desks in her classroom. She wants to put the desks in rows so that each row has the same number of desks.*

Now, ask students to take eight tiles and arrange them into rows. Remind students that each row must have the same number of tiles.

Ask students to describe their arrangements. On chart paper, draw a picture of each arrangement, as in the following example:

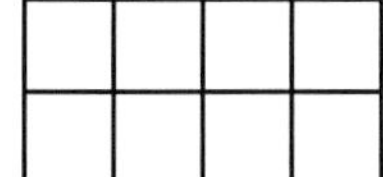

Explain to students that an array is an arrangement of objects into equal-sized rows. Tell students that this arrangement is a 2-by-4 array because there are 2 rows with 4 tiles in each row.

Activity: Part Two

Divide the class into pairs of students and give each pair at least twenty tiles. Have each pair use the tiles to make and describe:

- a 5-by-3 array
- a 2-by-9 array
- an array that has more rows than it has tiles in each row
- an array that has the same number of tiles in each row as the number of rows
- an array that has an even number of rows and an even number of tiles in each row
- an array that has an odd number of rows and an even number of tiles in each row

Activity: Part Three

Distribute to each student twenty-four tiles, coloured pencils, and a copy of Activity Sheet A (5.15.1). Have students use their tiles to make as many arrays as they can for each number. Have students use coloured pencils to record each array on the corresponding grid.

Activity Sheet A

Note: This is a two-page activity sheet.

Directions to students:

For each number, use tiles to make as many arrays as you can. Use coloured pencils to draw each array on the grid (5.15.1).

Extensions

- Add the term *array* to your classroom Math Word Wall.
- Have students use blank sheets of centimetre grid paper (included) to draw all the arrays possible for other numbers (5.15.2).

▶

- Challenge students to draw all the arrays possible for larger numbers. To provide space for larger arrays, have students tape together sheets of grid paper, or distribute sheets of graphed chart paper.
- Photocopy, and cut out a set of array/ product cards (included) for each pair of students. Have students play a version of "Concentration" ("Memory") in pairs. Tell students to sort their cards into array cards and product (number) cards. Then, have students place all their cards facedown in the centre of their playing space – the array cards on one side and the product cards on the other side. Ask students to take turns turning over one array card and one product card. If the cards match, players keep the cards and take another turn. If they do not match, players turn the cards over again. The player with the most matches at the end of the game wins (5.15.3).

Date: ____________________ Name: ______________________________

Making Arrays

12

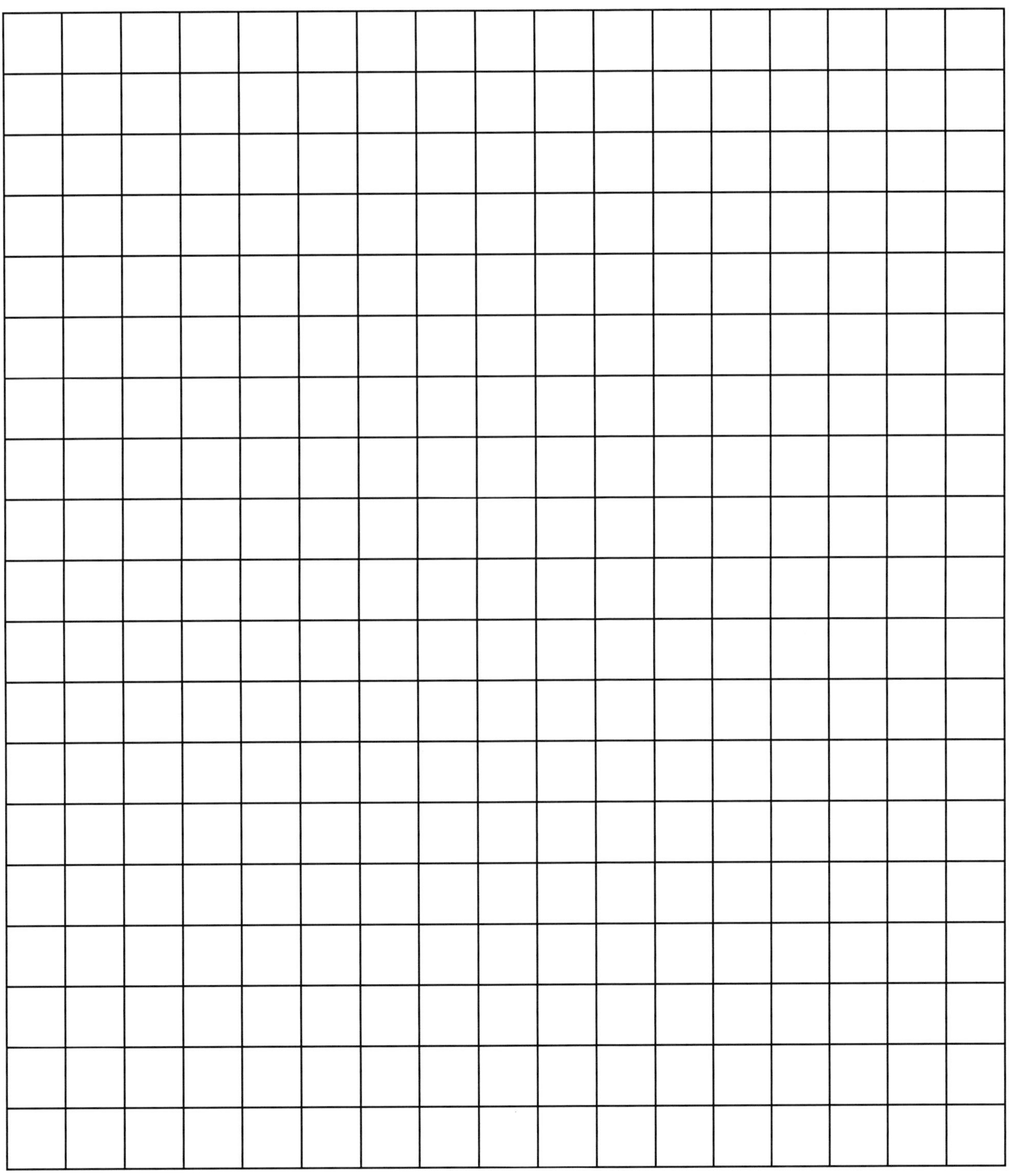

Date: ____________________ **Name:** ________________________________

24

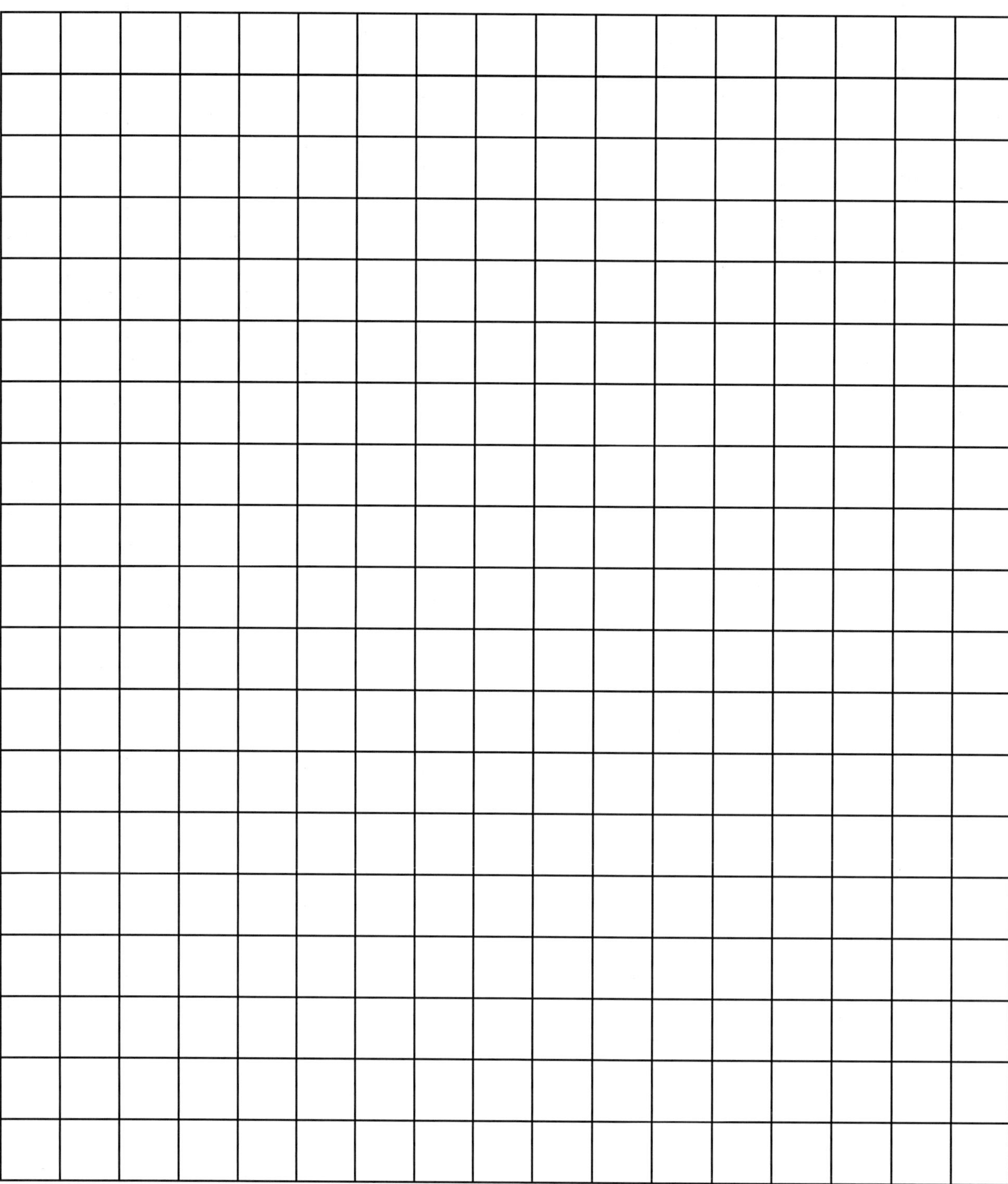

Date: ____________________ Name: ______________________________

Centimetre Grid Paper

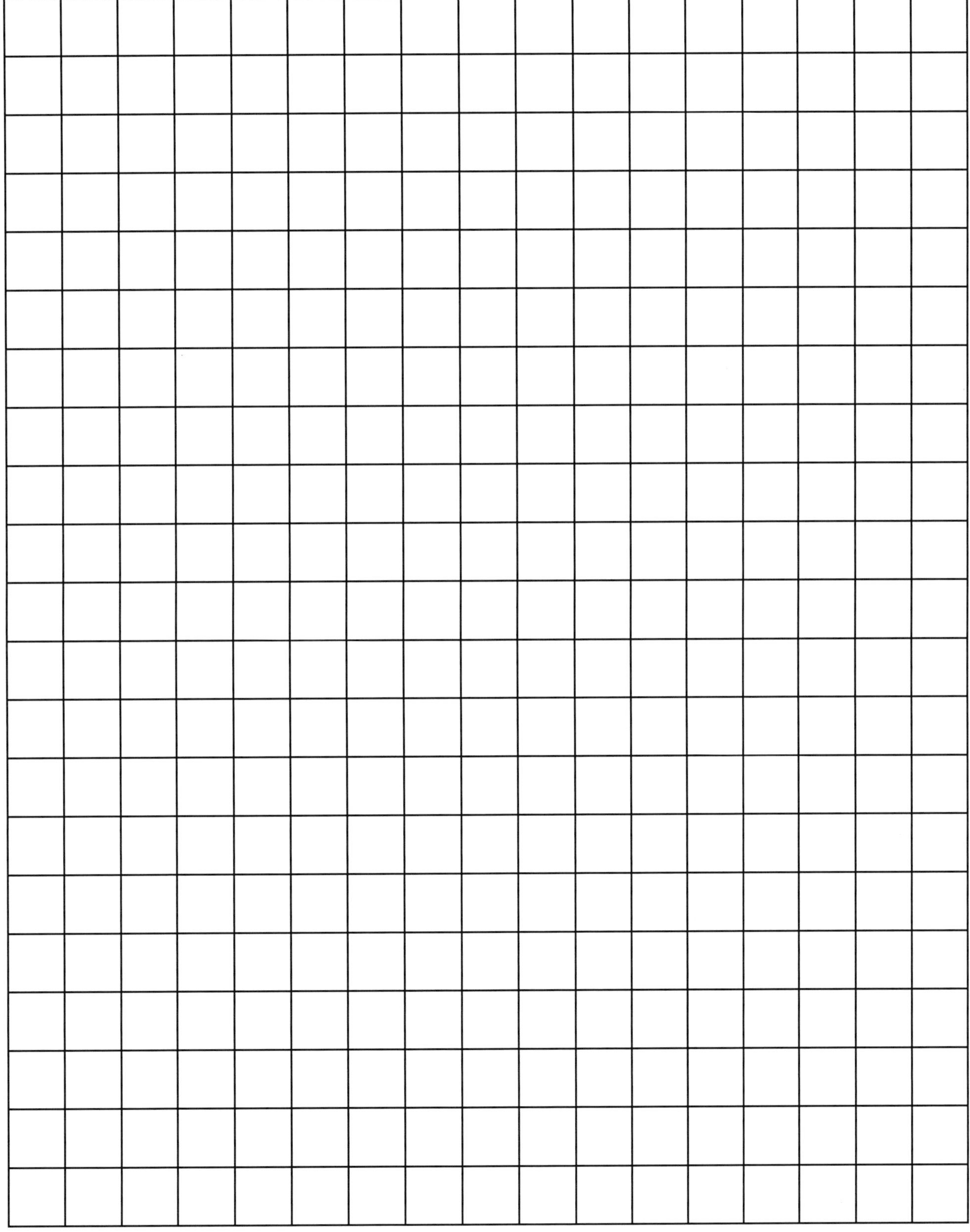

Array/Product Cards

Array Cards

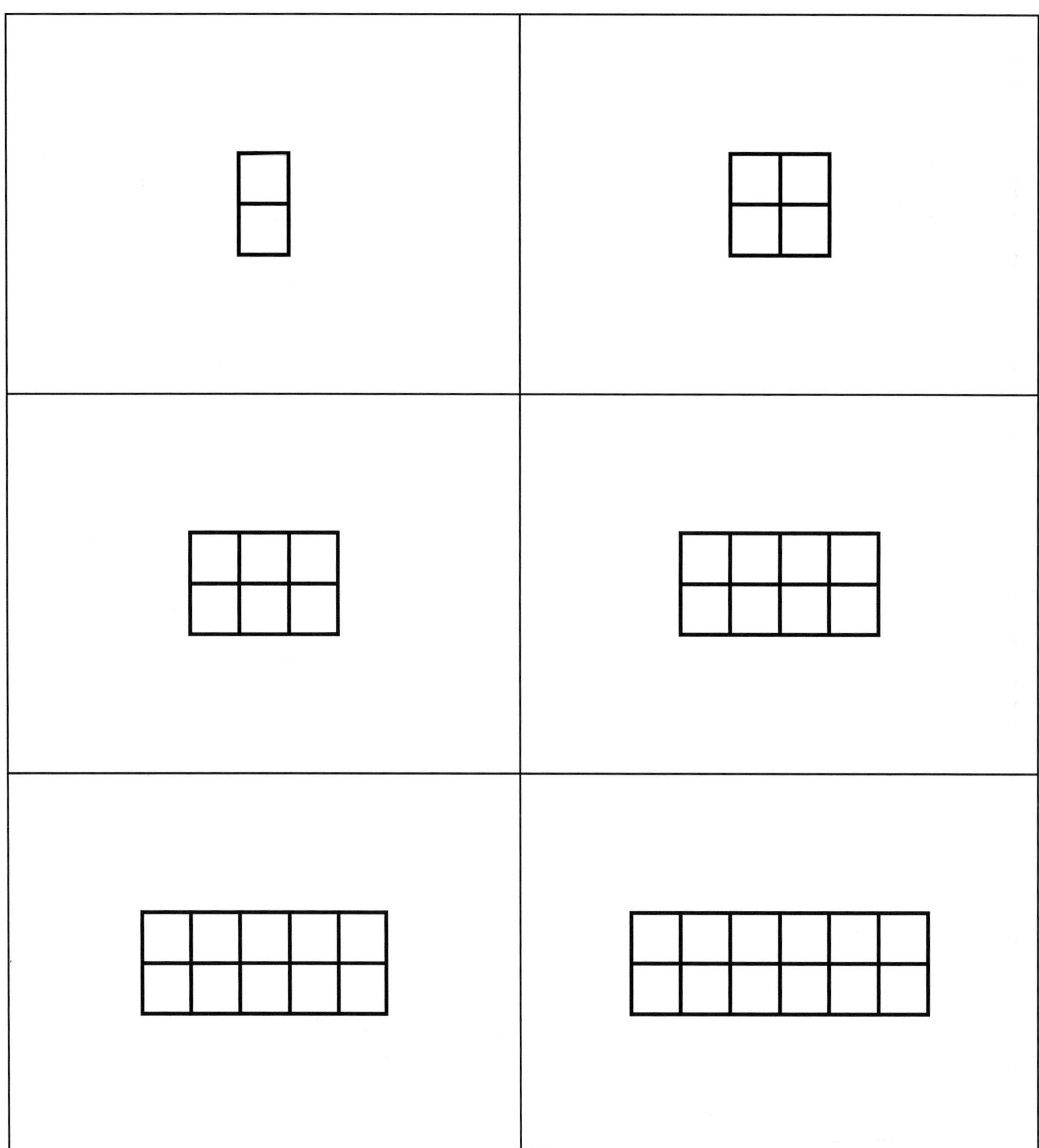

Array/Product Cards

Array Cards

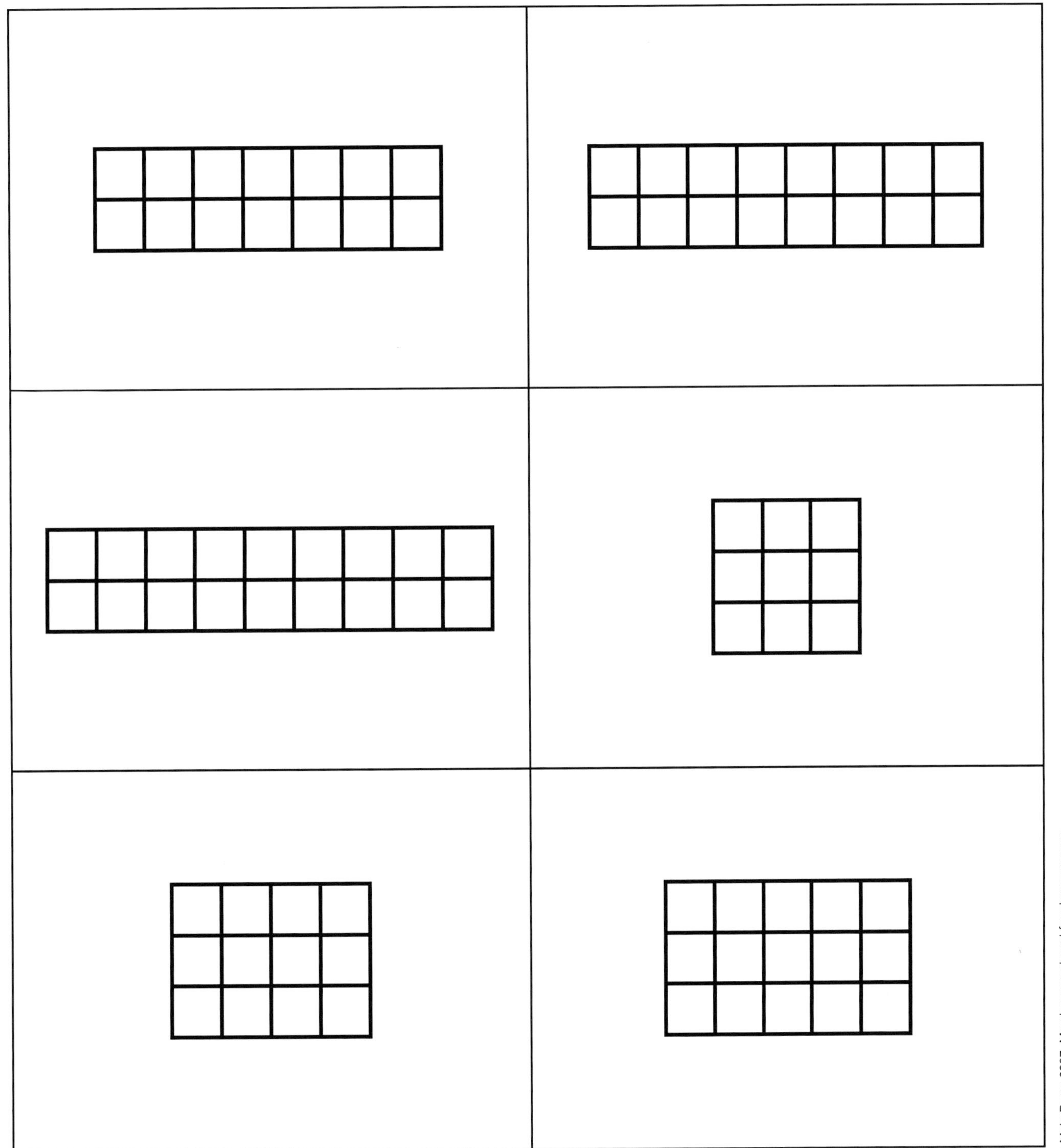

Array/Product Cards

Array Cards

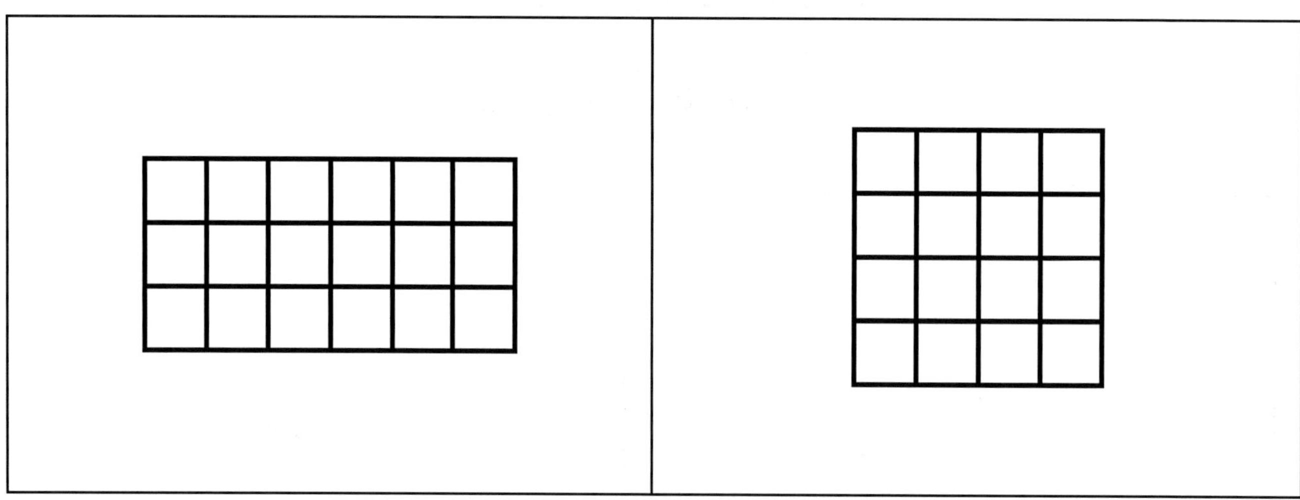

Product Cards

2	4
6	8

Extension B

Array/Product Cards

Product Cards

10	12
14	16
18	9

Array/Product Cards

Product Cards

12	15
18	16

16 Exploring Multiplication – Part Four

Background Information for Teachers

In this lesson, students are introduced to multiplication symbols and related number sentences.

Materials

- chart paper
- markers
- coloured tiles (several tiles for each small group of students)
- small paper bags
- centimetre grid paper (included with lesson 15) (5.15.2)
- coloured pencils

Activity: Part One

On chart paper, draw a 3-by-4 array, as in the diagram below, and ask students to describe it:

○ ○ ○ ○

○ ○ ○ ○

○ ○ ○ ○

Have students find the total number of objects in the array. Ask several students to explain how they calculated their answers.

Now, record the number sentence 3 x 4 = 12 below the array. Explain to students that this number sentence means "three rows of four" or "three groups of four."

Tell students that the x is called the *multiplication symbol*, and it means "groups of," "sets of," or "times." Explain that we can use multiplication to find the total number of objects in an array. Repeat the activity several times with students.

Activity: Part Two

Note: For this activity, you will need a small paper bag filled with tiles for each small group of students.

Divide the class into small groups of students, and give each group some centimetre grid paper, pencil crayons, and a small paper bag filled with tiles. Have students take turns removing a handful of tiles from the bag and making an array with some of the tiles.

Note: Students may have some leftover tiles from their handfuls, which do not fit into their arrays.

Ask each student to draw his/her array on the grid paper and write the corresponding multiplication sentence underneath.

Next Steps

- Ask students to use twelve tiles to make as many different arrays as they can. Have students use coloured pencils to draw each array they make on grid paper. Tell them to write the corresponding multiplication sentence underneath each array. Repeat the activity for other amounts of tiles such as thirteen, fifteen, and twenty-four tiles.
- Collect, and show students everyday examples of arrays such as a muffin tin, a sheet of stamps, and an egg carton. Have students create and then solve story problems that include these items.

16

Extensions

- Add the terms *multiplication, multiply*, and *times* to your classroom Math Word Wall.
- Read *What Comes in 2s, 3s, and 4s?* a book by Suzanne Aker. Use the concepts from the book to discuss the relationship and similarities between skip counting, repeated addition, and multiplication. Use manipulatives, diagrams, and empty number lines to demonstrate this for students.

Assessment Suggestion

Have students complete Student Self-Assessment sheets, found on page 21, to reflect on what they have learned about multiplication.

17 More Multiplication

Materials

- *Amanda Bean's Amazing Dream*, a book by Cindy Neuschwander
- food-picture cards (included. Make a photocopy of each sheet, and cut out cards.) (5.17.1)
- pocket chart
- chart paper
- markers

Activity: Part One

Read the book *Amanda Bean's Amazing Dream* with students. Ask:

- What did Amanda Bean know about multiplication?
- What did she *not* know about multiplication?
- Why did she decide to learn the multiplication facts?

Have students look at the illustration on the page of the book on which the story begins, and draw their attention to the lollipops in the candy store. Now, place the five lollipop food-picture cards (5.17.1) into the pocket chart so that you have the same number of lollipops as shown in the illustration (20). Ask:

- How many lollipops are there altogether?
- What multiplication sentence could you record to show this?

Have students share their solutions to the problem. On chart paper, record students' explanations of how they found the total number of lollipops in the pocket chart, along with the appropriate multiplication sentence. For example, if a student adds together five 4s, record, on chart paper, 4 + 4 + 4 + 4 + 4 = 20 and 5 x 4 = 20.

Activity: Part Two

Use the other food-picture cards to solve more problems related to illustrations in the book. For example, ask students:

- How many cakes are there in the bakery?
- How many loaves of bread are there on the baker's cart?
- How many cookies are there on the second shelf of the baker's cart?
- How many pickles are there in the jars in the cupboard?

Have students share their solutions and explain their reasoning. Then, encourage students to find alternate solutions for each problem and record a multiplication sentence for each solution they find.

Activity: Part Three

To reinforce the relationship between addition and multiplication, present addition sentences, and have students rewrite them as multiplication sentences, and vice versa. For example, on chart paper, record:

- 5 + 5 produces the same result as 2 x 5
- 3 + 3 + 3 + 3 produces the same result as 3 x 4

Next Step

Introduce the terms *product* and *factor*. Explain that the answer to a multiplication problem is called a product and that the numbers that are multiplied together to get the product are called factors. Show students several different multiplication sentences, and point out which numbers are the factors and which numbers are the products.

▶

17

Extensions

- Add the terms *product* and *factor* to your classroom math word wall.
- Together with students, create a list of everyday situations in which students could use multiplication.
- Have students create, and solve, multiplication story problems that involve everyday situations.

Food-Picture Cards – Lollipops

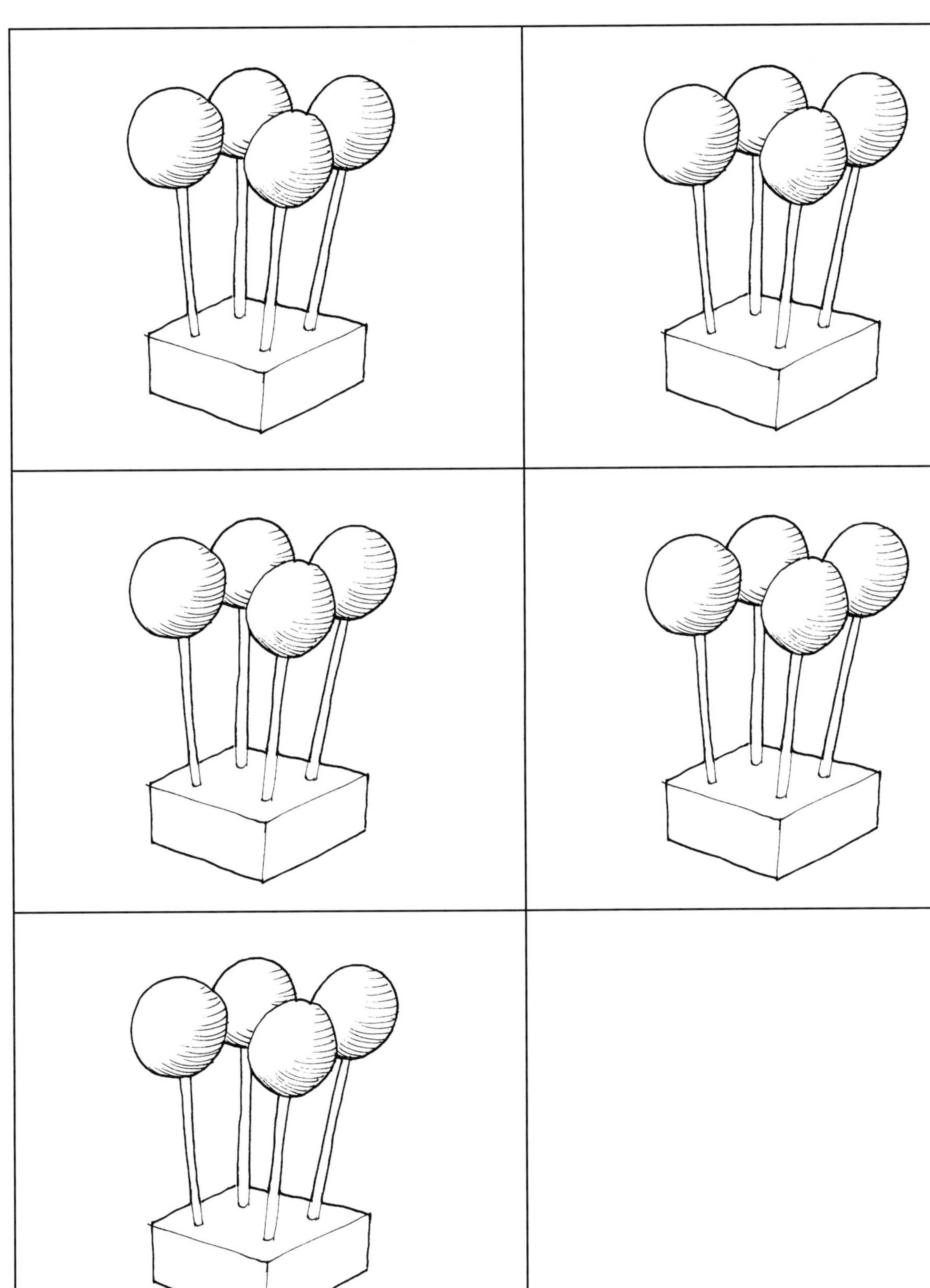

Food-Picture Cards – Cakes

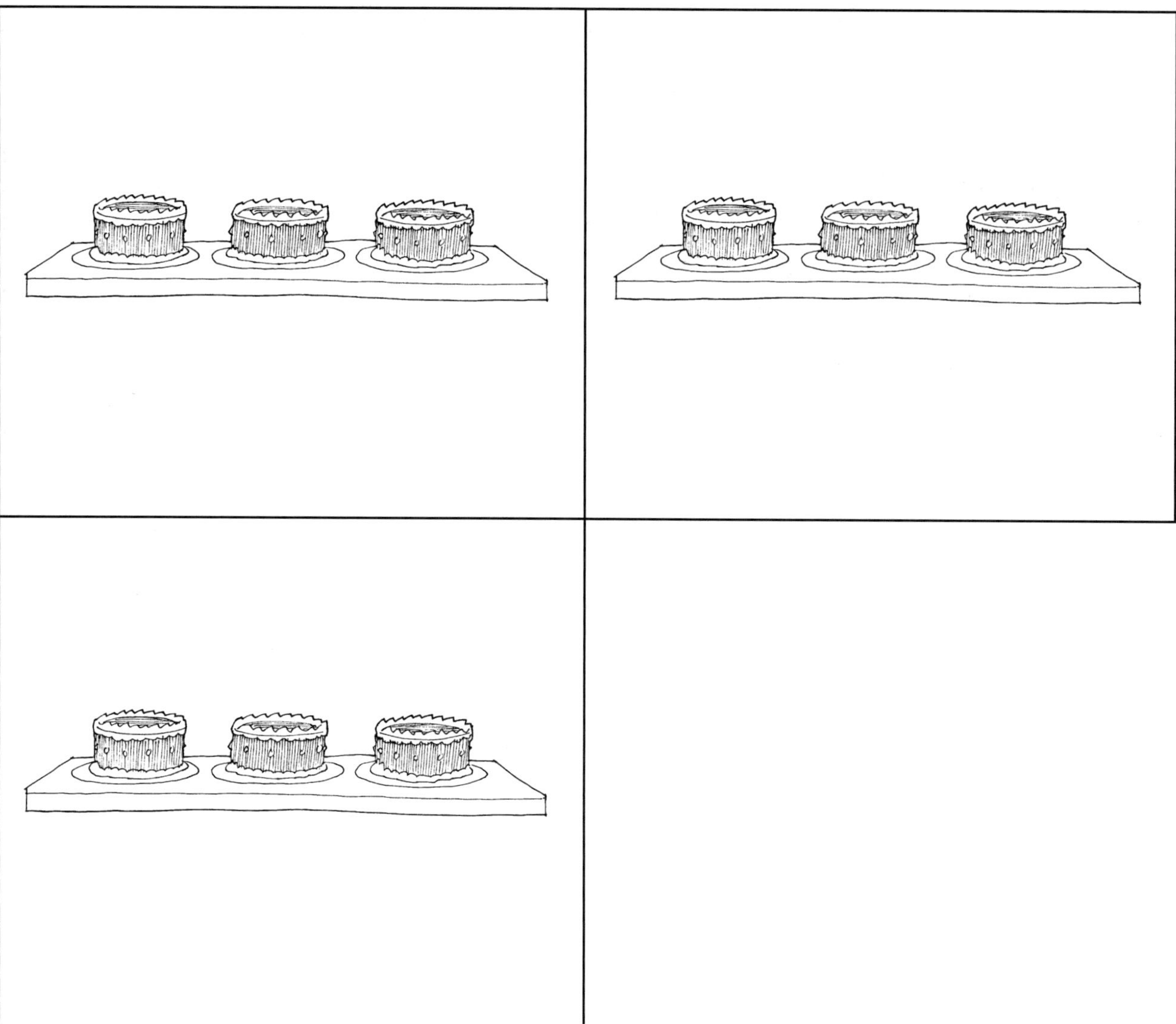

Food-Picture Cards – Bread

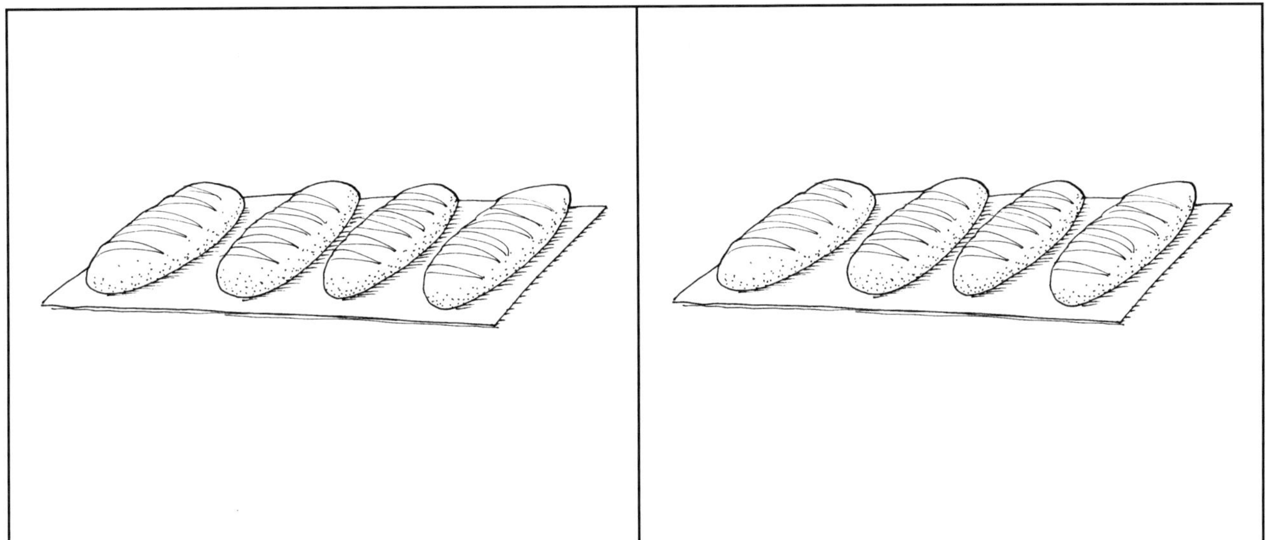

Food-Picture Cards – Cookies

Food-Picture Cards – Pickles

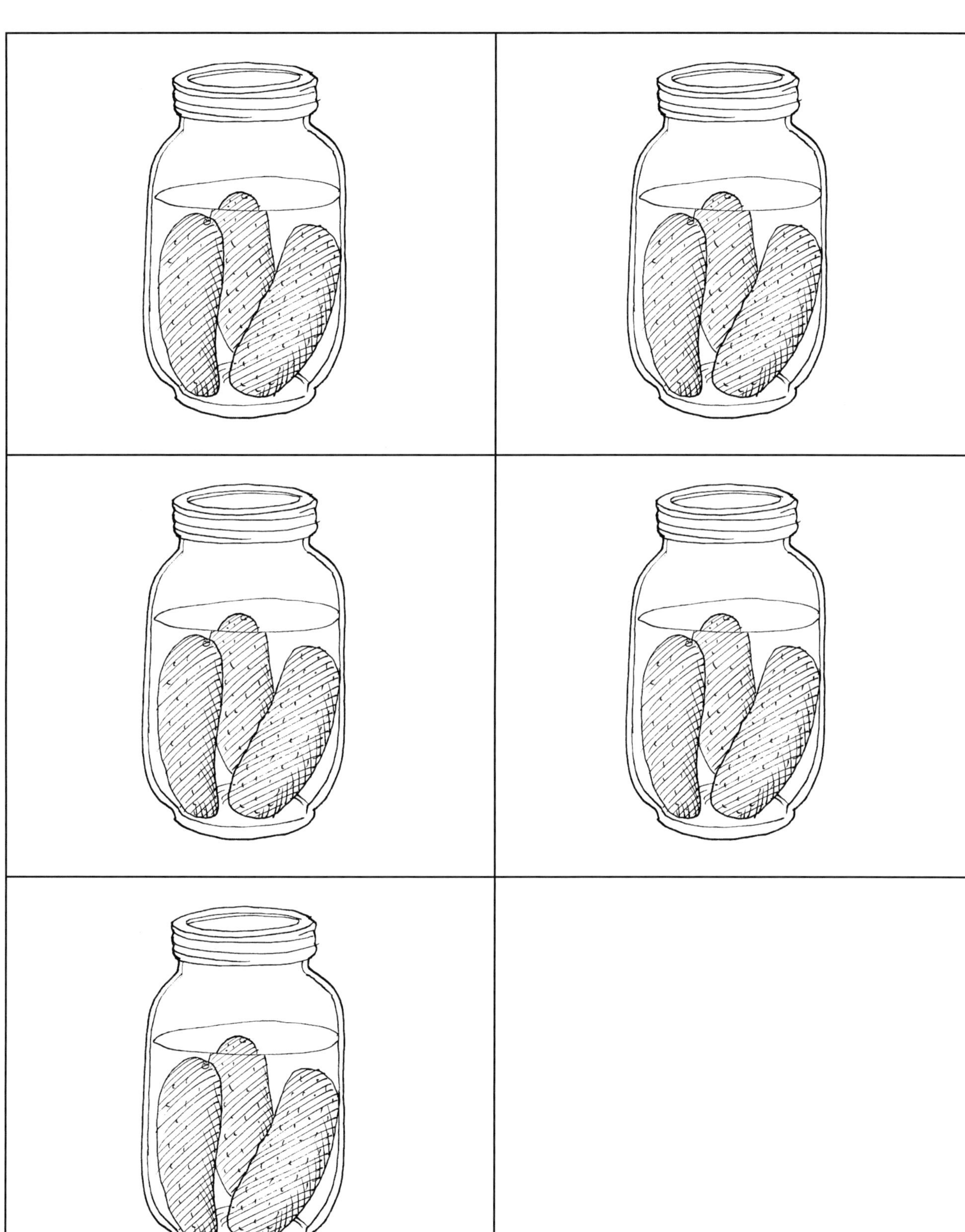

18 Commutative Property of Multiplication

Background Information for Teachers

The commutative property of multiplication allows two or more factors to be arranged in any order without affecting the product. For example, a x b = b x a. Understanding this property is an important precondition to properly learning the multiplication facts.

Note: For the grade-3 level, arrays should be limited to 5 x 5.

Materials

- overhead projector
- nonpermanent overhead markers
- centimetre grid paper (included. Make an overhead transparency of this sheet.) (5.18.1)
- coloured tiles (several tiles for each student)
- blank paper
- chart paper
- markers
- calculators (one for each student)
- number cubes (two for each pair of students)

Activity: Part One

On the overhead, use the centimetre grid paper transparency (5.18.1) and overhead markers to draw a 3-by-5 array, as below:

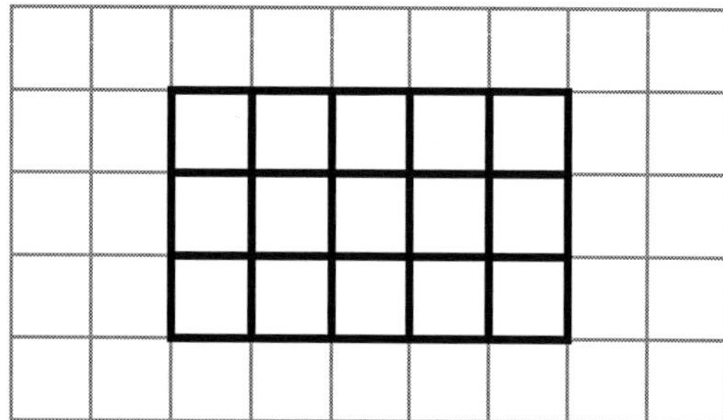

Distribute several coloured tiles and a blank piece of paper to each student. Have students use their coloured tiles to create similar 3-by-5 arrays on their pieces of paper. On chart paper, have a student record the multiplication sentence that describes the array.

Now, have students rotate their pieces of paper 90° so that their arrays look like this:

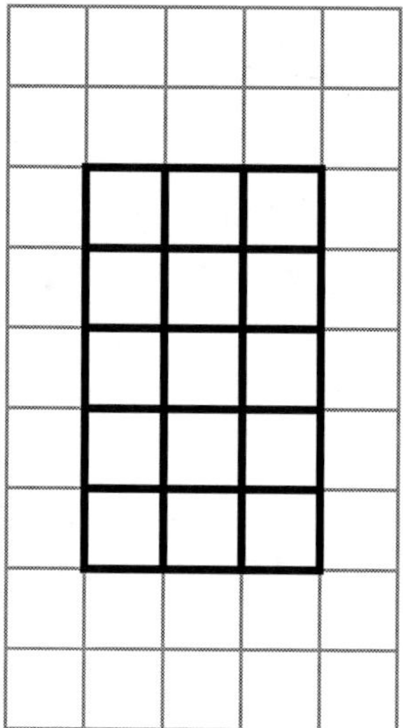

Model this on the overhead as well, by turning the grid paper. Ask students:

- What multiplication sentence describes this array? (Have a student record the number sentence on chart paper).
- How are the sentences 3 x 5 = 15 and 5 x 3 = 15 alike?
- How are they different?

Provide additional examples and repeat the same procedure by drawing the following arrays: 4 by 2 (and 2 by 4); 3 by 2; 4 by 5; 1 by 5; 4 by 1; and 5 by 3.

Check students' understanding of the commutative property of multiplication by asking:

- If 4 x 3 = 12, what does 3 x 4 equal? How do you know?
- If 4 x 5 = 20, what does 5 x 4 equal? How do you know?

Next Step

To further challenge students' understanding of the concept, ask:

- If 15 x 7 = 105, what else do you know? Why?
- If 13 x 21 = 273, what is 21 x 13? How do you know?

Distribute calculators, and have students use them to verify their answers to the questions.

Distribute Activity Sheet A (5.18.2). For each multiplication problem, have students follow the model by drawing a simple picture to illustrate the problem, recording a description of the picture, and then solving the problem. Then, tell students to record the problem's turnaround fact, draw a simple picture to illustrate the fact, and record a description of the picture.

Activity Sheet A

Directions to students:

For each multiplication problem, follow the model by drawing a simple picture to illustrate the problem, recording a description of the picture, and then solving the problem. Then, record the problem's turnaround fact, draw a simple picture to illustrate the fact, and record a description of the picture (5.18.2).

Extension

Have students use counters to determine whether or not division facts can be "turned around" in the same way multiplication facts can be.

Centimetre Grid Paper

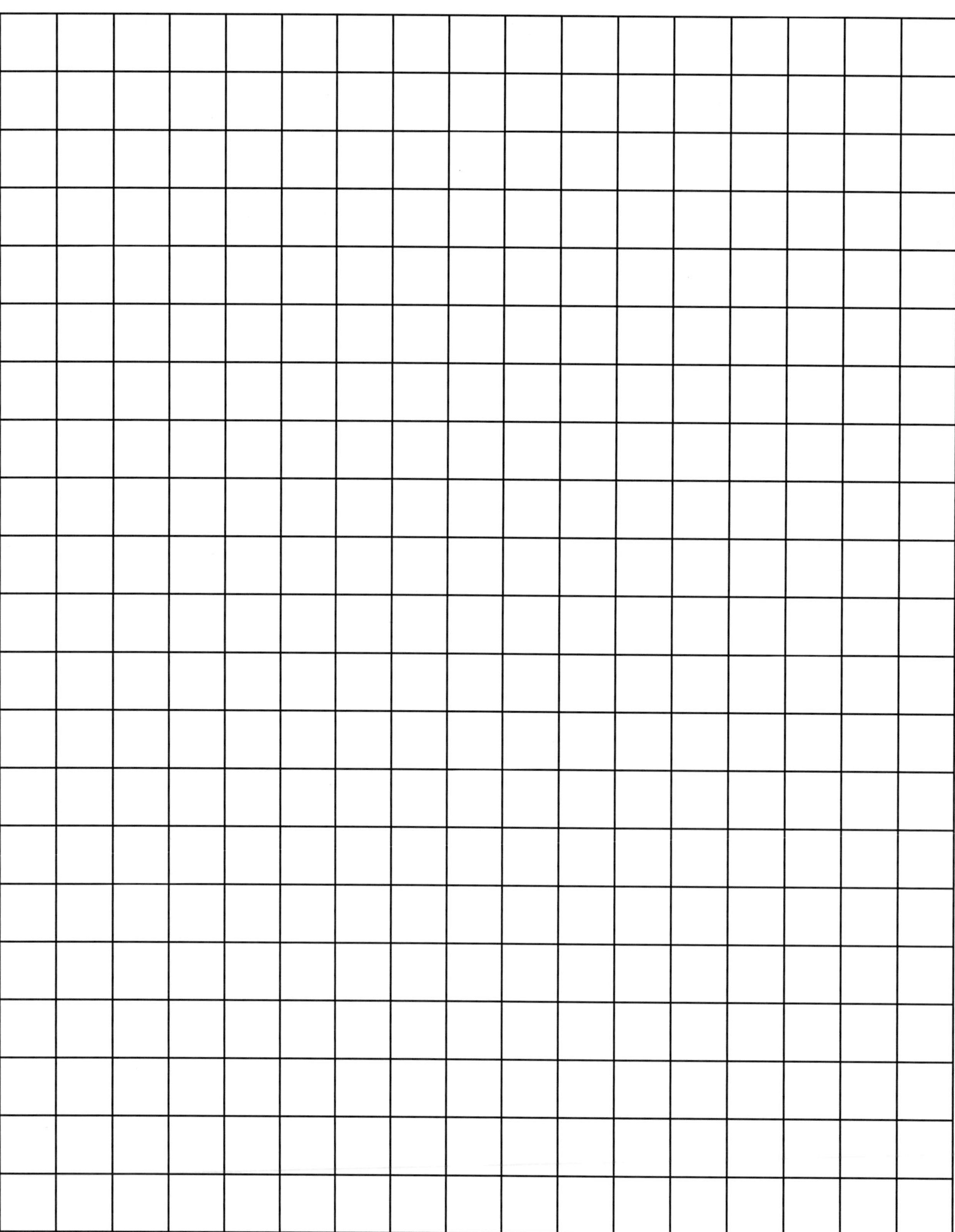

Date: ____________ Name: ____________________

Solving Multiplication Problems

Problem	Turnaround Fact
2 x 3 = 6	3 x 2 = 6

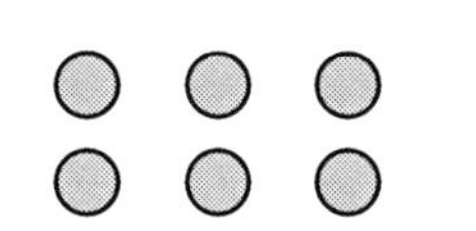

two groups of three

three groups of two

4 x 5 = ______

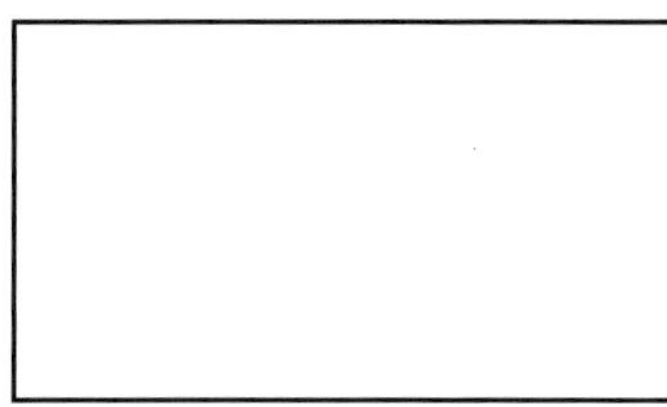

______

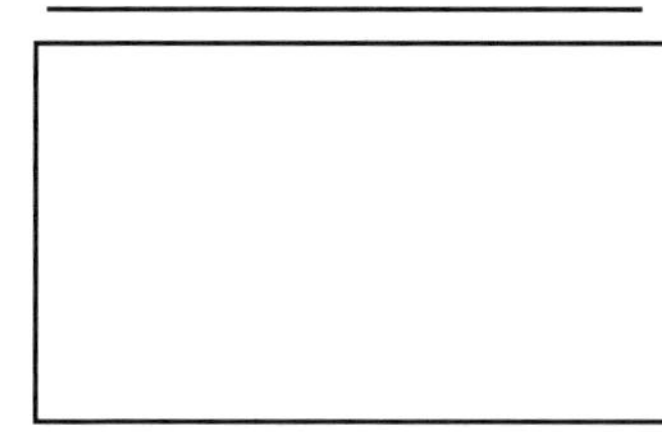

5 x 1 = ______

______

1 x 3 = ______

______

2 x 4 = ______

______

Date: ________________ Name: ____________________________

Problem | **Turnaround Fact**

5 x 2 = ______

____

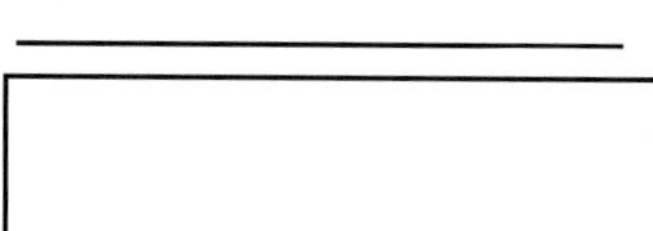

4 x 3 = ______

____

5 x 3 = ______

____

4 x 1 = ______

____

2 x 1 = ______

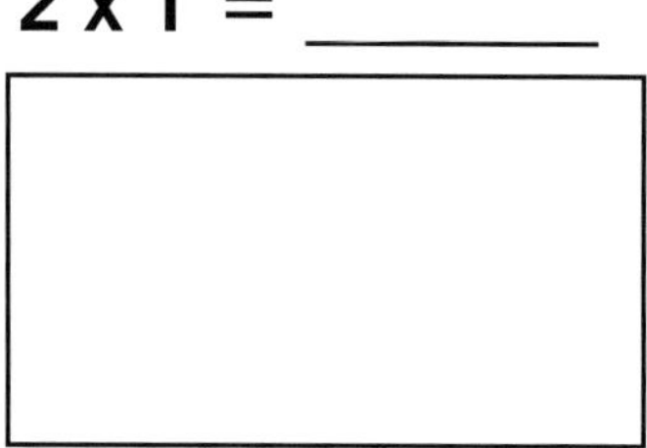

____

19 Multiplying by 1 and by 0

Materials

- grid paper
- pencils
- scissors
- counters
- paper plates

Activity: Part One

Distribute grid paper and pencils, and have students draw the following arrays on their paper:

5 rows of 3	1 row of 5
1 row of 3	9 rows of 1
6 rows of 2	8 rows of 1
4 rows of 1	1 row of 7
4 rows of 7	1 row of 6
3 rows of 2	6 rows of 6

For each array they have drawn, ask students to determine how many squares it has and then record on it the multiplication sentence it illustrates. For example:

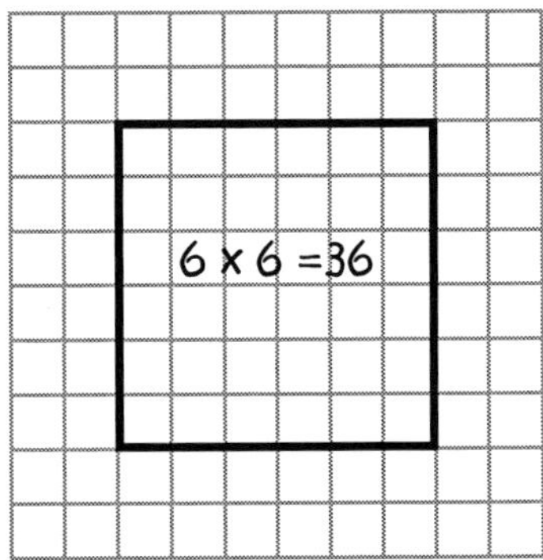

Next, distribute scissors, and have students cut out their arrays and sort them into two groups: arrays that have a dimension of 1 (for example, 1 row of 7 or 7 rows of 1) and arrays for which both dimensions are greater than 1. Have students compare their two groups of arrays.

Ask:

- What happens when you cut out an array with a dimension of 1 (1 x ___ or ___ x 1)?
- How can you quickly find out the number of squares in an array that is 1 row by another number or another number by 1?
- What do you know about the product of two numbers when one of the factors is 1?

Activity: Part Two

Distribute Activity Sheet A (5.19.1), and present the following situation to students:

Sergio says he will never be able to finish his math assignment in time to play hockey. He thinks there are too many problems on the activity sheet. He completes the first problem, and then looks at the other problems again. "I'm wrong," he says, "these problems are easy. It will only take me a few minutes to do them." Why did Sergio change his mind?

Have students offer their suggestions and then complete the activity sheet.

Activity Sheet A

Directions to students:

Finish Sergio's math assignment. Answer the questions at the bottom of the page (5.19.1).

Activity: Part Three

Distribute grid paper to students. Introduce multiplication by 0 by asking students to try to draw the following arrays on the paper:

- 0 rows of 3
- 5 rows of 0
- 0 rows of 4
- 8 rows of 0

19

Distribute counters and paper plates, and have students use them to explore multiplication with 0. Present students with the following problem:

Jeremy has 3 paper bags. There are 0 cookies in each bag. How many cookies does Jeremy have?

Discuss what students know about the product of two numbers when one of the factors is 0.

Distribute Activity Sheet B (5.19.2), and have students finish Sergio's second math assignment. Tell students to also answer the questions at the bottom of the page.

Activity Sheet B

Directions to students:

Finish Sergio's second math assignment, and answer the questions at the bottom of the page (5.19.2).

Date: ________________ Name: ____________________________

Sergio's Math Assignment

8 x 1 = ______	3 x 1 = ______	1 x 12 = ______
24 x 1 = ______	1 x 98 = ______	35 x 1 = ______
1 x 40 = ______	66 x 1 = ______	73 x 1 = ______
5 x 1 = ______	1 x 25 = ______	100 x 1 = ______

Why did Sergio decide that the problems above are easy?

____

____

What multiplication rule can you record to describe the product of two numbers when one of the factors is 1?

____

____

Date: ____________ Name: ____________

Sergio's Second Math Assignment

18 x 0 = ______	31 x 0 = ______	0 x 12 = ______
4 x 0 = ______	0 x 98 = ______	35 x 0 = ______
0 x 44 = ______	69 x 0 = ______	73 x 0 = ______
54 x 0 = ______	0 x 25 = ______	100 x 0 = ______

Why does Sergio think the problems above are easy too?

____

____

What multiplication rule can you record to describe the product of two numbers when one of the factors is 0?

____

____

20 Multiplication Facts

Materials

- overhead projector
- mixed-up multiplication table (included. Photocopy the table onto an overhead transparency.) (5.20.1)
- nonpermanent overhead marker
- number cubes (two number cubes for each group of four students)
- four colours of bingo chips (Each group of four students will need nine bingo chips in each of the four colours.)

Activity: Part One

On the overhead projector, display the mixed-up multiplication table (5.20.1). Explain that the table is "mixed-up" because the factors that go across the top and down the left-hand side are not in consecutive order. But, when the correct numbers are filled in along the top and down the side, one factor from the top row multiplied by one factor from the left column will equal the corresponding product already in place. Tell students that their job is to fill in the correct factors across the top and along the left-hand side. Help students begin to identify the missing factors by asking:

- What do you notice about the numbers in the fourth, filled-in row?
- What two numbers can you multiply to get a product of 25? A product of 20?
- What factor belongs on the far left (first column) of the bottom row? How do you know?

Continue asking questions in this way until students find all the missing factors. Use a nonpermanent overhead marker to record each factor on the chart as students identify it.

Distribute Activity Sheet A (5.20.2), and tell students that you have another mixed-up multiplication table for them to complete. In this table, however, only some of the products are already filled in. Have students complete Activity Sheet A.

Activity Sheet A

Directions to students:

Complete the mixed-up multiplication table by recording the correct factors along the top and down the left-hand side. Also, fill in the missing products (5.20.2).

Mixed-Up Multiplication Table

X					
	20	12	8	4	16
	5	3	2	1	4
	15	9	6	3	12
	25	15	10	5	20
	10	6	4	2	8

Date: ____________ Name: ____________

Mixed-Up Multiplication Table

x				3	
	8			6	
		5			
1			2		5
			6		
	16				

21 Exploring Division – Part One

Background Information for Teachers

There are two types of division problems: partition problems and measurement problems.

In *partition problems*, both the total number of objects and the number of groups are known, and the size of the groups must be determined. For example, Alison has 12 candies. If she gives candy to 3 friends, how many pieces of candy does each friend get?

Measurement problems involve finding the number of groups when both the total number of objects and the size of each group are known. For example, Alison has 12 candies. If she gives 3 candies to each friend, how many friends does she give candy to?

Be sure to provide students with opportunities to solve both types of problems.

In this lesson, students use manipulatives, diagrams, and symbols to illustrate the process of solving partition-division problems.

Note: Focus on division problems that are related to multiplication facts to 5 x 5.

Materials

- *The Doorbell Rang*, a book by Pat Hutchins
- bingo chips (several for each pair of students)
- paper plates or cups (several for each pair of students)
- paper
- pencils
- counters (twenty to thirty for each pair of students)
- six-sided number cubes (one for each pair of students)
- small paper bags (one for each pair of students)

Activity: Part One

Read *The Doorbell Rang* with students. Have students describe situations when they shared things with their friends or family members. Ask students to tell how they made sure everyone got the same amount and what they did with any leftovers.

Now, divide the class into pairs of students, and distribute bingo chips and paper plates to each pair. Read the story again, and have students use their bingo chips and paper plates to represent each division situation that happens in the story. For example, if 12 cookies are shared between 2 people, tell students they must place an equal number of bingo chips onto each of 2 plates.

Next Steps

- Have students use bingo chips and paper plates again to represent each division situation in the story *The Doorbell Rang*, but this time, change the numbers from the story to reflect related facts to 5 x 5. For example:

  Problem: If you have 12 cookies to share among 5 people, how many cookies does each person get?

Note: The previous problem requires an explanation of the word *remainder* for students. Tell students that a "remainder" is the number left over when one number is divided by another number. In this case, 5 cannot be divided into 12 an equal number of times; there is a remainder of 2.

22 Exploring Division – Part Two

Background Information for Teachers

In this lesson, students use manipulatives, diagrams, and symbols to illustrate the process of solving measurement-division problems.

Materials

- bingo chips or counters
- paper plates or cups
- paper
- pencils

Activity

Divide the class into small groups of students, and distribute bingo chips, paper plates, paper, and a pencil to each group. Have groups discuss and solve each of the following problems. Allow each group to determine the strategy they will use to solve each problem. Some groups may choose to use bingo chips and paper plates, while others may choose a more abstract strategy such as drawing pictures or using symbols to repeatedly subtract a number.

Note: Two of the following measurement problems involve remainders. Tell students how they should deal with the remainders.

- Coach Saunders needs 15 tennis balls for the tournament. If tennis balls come in packages of 3, how many packages does Coach Saunders need to buy?
- Maria buys 12 eggs. If she needs 3 eggs to make 1 omelette, how many omelets can Marie make?
- Alex has 15 stickers. If he gives 5 stickers to each friend at his party, how many friends will he give stickers to?
- Twenty-five children sign up to play flag football. If there are 5 players on each team, how many teams will there be?
- Courtney and John picked 20 apples. If they put 4 apples into each bag, how many bags of apples will Courtney and John have?

Have students in each group share their solutions for each problem and explain their reasoning.

Note: Reproducible masters for these problems can be found on pages 614 and 615.

23 Exploring Division – Part Three

Background Information for Teachers

In this lesson, students use manipulatives, diagrams, and symbols to solve division problems.

Materials

- "Sharing Game" number cards (included. Photocopy, and cut out one set of cards for each group of three students.) (5.23.1)
- small paper bags (one for each group of three students)
- bingo chips or counters
- "Sharing Game" score sheet (included. Make one photocopy for each student.) (5.23.2)
- counters (at least twenty-four for each pair of students)
- chart paper
- markers

Activity: Part One

Before beginning this activity, place a set of "Sharing Game" number cards into each paper bag. Divide the class into groups of four students, and provide each group with several bingo chips, a bag of cards, and copies of the "Sharing Game" score sheet (5.23.2). Have students play the "Sharing Game."

Tell Player *A* in each group to pull a card out of the bag, record this number in the "Number Drawn" column on the score sheet ("Round 1"), and take as many bingo chips as the number on the card. Then, ask this player to divide the bingo chips equally among all three players. Have this player record the number of chips each player receives in the "Score" column on the score sheet. Also have him/her record a diagram of the sharing process.

For example, if Player *A* draws the "12" card, he/she counts out 12 chips and gives each player 3 chips. He/she then records 12 in the "Number Drawn" column, "3" in the "Score" column, and draws a diagram of the sharing.

Ask Player *A* to return the card into the bag. Then, have Player *B* pull a card out of the bag and complete "Round 2" on the score sheet. After five rounds, have players add up their scores. The group with the highest total score wins the game.

Next Steps

- Vary the game by changing the numbers on the cards. For example, use multiples of 3 or 5.
- Have students associate division with arrays. For example, divide students into pairs, and give each pair twenty-four counters. Ask them to use all the counters to find the number of rows in an array that has 4 counters in each row. Have students describe the corresponding division problem. Vary the activity by asking students to determine how many counters are in each row of an array that has 4 rows.

Activity: Part Two

Present to students the following story problem:

- Jeremy has 8 strawberries. There are 4 plates on the table. How many strawberries will Jeremy put onto each plate?

Draw the four plates on chart paper. Explain that the strawberries must be divided evenly among the plates. Remind students that the term *divide* means to share *equally*. Draw one strawberry on each plate. Have students count aloud as you draw each strawberry. Now, draw a second strawberry on each plate. Have students continue counting aloud until you have drawn eight strawberries, as in the following diagram:

   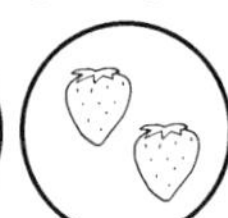

Discuss the diagram, explaining that 8 strawberries shared among 4 plates means there are 2 strawberries on each plate. On chart paper, record the number sentence for this story problem:

$8 \div 4 = 2$.

Explain to students that this number sentence means "Eight divided by four equals two." Repeat this procedure using similar problems involving both measurement and partition. Draw a diagram, and record a number sentence for each story problem.

Distribute Activity Sheet A (5.23.3), and have students draw sets to find the answer to each division problem. Then, tell students to record the answer in the space provided. Finally, have students write a story problem to go with one of the problems.

Activity Sheet A

Note: This is a two-page activity sheet.

Directions to students:

For each division problem, draw sets to find the answer. Then, write the answer in the space provided. Finally, write a story problem to go with one of the questions (5.23.3).

Extension

Add the terms *divide, division*, and *divided by* to your classroom Math Word Wall.

Assessment Suggestions

- Observe students as they work together to play the "Sharing Game." Focus on each student's ability to work in a group. Use the Cooperative Skills Teacher-Assessment sheet, found on page 20, to record your results.
- Have students complete copies of the Cooperative Skills Self-Assessment sheet, found on page 22, to reflect on their abilities to work together.

Sharing Game Number Cards

4	8
12	16
20	

Date: ____________________ Names: ______________________________

____

____

Sharing Game Score Sheet

Round	Number Drawn	Score	Diagram of Sharing
1			
2			
3			
4			
5			
Total Score			

Date: ______________ Name: ______________________

Solving Division Problems

Problem	Sets
1. 8÷4= 2	
2. 9÷3= ____	
3. 8÷1= ____	
4. 16÷4= ____	

Date: ____________ Name: ____________

5. 25÷5= _____	
6. 5÷5= _____	
7. 15÷3= _____	
8. 10÷5= _____	

Story Problem for Question Number _____ : ____________

____

____

____

24 The Inverse Relationship between Multiplication and Division

Materials

- scrap paper
- pencils
- counters
- coloured tiles
- grid paper
- chart paper
- markers
- index cards

Activity: Part One

Distribute scrap paper and pencils, and ask students to use only the numbers 3, 5, and 15 to record four multiplication and division facts. Have materials such as counters, coloured tiles, and grid paper available for students' use, and tell students to use strategies of their own choice to find the facts.

Have students share the multiplication and division facts they found and explain how they found them. Ask students:

- What do you notice about the facts?

Distribute coloured tiles (or grid paper and pencils), and have students use them to create arrays that are 3 rows of 5. Ask:

- Which multiplication facts does this array describe?
- Which division facts does this array describe?

Tell students that multiplication and division are *inverse* operations. Explain that this means one operation undoes the other. For example, when we multiply 3 by 5 (or 5 by 3) to get 21, we can *undo* the multiplication by dividing 15 by 5 to get 3 (or by dividing 15 by 3 to get 5).

Provide students with more examples of the inverse relationship between multiplication and division. Ask students to identify the inverse of the following number sentences:

- 3 x 5 = 15
- 6 ÷ 2 = 3
- 10 ÷ 2 = 5
- 4 x 5 = 20

Activity: Part Two

Show students how to use the relationship between multiplication and division to solve division problems. Tell students that if they do not know what the answer to 12 divided by 4 is, they can think, what number times 4 equals 12?

Next, have tiles, counters, and grid paper available for students' use, and tell them to solve the problem ____ x 4 = 12. Ask:

- What division facts do you see when you look at your tiles, counters, or array?
- How are these facts related to the multiplication facts?

Explain that since 3 x 4 = 12, then 12 ÷ 4 must equal 3. On chart paper, record the steps to the following strategy as you describe them:

12 ÷ 4 = ______

Think: _____ x 4 = 12

3 x 4 = 12

So, 12 ÷ 4 = 3

Repeat the process using two or three more examples. Then, distribute counters, coloured tiles, or grid paper, and have students use the manipulatives to help them solve each of the following problems. Encourage students to use multiplication and the same steps demonstrated to them:

- 25 ÷ 5 = ______
- 16 ÷ 4 = ______
- 15 ÷ 3 = ______

As students solve each problem, discuss, and have students explain, how multiplication helped them solve the problems.

Distribute Activity Sheet A (5.24.1). For each division problem, have students use multiplication to help them find the solution, draw an array to show how they solved it, and record the matching multiplication fact.

Then, distribute Activity Sheet B (5.24.2). For each division problem, have students use multiplication to help them find the solution, draw groups to show how they solved it, and record the matching multiplication fact.

Activity Sheet A

Directions to students:

For each division problem, use multiplication to help you find the solution, draw an array to show how you solved it, and record the matching multiplication fact (5.24.1).

Activity Sheet B

Directions to students:

For each division problem, use multiplication to help you find the solution, draw groups to show how you solved it, and record the matching multiplication fact (5.24.2).

Activity: Part Three

Distribute several index cards to each student. Select a group of multiplication facts (to 5 x 5), and have students record the facts on the index cards, one fact per card, as in the diagram below:

3 x 4 = 12

On chart paper, record a division problem that is related to one of students' multiplication facts. Have students hold up their matching multiplication fact (recorded on an index card). For example, if you record 12 ÷ 4 = _____ on chart paper, each student should hold up an index card with 3 x 4 = 12 recorded on it.

Activity Centre

At a centre, place decks of fifty-two Related-Facts Rummy cards (included. Photocopy, and cut out, cards, and consider mounting them onto sturdy tagboard.)

Note: Each deck of cards is comprised of 13 "books"; a "book" is a set of four related multiplication and division facts. For example: one book would consist of cards with 3 x 4 = 12, 4 x 3 = 12, 12 ÷ 4 = 3, and 12 ÷ 3 = 4.

Have groups of three to five students play Related-Facts Rummy. Designate one player in each group as the dealer, and have the dealer give five cards to each player. Tell the dealer to place the remaining cards, facedown, in the centre of the playing area, forming the "draw pile." Also, ask the dealer to turn over the top card and place it, face up, next to the draw pile to begin the "discard pile."

24

Tell players they are looking for "books" (sets) of related multiplication and division facts. Have player *A* take either the top card from the draw pile or the top card from the discard pile. Then, tell player *A* to either keep the drawn card and place one of his/her original five cards, face up, onto the discard pile, or place the drawn card onto the discard pile.

After the first play (player *A*), tell players to take turns drawing either one card from the draw pile or up to four cards from the discard pile. If, for example, a player wants the third card in the discard pile, he/she must take the first and second cards too. After each draw, a player must put one card into the discard pile.

Have players try to get rid of all their cards by doing any combination of the following:

- creating a four-card book of related multiplication and division facts and setting it down in the centre of the playing space
- creating a three-card spread of related multiplication and division facts and setting it down in the centre of the playing space
- playing a card onto a three-card spread in play

Players cannot play a card onto a three-card spread in play until they have created, and set down, at least one three-card spread or four-card book of their own. Only three- and four-card spreads can be set down for play (that is, a player must hold onto a two-card spread of related facts until a third related fact is drawn). If players run out of cards in the draw pile, have the dealer pick up, and shuffle, all but the top card from the discard pile and place the cards, facedown, to form a new draw pile. The first player to get rid of all cards in his/her hand wins (5.24.3).

Extension

Add the term *inverse* to your classroom math word wall.

Assessment Suggestion

Meet with each student individually, and provide counters, grid paper, blank paper, and a pencil. Ask students to solve the problem $20 \div 4 =$ ____ in as many ways as they can. Consider:

- whether each student can solve the problem correctly
- whether each student can use more than one strategy to solve the problem
- what strategies each student uses (arrays, groups of manipulatives, repeated subtraction or multiplication)

Record your results on the Individual Student Observations sheet, found on page 16.

Date: ______________ Name: ______________________

Multiplication and Division

Division Problem	Array	Multiplication Fact
1. 15 ÷ 3 = _____	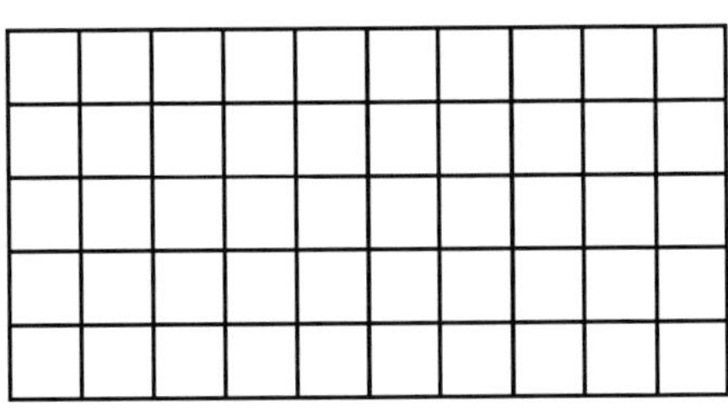	_____ x _____ = _____
2. 12 ÷ 4 = _____	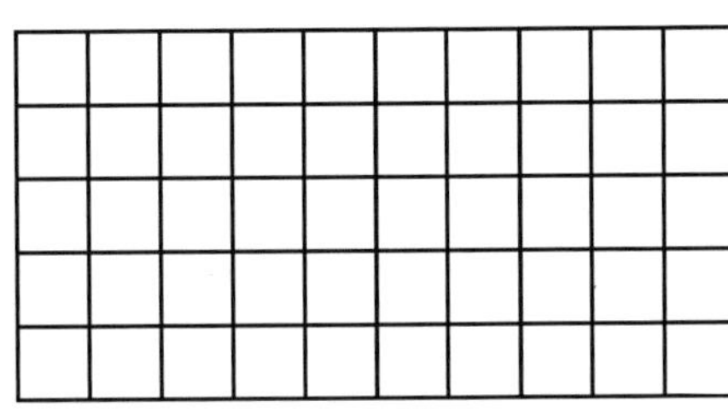	_____ x _____ = _____
3. 25 ÷ 5 = _____	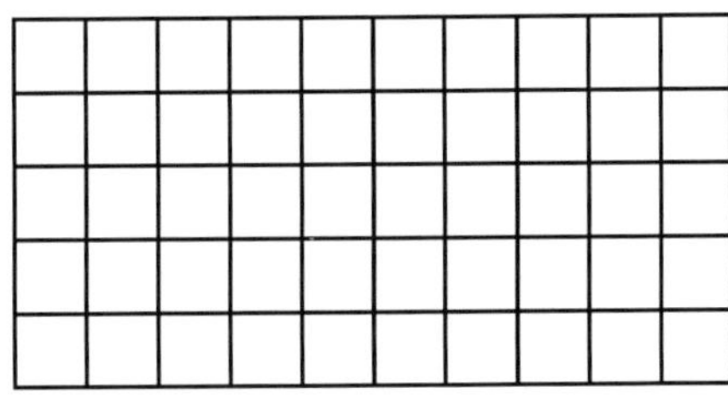	_____ x _____ = _____
4. 16 ÷ 4 = _____	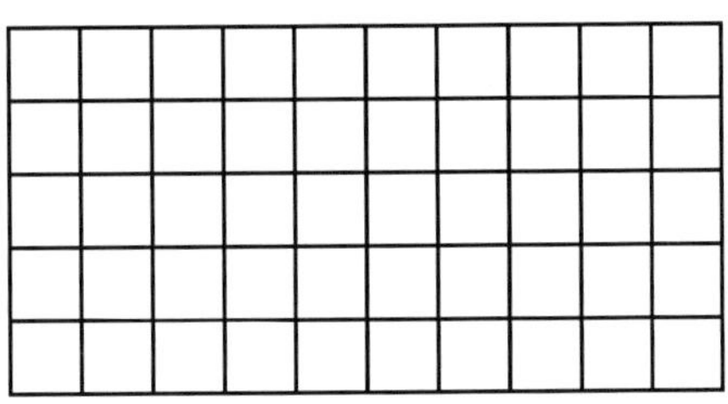	_____ x _____ = _____

Date: ____________ Name: ____________________

More Multiplication and Division

Division Problem	Groups	Multiplication Fact
1. 8 ÷ 4 = ____		____ x ____ = ____
2. 9 ÷ 3 = ____		____ x ____ = ____
3. 10 ÷ 2 = ____		____ x ____ = ____
4. 20 ÷ 4 = ____		____ x ____ = ____

Related-Facts Rummy Cards

3 x 4 = 12	4 x 3 = 12	12 ÷ 4 = 3	12 ÷ 3 = 4
1 x 4 = 4	4 x 1 = 4	4 ÷ 1 = 4	4 ÷ 4 = 1
5 x 4 = 20	4 x 5 = 20	20 ÷ 4 = 5	20 ÷ 5 = 4
2 x 3 = 6	3 x 2 = 6	6 ÷ 3 = 2	6 ÷ 2 = 3
4 x 2 = 8	2 x 4 = 8	8 ÷ 2 = 4	8 ÷ 4 = 2

Related-Facts Rummy Cards

$5 \times 1 = 5$	$1 \times 5 = 5$	$5 \div 5 = 1$	$5 \div 1 = 5$
$2 \times 5 = 10$	$5 \times 2 = 10$	$10 \div 2 = 5$	$10 \div 5 = 2$
$3 \times 5 = 15$	$5 \times 3 = 15$	$15 \div 3 = 5$	$15 \div 5 = 3$
$2 \times 1 = 2$	$1 \times 2 = 2$	$2 \div 2 = 1$	$2 \div 1 = 2$
$1 \times 3 = 3$	$3 \times 1 = 3$	$3 \div 1 = 3$	$3 \div 3 = 1$

Problem-Solving Black Line Master: Number Operations

Copy the following 7 sheets onto overhead transparencies to present to students as daily problem-solving activities. Or, photocopy the pages, and cut them apart for students, problem by problem. Have students paste the problems into their math journals or agendas for completion independently.

Tony sold some newspapers on Monday, and he sold 8 newspapers on Tuesday. Altogether, he sold 17 newspapers. How many papers did Tony sell on Monday?

From module 5, lesson 1, page 504

Bruce and Robbie are playing cards. Robbie has 9 cards. Together, the two boys have 14 cards. How many cards does Bruce have?

From module 5, lesson 1, page 504

Gwen had 7 dimes. Nicky had 6 dimes and 3 pennies. Gwen's father gave her some more dimes. Now she has 13 dimes. How many dimes did Gwen's father give her?

From module 5, lesson 1, page 504

Jake found 7 seashells on the beach. He took them home and added them to the 28 seashells he collected last week. How many seashells does Jake have now? Use the bridge-to-ten strategy to solve the problem.

From module 5, lesson 3, page 516

There are 36 horses in the corral. Dario opened the gate and let in 8 more horses. How many horses are in the corral now? Use the bridge-to-ten strategy to solve the problem.

From module 5, lesson 3, page 516

✂ --

Sophie had 86¢. Her brother Ryan found 6¢, and he gave it to Sophie. How much money does Sophie have now? Use the bridge-to-ten strategy to solve the problem.

From module 5, lesson 3, page 516

✂ --

Forty-seven third-grade students go to summer camp. Nine fourth-grade students also go to camp. Altogether, how many third- and fourth-grade students go to summer camp? Use the bridge-to-ten strategy to solve the problem.

From module 5, lesson 3, page 516

✂ --

Mel is 18 years old. Her brother is 6 years older than she is. How old is Mel's brother? Use the bridge-to-ten strategy to solve the problem.

From module 5, lesson 3, page 516

✂ --

Bill is using centimetre blocks to build a tower. On Monday, the tower was 38-centimetres high. On Tuesday, he added another 5 centimetres to the height of his tower. What is the total height of Bill's tower now? Use the bridge-to-ten strategy to solve the problem.

From module 5, lesson 3, page 516

✂ --

Use a calculator to solve this problem: Using *only* the 5, the 3, the +, and the = keys, which numbers from 3 to 30 can you make?

From module 5, lesson 4, page 521

▶

Use a calculator to solve this problem: How can you make the calculator show 756 if the 7 key and the 5 key are broken? How many *different* ways can you make the calculator show 756? What are they? For example, press: "300 + 400 + 30 + 20 + 6."

From module 5, lesson 4, page 521

Use a calculator to figure out how to make each of the following number sentences true by putting the correct addition and subtraction signs between the numbers:

76 ☐ 13 ☐ 10 = 73

82 ☐ 17 ☐ 19 ☐ 9 = 89

34 ☐ 24 ☐ 25 ☐ 12 = 21

From module 5, lesson 4, page 521

Carl sold 128 tickets for the school play. Joseph sold 75 tickets. How many tickets did the two boys sell altogether?

From module 5, lesson 7, page 538

Fern wants to watch one movie that is 95 minutes long and another movie that is 153 minutes long. How long will it take Fern to watch both movies?

From module 5, lesson 7, page 538

Mr. Peters tagged 352 butterflies last week and 241 butterflies this week. How many butterflies did Mr. Peters tag altogether?

From module 5, lesson 7, page 538

William made 125 chocolate-chip cookies, 145 oatmeal cookies, 115 peanut-butter cookies, and 75 doughnuts for the school bake sale. How many cookies did William make?

From module 5, lesson 7, page 539

▶

Matthew accidentally tore a page out of his social studies book. He told his teacher that the sum of the page numbers (on the front and the back of the page torn out) is 189. What are the page numbers on the page Matthew tore out?

From module 5, lesson 8, page 541

Francine has six boxes of pears to load into her truck. The first box has 118 pears in it. The other boxes have 117, 119, 116, 117, and 115 pears in them. Francine makes three trips to her truck. On each trip, she loads two boxes, with a total of 234 pears, into the truck. Which two boxes does Francine load on each trip?

From module 5, lesson 8, page 541

Sarah found 15 shells at the beach. Andrew found 9 more shells than Sarah. Altogether, how many seashells did Sarah and Andrew find?

From module 5, lesson 9, page 546

Yale went to the store to buy some groceries. A package of cheese costs $4 and a bag of apples costs $5. Yale bought 2 bags of apples and 1 package of cheese. How much money did Yale spend on groceries?

From module 5, lesson 9, page 546

Peter put his hockey cards into three piles. There are 8 hockey cards in his first pile. The second pile has 6 more cards than the first pile. The third pile has 5 fewer cards than the second pile. How many hockey cards does Peter have?

From module 5, lesson 9, page 546

Natasha has 12 marbles. She lost half of them, so she bought 12 more. How many marbles does Natasha have now?

From module 5, lesson 9, page 546

▶

On Saturday, 187 children went to the circus. On Sunday, 74 children went to the circus. How many more children went to the circus on Saturday than on Sunday?

From module 5, lesson 10, page 548

✂ ---

Dana has 345 stamps in her collection. She gives away 129 stamps. How many stamps does Dana have in her collection now?

From module 5, lesson 10, page 548

✂ ---

Charles is saving his money for some new hockey equipment. He needs $209 to buy the skates, helmet, and jersey that he wants. He has $150 saved up already. How much more money does Charles need to save?

From module 5, lesson 10, page 548

✂ ---

Sarah's mom has 463 photos in her photo album. If Sarah is in 284 of these photos, how many of the photos is Sarah not in?

From module 5, lesson 10, page 548

✂ ---

Paul works at the ballpark refreshment stand, which sells hotdogs, hamburgers, and boxes of popcorn. At the last game, Paul sold 268 hotdogs, 143 hamburgers, and 75 boxes of popcorn. How many more hotdogs than hamburgers did Paul sell?

From module 5, lesson 10, page 548

✂ ---

There are 168 boys and 165 girls who attend Marshall Elementary School. On Monday, 109 students were away from school on a field trip. How many students went to school on Monday?

From module 5, lesson 11, page 550

▶

Todd, Chris, and Paul all live east of Pattersville on Highway Road. Todd lives 178 kilometres from Pattersville. Chris lives 59 kilometres closer to Pattersville than Todd does. Paul lives 163 kilometres from Chris. How far does Paul live from Pattersville?

From module 5, lesson 11, page 550

✂ ---

Five owls go hunting at night. Each owl catches 3 mice. How many mice do the owls catch in total?

From module 5, lesson 13, page 560

✂ ---

Jennifer has 3 paper bags. There are 4 marbles in each bag. How many marbles does Jennifer have altogether?

Module 5, lesson 17

✂ ---

Barry made sandwiches for the party. He has 5 paper plates. He put 3 sandwiches onto each plate. How many sandwiches did Barry make?

Module 5, lesson 17

✂ ---

Coach Saunders needs 15 tennis balls for the tournament. If tennis balls come in packages of 3, how many packages does Coach Saunders need to buy?

From module 5, lesson 22, page 595

✂ ---

Maria buys 12 eggs. If she needs 3 eggs to make 1 omelette, how many omelets can Maria make?

From module 5, lesson 22, page 595

✂ ---

Alex has 15 stickers. If he gives 5 stickers to each friend at his party, how many friends will he give stickers to?

From module 5, lesson 22, page 595

▶

Twenty-five children sign up to play flag football. If there are 9 players on each team, how many teams will there be?

From module 5, lesson 22, page 595

Courtney and John picked 20 apples. If they put 4 apples into each bag, how many bags of apples will Courtney and John have?

From module 5, lesson 22, page 595

References for Teachers

Burns, Marilyn. *About Teaching Mathematics, A K-8 Resource*. Sausalito, CA: Math Solutions Publications, 1992.

Burns, Marilyn, and Robyn Silbey. *So You Have to Teach Math? Sound Advice for K-6 Teachers*. Sausalito, CA: Math Solutions Publications, 2000.

Burns, Marilyn, and Bonnie Tank. *A Collection of Math Lessons from Grades 1 through 3*. Sausalito, CA: Math Solutions Publications, 1988.

Fennell, Francis, et al. *Connect to NCTM Standards 2000: Making the Standards Work at Grade 3*. Chicago, IL: Creative Publications, 2000.

Hope, Jack A., et al. *Mental Math in the Primary Grades*. Lebanon, IN: Dale Seymour Publications, 1988.

O'Daffer, Phares G. *Problem Solving Tips for Teachers*. Reston, VA: The National Council of Teachers of Mathematics, Inc., 1988.

Reys, Robert, E., et al. *Helping Children Learn Mathematics, 7th Edition*. Hoboken, NJ: John Wiley & Sons, 2004.

______. *Helping Children Learn Mathematics, 2nd Edition*. Englewood Cliffs, NJ: Prentice Hall, 1989.

Ronfeldt, Suzy, and Marilyn Burns. *Third Grade Math: A Month to Month Guide*. Sausalito, CA: Math Solutions Publications, 2003.

Skinner, Penny. *It All Adds Up! Engaging 8-12-Year-Olds in Math Investigations*. Sausalito, CA: Math Solutions Publications, 1999.

Van de Walle, John A. *Elementary and Middle School Mathematics*. Don Mills, ON: Addison Wesley Longman, 2001.

Western Canadian Protocol for Collaboration in Basic Education. *The Common Curriculum Framework for K-12 Mathematics* – Grade 3, 1995.

Wright, Robert J., et al. *Teaching Number, Advancing Children's Skills and Strategies*. Thousand Oaks, CA: Paul Chapman, 2002.